CHRIS
HUTCHINS

JOHN BLAKE

Published by John Blake Publishing Ltd,
3, Bramber Court, 2 Bramber Road,
London W14 9PB, England

www.blake.co.uk

First published in hardback in 2005

ISBN 1 84454 146 0

British Library Cataloguing-in-Publication Data:

A catalogue record for this book is available from the British Library.

Design by www.envydesign.co.uk

Printed in Great Britain by Creative Print and Design (Wales),
Ebbw Vale, Gwent

1 3 5 7 9 10 8 6 4 2

Papers used by John Blake Publishing Ltd are natural, recyclable products
made from wood grown in sustainable forests. The manufacturing processes
conform to the environmental regulations of the country of origin.

Every attempt has been made to contact the relevant copyright-holders,
but some were unobtainable. We would be grateful if the appropriate people
could contact us.

My lasting memory of that April day in 2005 when Prince Charles married Camilla Parker Bowles is of standing with a television crew on a platform perched precariously on the roof of a building opposite Windsor Castle and, ironically, high above a Thresher's off-licence. My fellow *Fox News* presenter was inserting his blue contact lenses, and Gerri, my wife, was applying the required make-up to my face. At our feet lay two uninvited guests – police marksmen clad in black nylon body suits, surveying the crowd below through the sights of their high-powered rifles while a burst of organ music drifted down from St George's Chapel.

As I looked at the policemen's guns, I thought about a telephone call I had received the previous evening from a dear friend who had bumped into the Russian oligarch Roman Abramovich. She had asked him if he was going to have me shot because of the unauthorised biography of him I had written with Dominic Midgley.

'No,'replied Abramovich with a smile, 'I'm not going to have him shot.'

It is to such a diverse cast of characters who have so enriched my life that I dedicate this book. In short, everyone. But in particular Dominic Midgley who so skilfully helped put these recollections down on paper.

CONTENTS

Foreword   ix

Chapter One: One stuffed lion   1

Chapter Two: Music and mayhem   29

Chapter Three: Marriage v Beatlemania   43

Chapter Four: The man in the corner is Elvis   73

Chapter Five: Me and Mr Jones   85

Chapter Six: When a Prime Minister calls…   107

Chapter Seven: Pop stars not gangsters   139

Chapter Eight: Royals behaving oddly   151

Chapter Nine: The Forsyth saga   163

Chapter Ten: One yellow watch   173

Chapter Eleven: What Murdoch's butler saw   213

Chapter Twelve: Nobody's Virgin   231

Chapter Thirteen: In sickness and in health   251

Chapter Fourteen: With the parting of the ways   277

Epilogue   289

FOREWORD

When you join a newspaper as a fairly green journalist, it's hard not to be impressed by the anecdotes of the older hands. At the *Daily Mail*, I remember being particularly taken by a reporter who told me how he got the world exclusive on Baby Doc's wedding in Haiti by bluffing his way into the church posing as the man from the Miami-based wedding-cake manufacturer. But it was when I joined *Today* newspaper in the early 1990s that I came across a journalist whose fund of stories was richer than anyone else's. I sat opposite Chris Hutchins on the features desk there for four years and in that time I gradually filleted him of the highlights of what turned out to be a pretty extraordinary life. As a young journalist on the *New Musical Express*, he had befriended the Beatles when they were nobodies and went on to introduce them to Elvis Presley. When he moved into PR, he spent an eventful decade acting as publicist for Tom Jones, the Bee Gees, Engelbert Humperdinck and Gilbert O'Sullivan among others before returning to journalism as a gossip columnist who broke some of the biggest stories around. What struck me early on was that the background to the scoops was often more fascinating than the stories themselves: the painstaking cultivation of Elvis Presley's manager, the relationship with Rupert Murdoch's mischievous butler, the lunches with the Palace maid who had had an affair with Prince Edward, the chance encounter with a senator at an AA meeting that led to an invitation to Bill Clinton's inauguration. When *Today* folded in 1995, we started to write books together and it soon occurred to me that one of the most fascinating books Chris could write would be his own life story. After all, I reasoned, while Chris may be largely unknown to the general public, his life has revolved around some of the very biggest names in showbusiness and big business, and he was in a unique position to write the inside story of his dealings in much the same way Julia Phillips did in her brilliant exposé of Hollywood, *You'll Never Eat Lunch in This Town Again*.

What makes Chris's experience particularly unusual is that, instead of switching from journalism to public relations and staying there, he returned to newspapers. This gave him valuable insight. Having spun lines for a decade, he knew just how to unravel them when they were pitched to him as a reporter. In this book, apart from a host of revealing anecdotes, he offers us what I think is a fascinating look at the anatomy of celebrity.

Chris's book is also the very human story of a how a boy born in poverty and reared by a widow who took out her bitterness at her lot on her children succeeded in making it in a highly competitive field. It was, however, a career that was achieved at great personal cost. The music business had long been awash with drugs and, as a music writer, Chris was soon addicted to downers as well as uppers. Tom Jones presented a different problem. While he is one of the most prominent anti-drug campaigners in the business, he certainly wasn't then – and isn't now – averse to a drink or two. Chris's attempts to keep up with Jones later helped turn him into an award-winning boozer. When he returned to journalism, life was no less stressful. As he recalls in Chapter Nine, on the first day of embarking on a gossip column that was to appear six times a week swallowing 13 stories every day, he woke up with just one lead: Terry Wogan wore a toupee. While he did succeed in kicking the booze for a number of years, the drinking and drug-taking later resumed in earnest and eventually cost him his marriage.

It's a mellow man who has written this story but there will be many philandering singers, pompous lawyers, adulterous royals, dodgy politicians and, of course, wig-wearing celebrities who may never forgive him.

Dominic Midgley,
June 2005

Chapter One

ONE STUFFED LION

It was on a grim day in November 1954 that I found out the truth about my father. Mum had always said he'd died from his wounds during his RAF wartime service, but as I grew older I began to doubt that. There was something about the way that the neighbours – in Empire Road, Torquay – acted towards us. Was it the early onset of paranoia or were some of the kids discouraged from playing with me? Even those who were friendly, like Kenny Clark and his twin sister Marilyn at number 57, would behave differently if their parents were with them as they passed by on Sunday-afternoon walks. I tried to find out what it was all about from my older siblings, Joan and Philip, and aunts and uncles on my father's side of the family, but they talked of dark secrets that were best left that way. My mother's relatives were so forbidding I could never bring myself to raise the matter with them.

Then came that grey day when all was revealed. When I got back from school to find the house empty and a note from my mother saying she had gone shopping, I knew I had a rare

1

opportunity to search for a clue to the great mystery. In my 13 years, I had often snooped around before, but without success. Inch-by-inch searches of the indoor coal cupboard, converted into a toy and storage room when the council provided outdoor bunkers, had proved fruitless. In the run-up to Christmas on previous years, I had breached the sanctuary of my mum's bedroom and rifled through lavender-scented drawers in search of the presents. I'd even taken the backs off framed pictures to find out what might have been concealed there. But there was one locked cupboard above the mirrored door of what seemed like a huge wardrobe that I had never been able to delve inside. Apart from its size, the wardrobe had taken on a sort of mystical status thanks to Mum's habit of covering the mirror with a blanket when thunderstorms loomed. This, she assured me as we hid in the cupboard under the stairs, would prevent it attracting lightning. Two days earlier, I had found a set of keys and was convinced that one would open the door to the forbidden cupboard. After carefully carrying the old brown kitchen chair she kept by her bedside to support a glass of water and the ever-ready bottle of tiny pink sleeping pills, and placing it in front of that wretched wardrobe, I climbed on to it, inserted a key in the lock and – hey presto! – it opened. It was stuffed full of papers: an eccentric collection of old rent books, letters from my father and pictures of old boyfriends.

And there was a faded cutting from a copy of the *Torquay Times* dated 1944. It was a single-column story just a few inches long – the report of an inquest into the death of a local man who had been discharged from the RAF on medical grounds and who had taken his life by putting his head into a gas oven in the kitchens of the school where he worked as caretaker. In recording a verdict of suicide, the coroner had taken the unusual step of criticising the conduct of the deceased's wife, who had apparently contributed to his distress by being unfaithful to him when he was away from home on active service. The dead man's name was Edward Victor Hutchins. My dad.

So how did I feel? Numb, just numb. No tears came. I wasn't angry with him for taking the easy way out and have never felt that way since, although some years later it was to cause an unpleasant altercation with a Harley Street psychiatrist who insisted I must have been. No, I was a bit cross with my mother for not having told me the truth, but the main legacy of this somewhat bizarre discovery was that I decided there and then that if ever I got married – and Mum had already told me a number of times that I shouldn't even entertain the thought – it would have to be to a girl who had never, ever been anyone else's girl. Someone who would be eternally faithful; always to be just mine.

My father's suicide remained a taboo subject for the rest of Mum's life, rather like sex was. In the years that followed, however, I eventually pieced together the story of my parent's dysfunctional background. Mother, Kathleen Ness, was the third of five children of a pharmacist from Turnham Green, west London, who had moved to Torquay for his health and opened three chemist shops in the area. There were rumours that there was some distant connection to a Lord Neville Ness and certainly my mother always gave that as the reason for giving me Neville as a middle name. Whatever the truth of the matter, Mr Ness expected his daughter to marry well. Unfortunately for him, at the age of 17 she fell for Edward Hutchins, 22, one of 13 children of a local fisherman, who worked as a maintenance man – not at all the sort of husband her father had in mind for her. Within months of meeting, in November 1927, they married in the teeth of fierce opposition from the Ness family. The rift that resulted between her and her parents and siblings rumbled on, in the case of one particular family member, for more than 50 years.

Joan was born 18 months after the wedding and Phil eight years later. Mum had made a grudging peace with her mother by the time I came along in 1941 and I was pally with my cousins throughout my childhood but her brothers Teddy, Jack and Cyril and her sister Mabel refused to speak to her for years. It was my uncle Teddy who held out the longest. When I was a child he was already successful, with a flourishing business. His Outsize Shop on Clapham Common was, by all accounts, a local landmark. On his visits to Torquay to see his widowed mother, Teddy would park whichever big American car he was driving at the time outside her house on Marnham Road, opposite the Torquay United football ground. Mum was forbidden to visit when he was in town and I was only allowed to turn up to stare longingly at the car – out of touching distance. It was not until 1992 that I was able to organise a reconciliation between them. The only concession Uncle Teddy made in my childhood years was to come out on one occasion with a cream bun after he had spotted me admiring his Pontiac. As he handed it to me, he muttered, 'Don't tell your grandmother.' I don't think it's overegging the pudding to say that incidents such as this and being ostracised by the neighbours filled me with a nameless guilt and feelings of inadequacy that had an effect on my life and linger to this day.

Growing up without a father probably marked me more profoundly than anything else that happened to me before I left home. I was barely three when he died, and I have no memories of him. My mother dominated my young life. She was a tall woman, with long legs that she showed off on every possible occasion. She was generous with what little she had, had a great sense of humour and a wonderful laugh on good days. She never had a regular job while I was a child but worked part-time in local hotels and boarding houses as a cleaner or washer-up whenever there was work to be had. She was a very good singer and pianist and accompanied herself on an upright piano that was so old it had candlestick holders on either side of the music stand. In my mind I can still hear her playing 'In A Monastery Garden' and singing along to 'You Made Me Love You'. A brilliant cartoonist too, she was especially keen on drawing likenesses of Jane, the scantily clad star of a hugely popular post-war cartoon strip in the *Daily Mirror*, which she pinned all over the walls in the front room. In physical terms, they became my view of the perfect woman, although, by the flirtatious nature of the poses, very much at odds with the girl I had dreamed of from the night I learned how and why Dad killed himself.

These then were her good points. But Mum was hopeless with money and was always in debt, buying things on the never-never. Her reaction to the problems this caused was a combination of manipulation and vicious temper. Joan, Phil and I, along with several neighbours, were the victims and it was almost a relief when things became too much for her and she took to her bed with a couple of the 'pinks' from the bottle on the kitchen chair. Then we would have to creep around a totally silent house: woe betide us if we ever woke her from a drugged sleep.

Being brought up by a single mother in the 1940s and 1950s presented a far more grim reality than it does today. We lived in a three-bedroom, semi-detached council house built in the 1930s that was damp and – unless there was enough cash to buy coal for the fire – horribly cold in winter. It was bordered on three sides by a small garden. In the back we grew a few vegetables, which we ate on Mondays when the widow's pension Mum collected from the GPO every

Tuesday had run out. Mondays were depressing for another reason too. It was the day everyone in the class was called to the teacher's desk to hand over the week's dinner money. Everyone except me, that is. I was the one who got free school meals. This was embarrassing enough but there were plenty of other reminders of how things were tougher for me than they were for my few pals. The blankets on the bed all had Red Cross labels, most of my clothes came from charities and Mum was forever dragging me round to organisations like SAAFA (the Sailors And Airmen's Family Association) to plead for 'grants'. Despite this, I can never recall there being enough money to last the week, something I knew all too well because, from an early age, I did the weekly shop. When once I complained that ten shillings wouldn't be enough to pay for all the items on her shopping list, Mum snapped, 'Well, I haven't got any more so *you* decide what we do without.' Now that was a lot of pressure to put on a seven-year-old.

We were also constantly dodging debt-collectors, mainly from clothing clubs. It meant learning to lie low below the windowsill when they came knocking. They got wise to that and would come back a few minutes later in the hope of catching us unawares. I think that qualified me as the most neurotic kid on the street.

Things weren't helped by the fact that by now I had developed a deep and abiding fear of the dark. This dates from visits to my paternal grandmother's two-bedroom cottage opposite a fish-and-chip shop in nearby Babbacombe. Two of my father's sisters, Frances and Grace, were spiritualists. They would hold séances in the tiny front room of this very dark house as I sat in the next room listening to the scratching of the glass being moved around the table. Every now and again, I'd hear an eerie voice asking, 'Who do you want to speak to?' When I was allowed to rejoin them it was to listen to ghostly tales of frightening things they had experienced on their journeys into the supernatural with terrifying consequences. The sisters were forever trying to contact my father. On nights such as those I could never sleep – a problem that lingers to the present day.

My sister didn't help matters when she took me to see my first film at the age of six. It was at a cinema called the Burlington, which my mother referred to as 'a fleapit' and made us take newspapers to sit on – again very embarrassing. But it was the film Joan chose to introduce me to the wonderful world of movies that I most remember about that night. The main feature was titled *The Beast with Five Fingers* and it was all about a disembodied hand that haunted a house by playing the piano at night. I lay awake for nights thereafter expecting to hear thunderous Beethoven chords coming from the room beneath my bedroom where the piano was kept.

Throughout my childhood, I never dared enter the house unless someone else was at home. Instead, when I got back from school on winter evenings I would stand outside under a street lamp and wait until one of the others came back. How crazy that sounds now but I would shake with fear of the unknown in those awful childhood days.

It was poverty that proved to be my earliest stimulus. In the absence of pocket money I became an entrepreneur at an early age. The only marketable resource to hand was my clotted-cream ration. In post-war Britain, milk was unpasteurised and fridges were unknown on council estates like ours, so the milk was boiled each night and the thick cream skimmed off in the morning. Clotted cream and jam were a treat but I wanted cash. At the age of five, I was obsessed with toy buses and learned to sell cream and jam buns to raise the money to buy them. I don't know whether it was my persistence or their gluttony, but the neighbours seemed happy enough to part with the few coppers I charged for the 'luxury' food I sold off an orange box parked by the gate. I thought of that years later when I heard Tom Jones say that as an equally small boy he earned coppers singing on an orange box at the corner shop in Laura Street, Pontypridd. Strange how our two lives were destined to meet.

By the time I was 11, I had a Saturday job delivering groceries for the Trewerns, who had a corner shop on Forest Road. Those to nearby houses I delivered on foot but at 1.30pm sharp a local taxi driver would pull up in a huge black Humber Imperial and the deliveries would be completed in style. In those parts the Imperial was the Rolls-Royce of its day. It was my first experience of being chauffeured around in a limousine – something I was to enjoy on a regular basis in years to come. Even now I can remember the smell of its rich leather upholstery. The shopkeeper, Ralph Trewern, paid me five bob a week but Mum obliged me to nick a packet of 20 Du Maurier cigarettes for her by way of a 'bonus' to her for my services. Trewern – who had an unhealthy interest in young boys – was only too happy to look the other way when I went to the cigarette shelf.

In my teens I took summer holiday jobs. Torquay – like most seaside resorts out of season – always seemed a depressing place, especially when rain lashed the seafront and there was often no one to be seen on the streets. In the summer, however, it was as much a paradise for me as it was for that breed Mum so despised – 'the visitors'. When the holidaymakers arrived, the gift shops – Aladdin's caves of glittering junk – would open along with the ice-cream kiosks and coffee houses, and those who ran them were always on the lookout for cheap labour. I'd have a day job in a gift shop on the harbourside and serve 'throffy coffee' – that's what cappuccino was called in those days – at the Palm Court Hotel on the front in the evenings. It brought in what seemed to me untold wealth.

The best form of escapism on days and evenings, particularly in the winter when I had to stay indoors, was the radio. Thank God for the BBC Light Programme (the 1950s version of Radio 2) which broadcast plenty of comedy and drama, then my staple diet of entertainment. Phil and I would sit in the dark (afraid that the shilling in the electricity meter would run out at a critical point), obsessively listening to *PC 49*, *Journey Into Space* and *Take It From Here*. Saturday nights were my introduction to variety with the appositely named *Variety Playhouse* hosted by Vic Oliver, who I was destined to meet in the flesh at the Torquay Pavilion – thanks to the pulling power of the *Monthly Mirror*.

The *Monthly Mirror* was born during a spell of boredom on a wet Sunday afternoon. I liked print and had bought one of the early John Bull printing sets out of the proceeds of the cream-bun trade. Seeing my name in print had been a thrill since it first appeared in the *Herald Express* in a list of the primary-school children taking part in a nativity play. Up to that point I had never got nearer to getting anything printed than pestering the people at Bellamy's, a small printing firm on Plainmoor, to give me estimates for stationery and calling cards on almost a weekly basis. Putting the *Mirror* together was a laborious process that involved first writing the stories in longhand in green hectographic ink. A jelly pad would then be laid on top of the page to pick up the ink and I could reproduce copies until the ink dried up. Then the stories would have to be written out again to produce a few more. It was a lot of effort for a small return but it was fun. I – naturally – was the editor and a handful of friends plus one cousin, David Redwood (the sports editor), were roped in as staff. Together we turned out the first (and probably the only) newspaper ever produced on the Westhill estate. Six copies of the first single-page issue were sold to long-suffering customers I had garnered back in the days of the cream-bun trade. Eventually the *MM* got up to eight pages and at one point the circulation was in three figures.

My semi-professional journalistic career had actually begun a year earlier, when I made it my business to highlight the story of Eric's missing fishing tackle. Eric was the husband of my sister Joan and the two of them were staying at Empire Road while they struggled to get a place of their own. Mum made the most of her ascendancy over her son-in-law, humiliating him at every possible opportunity. She insisted, for example, that Eric, an ex-sailor and keen angler, stored his fishing gear in a spare dustbin outside the back door. One day the inevitable happened: the dustmen emptied the wrong bin. Eric was distraught, but I convinced him that all was not lost. Years of observing my mother manipulate whoever she came across had already turned me into an accomplished operator. A famous newspaperman once defined the key attributes of the journalist as 'a plausible manner, a little literary ability and ratlike cunning'. Even in those days I relied on the latter rather more than most. I got on to the council and demanded they instigate a search for the missing fishing tackle, which led to a team of council workers scouring the dump. Then I called the BBC and the local evening paper to alert them to the story. Eric's gear was never retrieved but I made a couple of pounds selling the story.

The ability to hustle and the growing clout of the *Monthly Mirror*, following a glowing front-page story by a local author, Vian C Smith, in the *South Devon Journal*, led to some interesting encounters. I was contacted by a would-be politician called Peter Bessell who thought it would be 'cute' to have the support of the kids' newspaper in his hopeless campaign to win the Torbay seat for the Liberals. He took me on canvassing missions, usually in the company of John Arlott, the cricket commentator, who was a prominent Liberal supporter. I was mesmerised by Arlott's public-speaking ability and it was good grounding for what was to come in future years. Bessell's hopes of winning over the *Monthly Mirror* to his party were thwarted by my mother's strong Socialist beliefs. Alas, neither she nor I were able to spot that in any case Bessell was a wrong 'un. When the Liberal leader Jeremy Thorpe was put on trial for conspiracy to murder in the 1970s, Bessell gained considerable notoriety for agreeing a deal with a newspaper, under which he would receive £25,000 for his story if Thorpe were convicted. Since he was one of the main prosecution witnesses, the deal smacked of corruption and it brought scandal on the party hierarchy.

Another by-product of the *Monthly Mirror*'s growing popularity was access to the Pavilion. I got Bob Roberts, Torquay Council's entertainments manager, to take me on a tour of the theatre, at the end of which he offered me a pair of complimentary tickets for every Monday night's performance and a backstage pass. Did I accept? Who wouldn't!

And that was my introduction to showbusiness.

It was close to Christmas as I ventured behind the scenes during rehearsals for the pantomime *Sleeping Beauty*. Joining the *Monthly Mirror* bandwagon, the producer Pat McKay offered me a walk-on part as a shepherd's boy for the show's five-week run – a shrewd move since the story also made local headlines. Six nights a week I donned Highland costume and make-up for my solo spot walking a corgi down the winding path of a corny hillside set. The scene was designed to charm and, according to the reviews, it succeeded. But it got me into serious trouble at school where I was 'missing' on Wednesday afternoons – matinee day. Catching the last bus home every night also told on my homework. The publicity generated by McKay's canny decision to hire a local boy for his production brought me to the attention of Joe Harmer, the ultra-strict headmaster at Torquay Boys Grammar School. He was so annoyed that he took the unusual step of turning up at our house to remonstrate with Mum for letting me get involved in the first place. Looking round the dismal house we lived in, he said I had done well to pass the 11-plus examination and win a Grammar School education, but he went on to point out that it was still a privilege and not something to take second place in any boy's life.

Alas, I was to repeat the offence twice more that term, appearing with a professional company in two plays at the Pavilion on Bob Roberts' recommendation. This further enraged Harmer and after the second play he threatened me with suspension. So there ended my stage career. Strangely enough, the most enduring legacy of my short-lived career as an actor was not the dialogue of TS Eliot but two minor stage props: a white telephone and a long-stemmed wine glass. From the moment I set eyes on them I craved these two items for the sophisticated lifestyle they represented.

By now I had joined the choir at St John's Church, which towered over Torquay harbour and at night its huge neon cross made it a prominent landmark. The organist and choirmaster was one Francis Crute, also our school music teacher. Mr Crute – or Frank, as we called him – was not only a brilliant musician but also a charismatic individual who charmed pupils and congregations alike. Alas, he was not the sort of person who should have been given charge of a group of boys. Not long after I discovered the cutting from the *Torquay Times* about my father's suicide, we choristers heard that Frank was to be arrested for buggering one of our number. We turned up for choir practice as usual the evening before he was due to be taken into custody but he failed to appear. Eventually half a dozen of us cycled to his house on Parkhurst Road. We rang and rang the doorbell but there was no reply and when we peered through the windows at the front of the house he was nowhere to be seen. We walked around to the back of the house but there the kitchen window was set higher in the wall so, as the smallest and lightest in the group, I was hoisted on to the tallest boy's shoulders to look inside. The sight that greeted me remains imprinted on my memory: there was Frank Crute lying on the floor, with his head in the gas oven. It was as if God had determined that I should see the manner of my father's death for real.

Bob Roberts extended his generous 'free tickets' offer to include the Council's tiny concert hall at Babbacombe, just two minutes' walk from the house where my father had grown up. And that's where I met Bruce Forsyth. He and his wife, Penny Calvert, were appearing in a summer show called *Gay Time* and the first time I saw the aspiring comic on stage I couldn't believe how happy he was and how infectious that happiness was. Everybody who left the little theatre the first night I saw Bruce in action seemed to be laughing. I met him and Penny that night and the following day on the Downs outside the concert hall where they shared their sandwich lunch with me. Even to a 14-year-old it was obvious by the way they held hands and gazed into each other's eyes that they were very much in love. For me it was a defining moment: I wanted what Bruce Forsyth had – a happy nature, a blissful marriage to a woman who clearly only had eyes for him and the ability to make people laugh. From that moment I wanted nothing more than to be a comedian, to have a lovely wife and to follow in this happy man's footsteps.

Watching Bruce – and I went back to see his show night after night – whetted my appetite for variety of the showbusiness kind. I could not believe my luck when I heard from Bob Roberts that the West End impresario Harold Fielding was bringing his touring show *Music for the Millions* to the Pavilion. A different all-star cast every week. For the town it was a chance to see and hear such stars of cinema and radio as George Formby, Jimmy Edwards, Arthur Askey, Ted Ray, Peter Brough and Dick Bentley. For me it was an opportunity to meet and interview them.

It was not, however, one of the household names who was to make the biggest impression on me, but an up-and-coming 29-year-old whose name was quite low on the bill: a ventriloquist called Terry Hall. The big names who came to the Pavilion were probably more amused than anything by the kid who barged into their dressing rooms clutching a notebook and pencil. But Terry was more curious than most. He said he had an idea he wanted to discuss with me but first he wanted to meet my mother. His plan was to turn his newest dummy, a camp big cat called Lenny the Lion, into a household name via national television. To further the idea he needed publicity to raise his profile. He needed a fan club for Lenny – and someone to run it.

To his credit, Terry was first determined to persuade my mother to be a more responsible parent. He pointed out to her that there were many predatory homosexuals in showbusiness and delicately suggested that it might not be prudent to allow a 14-year-old boy to wander backstage unaccompanied. Mum seemed oblivious to the warning: she was too taken by the glamour of being in a theatre dressing room for the first time (with Lenny the Lion in a suitcase in the corner) to pay much attention to such words of caution. When Terry broached the fan club plan, she was elated. In fact, she loved the idea and, to my dismay, offered to help run it. And so, with her approval, a remarkable two-year association between me, Terry – a professional entertainer – and his motherly (to me) wife Kathleen began.

In February 1956, I ordered a thousand membership forms from a printer Terry knew in Burnley, Lancashire. They were displayed in the lobby of each theatre at which Lenny ('*with* Terry Hall', as they were billed) appeared, and also given to autograph hunters at the stage door. Soon about 50 applications a week were arriving at 42 Empire Road, each accompanied by the membership subscription of one shilling. Processing the orders meant commissioning membership badges, cards and other printed paraphernalia and so, at the age of 15, I suddenly had an account at Barclays Bank to pay in the subscriptions and write cheques for the merchandise. Terry and I wrote to each other two or three times a week as the enterprise grew alongside Lenny's increasing popularity and whenever there was something to discuss he would send a telegram (we had no phone) asking me to call him at whichever theatre he was appearing.

It was heady stuff and, in many ways, Terry – one of the nicest people I have ever met – became the father I'd never had. In fact, he was the first in a series of father figures I was to adopt as mentors. Apart from his paternal concern about my welfare backstage, he taught me much about life in general when I travelled to join him and Kath in their showbusiness digs. It was an education that proved invaluable in later life. If he was working in London, there would be precise instructions on how to take a train to Paddington, then a cab to the theatre or TV studio, how much to tip the driver and how to get past the doorkeeper. He taught me about food – 'eat less of that Devon cream and more salads and vegetables' – and did his best to help me rise above the never-ending family squabbles. The fact that someone cared enough to say these things meant a lot to me. My efforts were rewarded by trips to places like Blackpool and Great Yarmouth and they were a welcome respite from the remorseless psychological warfare that constituted life with my mother.

Terry's biggest brainwave was to suggest I write to the *Daily Mirror*'s Old Codgers' letters column to tell them about the fan club. It was particularly important, he said, to tell them my age. A few days later a photographer from the *Herald Express* called to say he had been asked by the *Daily Mirror* to take my photograph. Soon after, the letter Terry had had me write appeared with my picture as the lead item on the Old Codgers' page. It proved to be an early – and in some ways devastating – lesson in the power of publicity. Over the next several weeks, mail to 42 Empire Road was delivered not by the postman but by a man in a van who trudged down our front path carrying sacks of envelopes. Huge supplies of fan club material had to be ordered from the printer and the badge-maker as membership rose from a few hundred to more than 25,000 in a matter of weeks. Every night I was up at the kitchen table, filling out membership cards, addressing envelopes and filing the members' details until the early hours. By then I was also editing the fan club magazine, *Lenny's Fanfare*, and that entailed pressuring some of Terry's famous friends, including Max Bygraves, Tommy Steele and the boxer Freddie Mills, into writing articles. Joe Harmer despaired as once again my schoolwork went into sharp decline.

By now, however, there was another reason for this. Like most boys of 14, I found myself attracted to the opposite sex. Almost overnight, girls became mightily attractive beings. My pals and I would charge out of our school at four o'clock each day and cycle to theirs to catch them before they all dispersed. Then we found out about the weekly discos in the Co-op Hall and St Luke's church and, even more amazing, the rock 'n' roll music there was to jive to.

And that's where I discovered Elvis Presley.

Overnight, Lenny the Lion became a thing of the past. Sensing my declining interest, Terry had passed organisation of the fan club to Dr Barnardo's Homes who had plenty of volunteer helpers and were even able to make a small profit. Gone too was my interest in the fading comics who had so besotted me at the Pavilion. Now Elvis was everything, not only for me but also for most of my friends. We would fight the boys who sneeringly passed on their classical-music-loving parents' opinion that Elvis couldn't sing. My fifth-form pal Mickey Witherington had a record player in his house and, on the pretext that I was visiting my father's grave in the cemetery opposite, we took afternoons off school to play over and over again the few Elvis records he'd collected – early classics such as 'All Shook Up', 'Let's Have a Party', 'Gotta Lotta Livin' To Do', 'When My Blue Moon Turns To Gold Again' and 'Paralysed', learning by heart as many of the words as we could decipher from this man with the wonderfully curious accent. Then – usually with a couple of girls in tow – we'd go to the Odeon and immerse ourselves in the early Presley films, *Love Me Tender*, *Loving You* and *Jailhouse Rock*, sitting through two or even three showings back-to-back. This was a whole new world, exciting and far removed from anything I had previously known. But this new diversion took a further toll on my education and I managed just two feeble O-level passes at the first attempt and only another three at a second try a year later. As my 17th birthday approached, I decided the world had more to offer than exams, detention and nagging schoolmasters.

Given my background with the *Monthly Mirror* and *Lenny's Fanfare*, journalism was an obvious career path but it wasn't one I was particularly committed to. If nothing else, my experience as an amateur had taught me that journalists had access and I figured that a job on a newspaper would allow me to make a more informed choice later on. I had less than two months left at school when my mother's friend Connie, the new wife of Fred Waldron (a railway porter and one of my mum's many exes), tipped me off about a vacancy for a cub reporter at the *Mid Devon Times*, six miles away in Newton Abbot. The paper was edited by a man called AG Angel (I never did find out what the initials stood for) whose father, as luck would have it, had known my maternal grandfather.

I phoned Mr Angel and was duly summoned to an interview. At the offices of the *Mid Devon Times* on Albany Street, I was led into a cramped room which AG shared with the paper's three reporters. He was a big man who cut something of an Edwardian figure in his spats, braces and bow tie. He smoked a pipe that rarely left his mouth and the office ceiling was stained brown by years of accumulated fumes. Two other desks had typewriters but there was no such machine on AG's desk. He handwrote all his copy which was then decoded by the only person who could read his scrawl, a typesetter at the printworks in nearby Totnes. Impressed by my keenness, he offered me a five-year apprenticeship. He really needed someone to start straight away but he was a kind man and agreed to keep the £2-a-week post open until the school term ended six weeks later. Mickey Witherington was appalled. 'Two pounds a week? You're mad.' He had just landed a job as a commis waiter at a hotel on the harbour at £7 plus tips 'and a chance to meet a dozen new girls every week'. He had a point.

For me schooldays ended on the last Friday in June 1958. My first assignment for the *Mid Devon Times* was the very next morning, covering the annual garden show and fete at a tiny village called Ilsington. The chief reporter, Clive Angel – AG's son – told me to look up the previous year's report and model my piece on that. After the recommended hour's research in the *MDT* office, I kick-started my sky-blue Vespa scooter (bought with £25 borrowed from Fred Waldron) and pointed the handlebars in the direction of Dartmoor. A career that was to take my life in many unimaginable directions had begun.

While Mickey Witherington seemed to be taking out a different girl every night of the week, my love life was non-existent for the first few weeks at the *MDT*. Then something beautiful and totally unexpected happened. Riding my trusty Vespa along Torquay seafront on a particularly fine Saturday evening, I was flagged down by an ex-schoolfriend called Bernard. He had arranged a date with a lass from Yorkshire who was in town on holiday, but she'd turned up with a girlfriend and he wondered if I was up for a bit of 'escort duty'. I was taken by the prettier of the two, a slim dark-haired girl, but assumed she was Bernard's date. I couldn't believe my luck when it became clear that she was the unattached one. Her name was Janice Rowland. She was 14 and I soon decided she was the most wonderful person I had ever met.

We spent 20 minutes in a local amusement arcade and then the best part of three hours trailing Bernard and the other girl around the neon-lit beauty spots on what turned out to be the hottest night of the summer. Our family backgrounds were very different. Jan came from solid working-class stock. Both her parents, Alf and Nelly, worked in the steel industry: her father as a foundry worker, her mother as a cutlery polisher. While they never earned much, they created an enviably stable home life and Jan could always rely on coming home from school to good meals: fillet steak every Friday, roast on Sunday and hot pot every Monday.

Jan was due back at her parents' holiday digs at ten that night and by the time I got her there I was pretty sure that I had fallen in love, though I barely knew what that was. It's hard to put into words exactly what it is about someone that makes them special and different. I believe today that it's a lot to do with how the other person makes you feel about yourself. I told her she was the prettiest girl I had ever seen (she blushed!) and she told me I was 'very interesting'. It was more than a start. We may have been clumsy with words but deep inside we both felt a sort of chemistry going on that neither of us could adequately explain. We had never felt it before. Here then was the girl of my dreams, the girl who had never felt emotionally about any other man – the absolute I demanded on the day I'd discovered that my mother's infidelity had caused my father to take his life. She was going home to Sheffield the very next day and, when we said goodnight on the doorstep of her parents' digs, we wept. It was the kind of love Elvis sang about.

The following morning I was back early to wave her goodbye and exchange addresses. As they climbed aboard the coach, Alf and Nelly politely said they were pleased to meet me and Nelly added that she looked forward to us all meeting again some time in the future. Alas, I could not hope to reciprocate with an introduction of Jan to my own mother. It would never have done for Mum to know that I had a girlfriend; she had extracted solemn and oft-repeated promises from both Phil and I that we would never leave her, that she would always be our one and only girlfriend. The only address I could give Jan was 'Albany Street, Newton Abbot' – that of the *Mid Devon Times*. She wrote to me as soon as she got home and I received the letter in the first post on the Tuesday. It was the sweetest thing I have ever read. She pledged undying love and we wrote to each other in a similar vein twice a week while I got on with the garden fetes, parish council meetings and coroners courts that provided the stuff the *MDT* filled its pages with.

A year later, in 1959, the Rowlands returned for another holiday and I took most of the fortnight off to be with Jan – mostly taking her round my rural 'beat' on the back of the Vespa. Our teenage encounter had turned from the briefest of holiday romances into a deep and lasting love – by post, of course. That October I rode the Vespa to Sheffield (top speed 38mph: total travelling time ten hours) for my first stay at the Rowlands' home on East Bank Road in the city's Arbourthorne district. For five glorious days we explored Sheffield and the surrounding countryside and on the last afternoon, as we basked in autumn sunshine in one of the city's parks, I told her about my father and then I asked her to marry me and she accepted. Jan was 15 and I was two and a half years her senior. She chose and bought her own engagement ring (a row of garnets) and I reimbursed the £9 it cost in instalments. From that day on we were to write to each other every day until our wedding in March 1964 – always expressing undying mutual love, although neither of us could have known what fate had in store ...

I rode the 260 miles home, wondering all the way how I could let my brother in on the good news but have the strength to keep it from my mother. Phil was naturally delighted when I told him – he was secretly engaged himself too, to Rosemary, a local girl who became – and happily still is – his wife. He understood the dilemma only too well, bearing in mind the promises our mother had extracted from us.

Knowing I could only hope to see my schoolgirl fiancée a

couple of times a year, I expiated my loneliness by working harder than ever, scouring the office diary to grab every job going. There were few opportunities to excite the 4,000 readers of the *Mid Devon Times*, and the first chance I had to cause any trouble came when I won the office lottery to cover one of the biggest local stories of the year – a visit by the Duke of Edinburgh to the Outward Bound School at Ashburton on the edge of Dartmoor. Prince Philip arrived and departed at the controls of a Royal Navy helicopter and I had what was later described as 'the temerity' to describe his take-off as 'shaky'. It was soon made clear to me that I had broken the unspoken code of deference that persisted in those days and, following a complaint from Buckingham Palace, I was officially censured by the local branch of the National Union of Journalists. It was to prove the first of many brushes with the Royal Family.

My next clash with the local forces of conservatism came when I took the precaution of meeting Adam Faith off the train when he came to Torquay to perform at the new Princess Theatre. It was August 1961 and he was riding high in the charts. In a move to thwart the opposition (I was never a team player), I invited Adam and his agent Colin Berlin to go for a drive with me in a car I had borrowed for the day. They seemed bemused but agreed. After a scenic tour, I took them for a cream tea at a Dartmoor hotel, finally depositing them at the theatre with only minutes to spare before Adam's performance and no time to talk to rivals who had been waiting for him all afternoon. The magnitude of the offence I had caused to my fellow hacks was brought home to me as I rode to work the next day and saw an evening paper placard emblazoned with the words: 'POP STAR KIDNAPPED'. Once again I was censured and marked down as a trouble-making rule-breaker.

Happily, though, the meeting proved to be the start of a lifelong friendship with Adam (or 'Tel', as he was called, short for his real name Terry Nelhams). After that first encounter we kept in touch and he said I should give him a call whenever we were in the same area. When I discovered that a visit to Jan in Sheffield coincided with one of his appearances there, I wrote to Jan and told her that I had seats for the show and we were going backstage afterwards to say 'Hi'. In her reply she said she was looking forward to the show but could we forgo the backstage visit. It was an omen I failed to spot. This diffidence in the face of celebrity was something she never quite got over in all the years we were to be together.

Adam was one of several stars I got to know through the Torquay theatres. I became particularly good friends with Ken Dodd, then not only the most popular comedian on the circuit but also high in the charts with his record 'Love Is Like a Violin'. Despite the wealth that came with his fame, however, he was one of the meanest people I had ever met. Many people have a fear of ending up penniless but Ken took his financial insecurity to a neurotic degree. I discovered just how mean he was after accepting his offer of a lift north to visit Jan. Ken always drove home to Liverpool after his Saturday-night show and returned on the Monday afternoon. He suggested I join him and catch a train from Liverpool to Sheffield. On the weekend I took him up on the offer, he decided to go to an after-show party thrown by one of the chorus girls and it was 3am when we finally set off. I was asleep when he stopped off at a petrol station. But he shook me awake to tell me, 'I've just filled up with fuel and it cost £4, so your half is £2.' This time the comic wasn't joking and I paid up without a murmur but I never forgot the incident.

Many years later Ken's obsession with money (he kept huge

piles of cash in suitcases under the bed) almost landed him in prison when he was put on trial for tax evasion. Bearing in mind that his shows usually over-ran by an hour, I wrote a piece for the newspaper I was working on at the time saying the speculation was that he would get four years but do six. The judge was not amused and censured me in open court for predicting the outcome of the case. As it happened, the jury returned a verdict of 'not guilty'.

Another pal I made in Torquay at that time was a man called Vincent Waring, who had bought a small local cinema called the Empire. He was a thin, pasty-faced Londoner who always wore black suits and ties and looked more like a Victorian undertaker than a dispenser of entertainment. Vincent had no time for those who sought to impose authority. Ignoring petitions from the neighbours and rumblings of disapproval from the Town Hall, he had boosted the Empire's takings by showing French and Italian films featuring plenty of nudity – a definite no-no in Torquay at that time. He was required to pay the distributors a share of the takings but, when the time came to distribute the cash, he would post a note with a blank cheque to the movie distributors in Wardour Street, London, saying, 'I'm ashamed to tell you how little your film took last week. Make the cheque out for whatever your conscience allows.' They rarely took more than a fiver despite the roaring trade he was doing.

Seated on a couple of cushions, I'd learned to drive my brother's first car at the age of 14 and driving became one of my earliest obsessions. Aware of this and 'always anxious to please the press', Vincent Waring would occasionally loan me his run-down Ford Anglia when a job required posher transportation than the Vespa. One Saturday I had to cover the local wedding of two members of a popular singing group called the Mudlarks. Vincent offered me the use of his car and

I gratefully accepted but that morning I overslept and had to run to the Empire (later renamed the Binama when he introduced bingo) to collect the vehicle. When I got there, the sight that met my eyes was horrifying. Ever the enterprising entrepreneur, Vincent had covered all but the Anglia's windscreen and driver's side window with posters for a forthcoming soft-porn movie. I was now desperately late for the job and I had no choice but to take the motor. When I eventually got to the church there was nowhere to park the car but directly outside the main entrance. Few of those present will forget the sight that met the bride and groom as, to the accompaniment of the Wedding March, they walked out of the church to face waiting photographers... and a car plastered with posters proclaiming that *Une Nuit Excitante* was coming to the Empire.

That was an early schooling in how to make the most of free publicity.

Newton Abbot was an attractive English market town but the novelty of covering fetes, funerals, parish council meetings, court proceedings and inquests began to pale. As boredom got the better of me, I dreamed up ways to reduce it. When the proceedings of a parish council began to irk one evening, I told the chairman that it would not be possible to do justice to the proceedings unless they were brought to a close early, because the lights on my scooter had failed and I would have to leave before dusk. Mortified at the prospect of missing out on name-checks in the local bible, he and his fellow councillors hurried forward their votes on planning permission for a garage extension to a cottage and the granting of £15 to fund a traffic island, in order to fit in with my deadline. I was beginning to learn how to manipulate people in authority.

By now I was selling gossip items to the *New Musical*

Express, then the most influential weekly paper for rock fans. I loved the paper and was mightily impressed when I heard that its owner, Maurice Kinn, was such a powerful figure in the music business that, when he threw a party at his apartment in Knightsbridge, not even the biggest stars dared turn down an invitation. So when Don Wedge, the *NME*'s news editor, called to ask if I would be interested in a job as his assistant, I didn't hesitate, but took practically the next train to London where Don offered me the post. Then I was taken into the presence of the great man himself. Mr Kinn, as everybody was required to address him, was a distinguished-looking man with a splendid mane of wavy silver hair. He would decide the rate for the job. My weekly pay at the *Mid Devon Times* had risen dramatically in three years from £2 to £9, largely thanks to the NUJ negotiating a national minimum wage. Mr Kinn offered £18 and was not expecting any debate. But Vincent Waring had told me that whatever I was offered I should ask for part of it to be paid in non-taxable expenses. My prospective new boss was flabbergasted but agreed that two of the eighteen pounds would be for 'taxis'.

Back in Devon, two people were furious when I told them about the new job: my mother and AG Angel. Mum had hysterics at the prospect of her last child leaving home. After several devastating rows we reached a compromise: I would visit her once a month and return to live in Torquay after three years. Needless to say, I never had any intention of keeping the latter part of the bargain. The normally mild-mannered AG was appalled that I was breaking my indentures and fired off an uncharacteristically catty parting shot. He'd correctly assessed that Jan was essentially a provincial girl whose modest ambitions did not extended beyond being the wife of a small-town reporter. 'I'll tell you one thing,' he said. 'If you move to London, you can forget all about marrying that girl from Sheffield.'

But it was Vincent Waring's words that chimed most with the way I was feeling: 'You've got to get out of this wretched little town and away from these small-minded people who peer through net curtains. But, most of all, you've got to get away from that horrible mother of yours.'

Chapter Two

MUSIC AND MAYHEM

The offices of the *NME* were in Denmark Street, London's Tin Pan Alley. What Fleet Street once was to newspapers, Denmark Street remains to music publishers to this day. Barely a hundred yards long, it runs into the northern end of Charing Cross Road; most people walking up Charing Cross Road would be impressed by the scale of Foyle's bookshop on the left but few would notice the little turning on the right just after it. Yet this row of tall, narrow buildings, each the width of a small corner-shop grocers, housed the men who represented the world's greatest composers – the music publishers. In those days, they were almost exclusively Jewish. At lunchtime, those who could afford it would cross Charing Cross Road and walk deep into Soho to lunch at Isow's, a kosher restaurant where the most important customers had their names stamped in gold on the backs of high-backed, red leather chairs. Those not in that league were obliged to settle for a cafe ran by a fearsome woman with a foul temper. It was a dirty little place and diners ran a real risk of leaving with a sick belly, but the portions were cheap and generous. Cross the owner, as I once did, by complaining that there was more than one of her hairs in your meat, then – like me – you would be banished for life, exiled to the nearby Lyons Corner House and eating the blandest of the bland.

The editorial and advertising offices of the *NME* were halfway along Denmark Street above a musical instrument shop at no 23. The furniture was all second-hand, and cheap partition walls divided the rooms into cubicle-sized offices. The reception desk was manned by a formidable blonde called Sheila, whose many petty powers included control of the key to the lavatory half a landing up. If you wanted to use the loo or needed a fresh toilet roll, you had to be nice to Sheila.

To a 20-year-old from Devon, the atmosphere was, to say the least, intimidating. But the *NME* was the hippest paper around and, within days of my arrival, I became known – not very imaginatively, I thought – as 'the hick from the sticks'. Mike Hellicar, a senior features writer, was particularly cutting. On one occasion he opened my jacket to examine the label and declared, 'Old man, we don't wear Burton suits at the *NME*.' I had a different problem with Don Wedge. He was the most anally retentive man I had ever met, and was ever likely to meet. One of my tasks was to go through the newspapers and clip out the showbusiness stories. This would leave behind piles of newsprint, shredded to ribbons. If I screwed these up and stuffed them in the bin, Don's anal streak would go into overdrive. Without uttering a word he'd get up, skirt the desk and retrieve the newspaper from the bin. Then he would spread it out, smooth it flat, fold it and put it back into the bin like a freshly ironed shirt. Walking back to his seat he would fix me with a cold stare before getting on with his tedious work. He also had rules about which sort of papers should be stapled together and which should be attached with pins or paperclips. As if that wasn't enough, he came from Wolverhampton (no offence!) and had a particularly grating Midlands accent.

I had taken lodgings above the garage of a house on Peterborough Road, Parson's Green, seven or eight miles to the south west of my new workplace. The landlady, Mrs Butcher, charged me £2 a week for the dingy room with just a bed, a wardrobe and a gas ring on the floor. She forbade visitors, so when Jan – now a cashier with the Yorkshire Bank – came down from Sheffield to spend the occasional weekend with me, we had to creep in under cover of dark, remain desperately silent and carefully gauge visits to the loo to avoid encountering Mrs B on the landing.

On a poor diet and with no heating, I seemed to have a constant cold in that first miserable year, but the visits from my fiancée were always happy occasions and the naughtiness of our situation seemed to intensify the pleasure. We'd spend our evenings strolling along the King's Road through Chelsea and marvelling at the things people could buy in the designer shops if they had the money. Dinner would be a Wimpy (hamburger) and then it was back to 52 Peterborough Road. Mr and Mrs Rowland were assured that Mrs Butcher had a guest room which their daughter occupied on these occasions, but, even if she had, my budget would never have stretched to renting it. When the train pulled out from St Pancras Station to take her home to Sheffield on those Sunday evenings, she'd be weepy-eyed and say, 'Don't watch me go' but I would run alongside the train until she was out of sight. It was like a scene from *Brief Encounter*. Looking back, those were the halcyon days of our relationship.

Meanwhile, in Denmark Street my fledgling career as a rock

writer had run into a serious problem. I was finding it almost impossible to develop music-business sources – a vital step if I was to be anything other than Don Wedge's dogsbody for the next several years. At the *NME*, contacts were carved up on a roster system. If I spoke to Adam Faith – now a chum – I would get a roasting from Mike Hellicar. If I tried to contact Cliff Richard, I would get a bollocking from Derek Johnson and so on. The result was that my weekly information-gathering calls were to relative unknowns. (Though it has to be said, I could have worked a bit harder with David Jones, who did later find modest success as David Bowie.)

American artists, however, were a different matter. The paper's writers were only assigned to them when they were in the UK. Riding in to work one morning on the top of a 22 bus, it occurred to me that I might be able to establish a stable of my own contacts on the other side of the Atlantic, simply by working the phones. And why not start with the biggest of them all – Elvis Presley? Unlike my colleagues, I was always desperately short of cash, no proper home to call my own or much of a social life in this unfamiliar city. So why not stay in the warm office and try to reach Elvis's manager, the legendary 'Colonel' Tom Parker?

Parker always worked out of a suite of offices provided by whichever Hollywood studio Elvis was filming at. At that time it was Paramount, so at eight o'clock one evening – when everyone else had gone home – I put in a call to Paramount. It was lunchtime in LA, and I grew quite excited when a polite switchboard operator put me through to Parker's offices. There, however, I got a very different reception from the member of his elite staff (always male) who took my call. When I told him I was a writer calling from the *NME* in London, he told me firmly, 'The Colonel doesn't take calls from the press' and hung up.

I tried again the next night. And the next. It was, my diary recalls, on the 39th attempt that my luck changed. Again it was 8pm in London – 12 noon in California and the Presley management team were on their way to lunch. Parker was the last to leave the suite and picked up the ringing telephone. Recognising his voice from a much-played old radio interview, I told him I was calling from London and asked if I could have a few words from him for the *NME*. I didn't know it then but Parker was a notoriously mean man and his immediate reaction was to ask, 'From London? Is your call paid?' When I assured him it was, he said, 'Go ahead. What d'ya wanna know?'

We spoke for ten or 15 minutes, during which he interrupted me several times to tell me that it was the first interview he'd ever given to a British paper. Not that he told me much at that stage – it was mostly a piece of hype involving the unlikely story of how, when he heard that the producers of a forthcoming film, *Kissing Cousins*, wanted Elvis to play two roles (one with blond hair and one with dark hair), he had demanded they pay double the normal fee.

When the article appeared, I sent him a copy and to my surprise he wrote back, saying he liked the piece. Perhaps, on reflection, this wasn't so surprising, since I'd taken great care to make it as fawning as possible. Flattery obviously worked with Colonel Parker and we struck up a telephone relationship. I took to calling him once a week, often just for a chat. Mentor number two had arrived.

My other break came in the form of the promoter Don Arden. He and Maurice Kinn disliked each other intensely, so none of the established *NME* writers was particularly keen on dealing with him and he was handed over to me as the office junior. Arden was known as the man who handled the most troublesome artists – stars such as Jerry Lee Lewis,

Little Richard, Gene Vincent and Chuck Berry, and he had a reputation as something of a hard man. But, as two relative outsiders, we hit it off immediately. It was through Arden that I met the man who was to become one of my closest friends, Henri Henriod, known back then as 'king of the roadies', who worked for him. I was sitting in on a Brenda Lee rehearsal at the run-down Metropolitan Theatre on Edgware Road, when a grand piano began to roll downstage towards the orchestra pit. Two people rushed forward to stop it toppling over the edge: one was Henri, the other was me.

It was Henri, the son of a Swiss chef but with the accent of a Cockney barrow boy, who taught me to fear no one. As someone who had been brought up to touch his cap in deference to schoolmasters I met in the street, I found Henri a refreshing new influence on my life. No authority figure was safe when Henri was around. Over the years, I saw him make mincemeat of everyone from stage doorkeepers and policemen to council officials and even unco-operative theatre owners. He was not a huge man but he had all the physical confidence of the fairground boxer and wrestler that he had once been.

Henri drove Don Arden's powder-blue Studebaker around Britain, ferrying Gene Vincent to his gigs, and I took to travelling with them whenever I could escape the ties of Denmark Street. In the back clutching his daily ration (never less than a full bottle) of Jack Daniels invariably sat the man born Gene Vincent Craddock who wrote and recorded many international hits – none greater than 'Be Bop A Lula'. 'Not too fast, Henri,' he'd whine. 'Tyres are as bald as a baby's ass.' But Henri always drove fast because Gene Vincent was always late and always drunk. It was my first close encounter with alcoholism and I saw it on a daily basis wrecking the life and career of an enormously engaging entertainer. Drink was his obsession and he lived for it. At that time it held no interest for me and, however hard I tried to explain it to him, Gene could never understand why. The man who once loved rock 'n' roll had sold out entirely to John Barleycorn.

One autumn day in 1963, Henri drove Arden, Little Richard and me to a cinema in Doncaster for the opening night of Richard's British tour. It had always promised to be a controversial evening as the man known for pounding out songs like 'Rip It Up' and 'The Girl Can't Help It' had long forsaken rock music to become a preacher. When I had met him at Heathrow three days earlier and asked whether he was going to perform his old rock 'n' roll numbers, he'd replied, 'God would strike me down dead if I ever sang rock and roll again.' It was unclear, but most unlikely, whether the Little Richard fanatics in Doncaster were aware of this.

On the night, the excitement in the auditorium was almost tangible. Apart from Little Richard, the bill included Sam Cooke and Jet Harris, a recently departed member of Cliff Richard's group The Shadows, making his solo debut. The crowd was well warmed up by the time the main attraction, dressed all in white and – would you believe – clutching a Bible stepped on stage. To the total bewilderment of his audience, 'The Rev' Little Richard's opening number was a spiritual and, when this was followed by a second hymn, even his most die-hard fans became restless. The sound of foot stamping gradually swelled and more and more joined in a repeated chant of 'We want rock 'n' roll!' Richard turned to his keyboard player Billy Preston and told him to stop playing while he addressed what he clearly saw as his congregation, 'You don't understand, chill'en. I only sing the Good Lord's songs these days.' This pleased no one and the chant became a roar. He tried once more to placate the rockers crowded into the auditorium but again without success. Just as it looked as if a riot would break out, he flung his Bible to the floor and with a shout of 'Oh, what the hell' started belting out 'Long Tall Sally'. It seemed the roof would take off. It was a milestone night in rock 'n' roll history and the miracle that promoter Arden had been praying for. He'd installed his band, Sounds Incorporated – who knew Little Richard's act – on stage behind him ('just to dress the stage', he'd persuaded Richard in the car on the way up). The legend was back, and to the best of my knowledge God still hasn't struck him down.

By this time I was going to Arden's house on Angel Road in Brixton on Saturdays to earn some extra money typing provincial press releases for him. Occasionally, he'd ask me to stay on and baby-sit for his daughter Sharon – who later married Ozzy Osbourne and became a cult star through *The Osbournes* television show – and his son David. When Arden decided he was going to take his feud with Maurice Kinn one step further, I was the obvious choice to enlist – a Trojan horse, so to speak.

Despite their poor relations, Arden couldn't help admiring what Maurice had done with the *NME*. He had bought it ten years earlier when it was selling 10,000 copies a week and turned it into the publishing success story of the decade. By the time I joined it, the circulation had soared to more than 250,000 and climbing. Arden's plan was to capitalise on the popular-music explosion by setting up a rival title he hoped would topple the *NME*. I was to be its editor. For a 21-year-old cub reporter living in digs and cutting up the morning papers, it was a golden opportunity for career advancement.

Using the experience I'd gained producing *Lenny's Fanfare*, I set about finding printers, ordering estimates, planning layouts and working out which of my *NME* colleagues I might poach. Excited about the venture, I confided the detail of it to Jimmy Savile as we sat in his Rolls-Royce on Shaftesbury Avenue after returning to London from a late-night gig. What I didn't know then was that the disc jockey was a good friend of Maurice. When I got into work the next morning, I was told by a secretary to 'report immediately to Mr Kinn's office'. There, stern-faced, the boss asked me whether I had been talking to Don Arden about setting up a rival publication and, when I admitted I had, he gave me ten minutes to clear my desk and leave the building. I was never to darken his doorstep again – or so he thought...

Fifteen minutes later, with the aforementioned contents of my desk crammed into the same shabby hold-all in which I had brought all my worldly possessions up from Torquay, I was in a phone box on Trafalgar Square making a desperate call to Arden. I'd been fired, I told him, and was therefore available to start work early on the new title. The bottom fell out of my world when he told me he'd changed his mind and wasn't going to launch a paper after all. I was gutted. Stranded, almost penniless, on one of the great squares of what had suddenly become a hostile city, I took in the gravity of the situation. I couldn't afford to stay in London without a job and there was no chance of AG taking me back on the *Mid Devon Times*.

Then I had a brainwave. I called Gerald Marks, the editor of *DISC* (the *NME*'s main competitor), told him I was on the market and that I came complete with every phone number of every major artist and agent accumulated by the *NME*'s staff over the years. Almost without hesitation, Gerald offered me a job at £4 a week more than the *NME* had been paying me. What's more, he told me to take a fortnight's holiday before I started. I called Arden back with the news and, as I had two weeks to kill, he suggested I go to Hamburg with Little Richard, who was booked to appear at the Star Club. Arden promised to cover my expenses but he clearly wasn't in a mood to splash out. While Richard stayed at the smart Atlantic Hotel, I was put up in a two-star boarding house on the notorious Grosse Freiheit.

When we arrived at the club on the first night of Little Richard's two-week stint, his support act was already on stage and going down a storm with the German audience. It was a little-known British group from Liverpool called... the Beatles. Once off stage, all four members of the band turned up at Richard's dressing-room door to introduce themselves. Deferential at first, their native irreverence soon surfaced and, within minutes, they were being lairy. Clearly, they were worth getting to know. I got on best with John Lennon, who told me how outrageous you could be in Hamburg. He said he would pee from his bedroom window on to the heads of nuns heading for church on the street below. No wonder Richard later described him as 'the Devil's own child'.

EMI had just put out the Beatles' first single, 'Love Me Do', which had managed to scrape into the *NME* chart at no 19, but their Star Club fee did not reflect even that modest success and they were operating on a tight budget. I went with John when he played at strip clubs between sets to earn extra cash which he would post home each Friday to his wife Cynthia and their baby son Julian. Needless to say, when they discovered that Arden was paying Richard's bills, the Beatles would turn up at his dressing room each night just as he was ordering dinner. He would say to the waitress, 'I'll have a steak', and John would jump in and say, 'Make that five steaks.' Aware that I had a certain responsibility to Arden for Richard's spending during the engagement, I began to fret about the rising bills. John spotted the problem and handed me a pill. ''Ere, get that down yer gob.' The result was instant euphoria. Sod the bills, Arden could afford them.

After the club closed one night, Richard invited Ringo and me to supper back at the Atlantic with him and Billy Preston. Naive in the extreme, neither I nor Ringo had given any thought to the fact that both Americans were gay. Dinner turned out to be a plate of curled-up sandwiches in Richard's suite and he spent most of the time trying to talk the Beatle and me into getting into bed with him and Billy. Still a religious man, he even resorted to reading us some highly selective passages from the Bible that he claimed justified his approach. Happily, Ringo and I managed to repel boarders for a couple of hours before making our escape. As we walked back to our digs, Ringo said, 'What are you writing about him for anyway? You should be writing about us. Our manager, Brian Epstein, says we're going to be bigger than Elvis.'

During the week and a half I was in Hamburg, I spent a lot of time in the group's company, and was the grateful recipient of more and more of the pills John dispensed – their drug of choice at that time – a powerful stimulant called Dexedrine. Up to then I had only dabbled with the milder Purple Hearts, supplied to me, bizarrely enough, by my mother. She was prescribed them as slimming pills but they also acted as uppers and, when I complained that I found it hard staying awake on my late-night drives back to London after spending the obligatory monthly weekend with her in Torquay, she suggested I try one. I was hooked from the feel-good effect of the very first one and called Mum the next day to ask her to get me some more. She did and in so doing became, I suppose, my first drug dealer. The Beatles' 'Dexies', however, were twice as strong as Mum's slimming pills and, more remarkable still, helped to make me an equal member in the John Lennon Debating Society. Talk? On Dexies you couldn't stop.

There was a moment of light relief during my visit to Germany (my first trip abroad, incidentally): I went to a US Air Force base to see a pal of mine, the musician Laurie Jay. Always a rocker, he had been talked into playing drums in a band playing country music, which he hated. The band included the then 13-year-old Elkie Brooks, who had to wear pigtails and a straw boater for her act. I knew the gig had the kiss of death for Laurie and his fellow musos when I noticed the audience was made up almost entirely of black faces – certainly not lovers of the Dixie music they were about to hear. They listened in silence to the band's version of 'Orange Blossom Special' and the silence continued for at least one highly embarrassing minute after the number finished. Then a single voice called out in a low drawl, 'GET – OFF.' Laurie and the band did not need telling twice.

The next act was the 'blind' singer Gerry Brereton. The audience erupted when he was led on stage wearing dark glasses, a St Dunstan's badge on his blazer and a white stick clutched in his hand. Song after song, rendered in his rich tenor tones, was met with raucous applause. Finally, he all but brought the house down with his emotionally charged version of 'You'll Never Walk Alone'. There was hardly a dry eye in the house when, amidst a standing ovation he left, not by the wings, but by stepping into and striding through the still-applauding audience, sending drink-laden tables flying as he made his way to an exit at the back.

'That was some show Gerry put on,' I said to Laurie later.

'Not as good as the one he did in the loo,' my friend replied. 'He walked in, threw the stick down, took off the dark glasses turned to me and said, 'Hi, Laurie, good to see you again.'

One of my earliest introductions to the tricks of the showbusiness trade.

The short-term consequence of my budding friendship with the Beatles was an almost immediate upturn in the fortunes of *DISC*. Word spread quickly among their fans that if you wanted to get news of the band first – and that often meant getting concert tickets before they sold out – you had to buy that paper. To the delight of its publisher, Hulton Press, *DISC*'s circulation soared – a fact that did not go unnoticed back in Denmark Street, where Maurice Kinn fretted at the new-found success of a rival he had never considered of any consequence.

One morning I got a call from Percy Dickens, Maurice's advertising manager, close friend and, on occasions such as this, his emissary. 'I'm sure if you called Mr Kinn he would be pleased to discuss re-employing you,' Percy said.

'Oh, I don't think he would,' I said, mindful of the acrimonious nature of my dismissal a year earlier.

An agitated Percy called back several times that day to ask why I had not contacted Maurice but that only made me more aware he had the boss himself hovering in the background. Eventually, frustrated by my refusal to take the bait, the big banana himself picked up the phone and invited me to tea at the famous party apartment in Lowndes Square, SW1. Aware that I held all the cards, I drove a hard bargain. I wanted Don Wedge's job and double my former salary. Thanks to my new friends, the Fab Four, I got both and within days was on my way back to the paper I had been planning to topple.

When time permitted, I still travelled to gigs with the great American rockers Arden brought in and Henri somehow kept on the road. He usually managed to get them there on time and – in Gene Vincent's case especially – just about sober enough to go on stage. Henri's skills were tested to the limit one night in north London when Little Richard and Jerry Lee

Lewis – headlining the same bill – argued about who should close the show. Henri appeared to have resolved it when he quietened the raised voices of the competing piano-players by saying he would toss a coin for the coveted spot. Richard won the toss and was exuberant: 'Nobody follows me. I am unfollowable,' he declared. Jerry Lee went on before him and gave a barnstorming performance. What none of us knew was that, prior to his act, he had poured lighter fuel into the grand piano and, as he left the stage with the fans screaming for more, he tossed a match into the piano which instantly became a mass of flame.

Lewis glared at a shocked Richard waiting in the wings to go on and, in his inimitable southern drawl, called out, 'Follow that, black man.'

Chapter Three

MARRIAGE V BEATLEMANIA

A measure of my much-improved status when I returned to the *NME* was the freedom Maurice Kinn gave me to create an imposing new office for myself. Builders were called in to demolish a wall, converting two rooms into one, and a cabinet-maker was hired to make a huge table that would accommodate the entire editorial staff for my weekly editorial conferences. Self will run riot or not, it was going to work. Less than two years earlier, I had been the junior member of the team but now, at the age of 22, I was going to run it. This did not make life easy for the men who had been my peers but I was in no mood to be conciliatory. If it helped to make a point, then I was going to bang what soon became known as the Hutchins table and, fuelled by mother's little helpers, I pounded that table frequently. If someone deserved the kind of bollocking I'd once been given there, they got it in spades.

The editor, a mild-mannered Canadian called Andy Gray, was philosophical about the virtual hijacking of his paper.

43

He had prospered under Maurice because the proprietor was a powerful and domineering man whom it had suited to have a compliant editor. Through the success of *DISC*, Maurice had seen the value of my close relationship with the Beatles and, by now, their manager Brian Epstein too. Indeed, it seemed to generate an excitement in him. For once, *he* was being introduced to the biggest act of the day, rather than the other way round. It was me who had to haul the new stars along to Lowndes Square for his parties. It has to be said, however, that, while I was happy standing round the grand piano with such friends of his as Vera Lynn, Russ Conway, Alma Cogan and Lionel Bart, John, Paul, George and Ringo found the showbusiness protocol an utter bore and often let me know it.

Meanwhile, my change of status was also reflected in my lifestyle. Aware that Mrs Butcher's wrath might be as menacing as my mother's, I did a moonlight flit from Parson's Green and moved into a flat in King's House, which faced the most fashionable chunk of Chelsea from its windows on the King's Road. My landlady was an out-of-work actress who each morning served me breakfast (part of the deal for the princely sum of five guineas a week) wearing sunglasses to shield her eyes and then promptly went back to bed to nurse her eternal hangover. Next I went to the Beatles' tailor Dougie Millings and ordered half a dozen suits. (Deep down, I had always known that Hellicar was right about that Burton number.) And it wasn't long before I'd bought my first car, a Wolseley saloon, which I drove to work and parked behind Maurice's Rolls so that his obliging chauffeur could keep an eye on it.

Free now from all restrictions, I set about expanding my range of contacts. Don Arden – who was also going up in the world and had by now moved into offices in Soho –

introduced me to his new publicist, with the promise, 'He's brilliant – he'll make everybody sit up.' His name was Andrew Loog Oldham and he was just 19. Given the job of publicising Arden's Jerry Lee Lewis tour, Andrew sent out a press release saying, 'Come on, you Teds, get your blades out. Come and see Jerry Lee and, when he sings 'Great Balls of Fire', get to work on those seats.' Not surprisingly, Arden had to field an angry call from Johnny Hamp, controller of Granada Theatres, who threatened to cancel all his dates on the tour unless the press release was withdrawn.

Oldham did not hang around Arden for long. Soon afterwards he went to see a promising new band at the Crawdaddy pub in Richmond and instantly recognised that they could be as big as the Beatles. Within days, he had become not only their manager but also the band's record producer. Within months, they had had their first hit. It's a tribute to Andrew's judgement that, after one unsuccessful attempt to get them into matching hounds-tooth-patterned jackets, he allowed the Rolling Stones to be themselves. Brian Epstein had convinced the Beatles they would get nowhere without neat haircuts and smart stage suits and that left the Stones a clear run at being the bad boys of rock. During one late-night booze and Dexies session, I remember Lennon bemoaning, 'They've stolen our image. That's what we should look like.'

Appearances, however, can be deceptive. I sussed Mick Jagger out to be a snob from the start and, although the job required me to hang around them professionally and I saw much of Brian Jones socially, I never took to the Stones as I did to the four from Liverpool.

My relationship with Arden did not long survive my return to the *NME*. He probably felt that he could no longer confide in me now I was back working with his old enemy – Maurice.

Things came to a head late in the early hours of one morning when I was having drinks with Sounds Incorporated – the band he had subsidised and hoped to turn into hit-makers – in the lounge of the Royal Garden Hotel behind Kensington Palace. They were down in the dumps and going on about the slow progress they were making when the night porter came in to say there was a telephone call for me at his desk. It was a ruse to separate me from the group and in the lobby I was grabbed by a huge and very ugly-looking man who propelled me to a car waiting outside with the engine running. My captor turned out to be a man called Peter Grant, who later discovered Led Zeppelin (and, even later, how to consume inordinate quantities of cocaine) but was then a part-time minicab driver as well as working for Arden. This oversized and intimidating man drove me – protesting all the way, needless to say – to the Arden house in Brixton. There I was shoved into the same room where, in happier times, I had baby-sat for his kids David and Sharon (what a scene this would have made for *The Osbournes*).

The Crewe-born promoter who had adopted a strange sort of Anglo-American accent was beside himself with rage and I was scared witless. 'What are you doing with Sounds? Are they leaving me after all the money I've put into them? Are you involved?' he ranted.

The more I protested my innocence, the worse his temper got. I don't remember exactly what he threatened but I can still recall the air of menace and at one stage I wondered whether I would ever leave Angel Road in one piece.

The ordeal had started around two in the morning and it was almost five when, to my relief, Arden ordered Grant to drive me home. Maurice was furious when he heard about that night's events. He instructed the *NME*'s lawyer, a kindly man called Michael Balin who was to figure on both sides of the fence in later stages of my life, to frighten Arden off with threats of charges being pressed if anything like it ever happened again to a member of his staff. It worked. He duly received a meek apology from the Al Capone of rock.

The night of 18 April 1963 turned out to be especially memorable for more reasons than one. That was the day the Beatles' British tour opened in style at no less a venue than the Royal Albert Hall and it has gone down in pop-music history as the official start of Beatlemania. The crowd waiting outside after the concerts was so vast that the huge police presence was all but overwhelmed and it was some time before the Fab Four could be escorted safely to their waiting limousine. It was clear that they could not go to any of their usual haunts that night: places such as the Ad Lib were already surrounded by fans desperate for a glimpse of them. As luck would have it, my landlady and her hangover were away so we headed for my flat. There were eight of us in all: John, Paul, George and Ringo, the singer Shane Fenton – later better known as Alvin Stardust – his girlfriend Susan, the actress Jane Asher and me.

When we reached King's House around midnight, it dawned on me that I wasn't geared up to host a party. The result was that we sat in a circle passing round the only drink I had, a couple of bottles of wine, which we drank from the neck. Four of the others (guess which four!) had brought their Dexies and my own supply (prescribed by a shady doctor in nearby Pimlico) soon disappeared from the bathroom cupboard. John, who could be waspish at the best of times, was in lethal mood without the required amount of alcohol to dampen the effect of the uppers. 'Go on, love,' he said, turning to Jane Asher. 'Tell us how girls play with themselves. We know what we do, tell us what you do.'

The demure actress, who, years later, was to open a cake shop nearby, was cruelly embarrassed. Paul mounted his best charm offensive and quickly poured oil on troubled waters, putting a consoling arm around the flame-haired girl to whom he had previously paid only scant attention. The agony of that awful moment was pivotal in cementing a relationship between them and subsequently, of course, Jane almost became Mrs McCartney.

As well as getting to know Messrs Lennon, McCartney, Harrison and Starr, I began to see a lot socially of Brian Epstein. He had the charm as well as the tenacity of a great manager but he was totally without experience. Brian – or Eppie, as he was known to his band – had come across the Beatles when he was running the record department of NEMS, his parents' department store in Liverpool, and he had been on a steep learning curve ever since. Just as I had milked him for the stories that had brought me success, he started drawing on my contacts. The *NME* had a hotline to everyone who was anyone in the business and I was more than happy to help him meet producers, promoters, agents, lawyers and even other managers. He learned the hard way not to let me down. An agent I had introduced to him, Cyril Berlin, called me in tears one day to say that Brian had abruptly cancelled a Beatles tour of Australia and New Zealand that he had spent weeks arranging. Furious, I called Epstein on his private line. It was my turn to rant. 'You can't do this. If you behave in this way you'll be back in Liverpool in five minutes.'

Shortly afterwards, Cyril got a call from Brian telling him the tour was back on. Brian understood the importance of good relations with the *NME*. No other paper held as much sway with record buyers and concertgoers and he knew better than to alienate it.

But underpinning our relationship was a genuine friendship. I enjoyed his company enormously and the feeling seemed to be mutual, even though he was gay and he knew I was straight. We met once a week for dinner, usually at Overton's, a renowned fish restaurant in St James's. There was a ritual to the evening: having ordered everything from caviar to sea bass, Brian would then get out the little silver box he always carried and produce half a dozen Purple Hearts, which we would share. These may have lifted our spirits but they also destroyed our appetites and all too often the food went back to the kitchen untouched. After dinner, we might go to see one of his acts. His success with the Beatles had attracted other artists and by now his stable included Gerry and the Pacemakers, Billy J Kramer and Cilla Black, who, he admitted, he did not particularly like 'especially when she isn't getting her own way and gives me that Jack Palance look'. If none of them was working that night, we'd go back to his mews flat on the other side of Lowndes Square from Maurice's. There – high as kites – we'd listen over and over again to the latest recordings the producer George Martin had made with his acts.

On one notable occasion, he invited me to lunch at Le Caprice. His choice of venue (then London's most fashionable and expensive restaurant) indicated that he had something important to say and he didn't take long to get to the point: would I like to be the Beatles' press agent? John, Paul, George and Ringo, he emphasised, had suggested he approach me. It was not an unattractive proposal but I was convinced that working for the *NME* was the right way forward; it offered access to top people right across the business. Turning down Brian's offer did not affect my relationship with the Beatles and, in January 1964, I went with them to Paris where I witnessed a poignant exchange between their music publisher

Dick James and Paul McCartney. On the first night everyone had partied heavily and Paul and I were the only ones up and about when Dick arrived at their suite at the George V Hotel the next morning. Dick, once a singer himself and the voice on the theme tune of the *Robin Hood* television series, was making his first real fortune from Beatles' songs but he was a mercenary man and keen to add to his repertoire. When he asked Paul whether he had written any new songs, Paul said, 'Yes, listen to this,' and walked over to the upright piano they had had installed. After playing a few chords, he began singing, 'Yesterday, all my troubles seemed so far away...' A few seconds passed in silence after he had finished the song, then Dick smiled and said, 'Nice, nice, but have you got anything with 'yeah, yeah, yeah' in it?' Never had I seen Paul look so dejected.

A few days later two things happened. I received not one but two postcards (addressed to 'Crispy Hutch') from the Beatles – still in Paris, and an elated Brian called to reveal that 'the boys', as he called them, had been booked to appear on America's number-one television programme, *The Ed Sullivan Show*. The Beatles had yet to make it on the other side of the Atlantic and this was the big break they had been waiting for. *The Ed Sullivan Show* had an audience of 80 million and a slot on it guaranteed overnight fame.

There was pandemonium when the band arrived at New York's JFK Airport early in February. Thousands of screaming fans were waiting to greet them and the scale of the reception ensured that the arrival of the Beatles dominated that night's news bulletins and the following morning's front pages. Maurice was so impressed by the phenomenon that he booked me on the next flight to New York to cover the Beatles' historic visit. So keen was he to make sure I caught the plane, he picked me up from King's House in his Rolls and drove me to the airport. On the way he said, 'We've got to get behind that band even more now. They sell papers. You've got to work non-stop and wring every word you can out of them.'

Oh dear, this was the moment I had to tell him, 'Maurice, Jan and I are getting married next month. I'll need two weeks off for the honeymoon.' Then, to my everlasting shame, I heard myself add, 'But I'll put it off if you'd like.'

'Not at all,' Maurice replied. 'I'm very happy to hear it. I hope you're going to invite Berenice and I.'

The scene outside the Plaza Hotel where the Fab Four were staying was one of pandemonium. Crush barriers held back screaming fans who maintained a 24-hour vigil on the opposite side of the street throughout the Beatles' stay in the city. Cops refused to allow anyone through who couldn't prove they were either a resident or a guest at the Plaza. 'I'm with the Beatles,' I said, but, before allowing me past, the cop did what every cop I spoke to thereafter did: he asked me to get their autographs for his kids.

From the window of their suite on the 12th floor, John marvelled at the scale of the welcome but he clearly thought this was how New Yorkers greeted all pop stars. None of us realised then that this had never happened before in the history of celebrity adulation. Not even Elvis attracted this sort of hysteria.

Nevertheless, things were not quite what they seemed. I learned later that America's frenzied welcome for the Beatles had been carefully contrived. Capitol Records (who had initially resisted putting out their records until EMI played a contractual card) had put in an enormous effort behind the scenes to create the 'spontaneous' welcome. Large sums of money and enormous resources had been applied to the campaign. A New York disc jockey, Murray 'the K' Kaufman, had been persuaded to go on the air repeatedly imploring listeners to go to the airport and greet the British group whose records he played incessantly. It worked beyond Capitol's wildest dreams and Murray the K was rewarded with unprecedented access to John, George, Paul and Ringo, but without his part in the campaign few might have wanted the access. Some years later when I tried to discuss the hype with John, he was embarrassed and told me to 'drop it'. It was the first in a long line of lessons I was to receive (and subsequently to give) on how fan mania can be created but how those who benefit from such artificial stimulation are loath to admit it once the real thing comes along.

Elvis was never far from my mind all the time I was on American soil. Having cemented relations with what had become the biggest group on the globe, the world's most famous solo artist was the next target. Cynical though it may sound now, it occurred to me that I could use the Beatles as bait to attract Elvis. When I mooted the idea of introducing them to The King, John, Paul, George and Ringo were all enthusiastic. He was, after all, their hero – the rocker who had inspired them as teenagers. From their suite I put in a call to Colonel Parker 3,000 miles away on the other side of the country.

The Colonel, being the Colonel, first wanted to talk business. He asked how much Brian had negotiated for the Beatles' appearance on *The Ed Sullivan Show*.

'$10,000,' I replied.

'I knew that, I was just checking,' Parker said, before adding, 'I got $50,000 for Elvis back in '56.' When I got down to business and proposed a meeting between Elvis and the Beatles, he said more by way of observation than enquiry, 'You know those guys pretty well, huh?' But it was clear that he still felt there was something of a gulf in status between his client, who had been a megastar for eight years, and the new kids on the block.

After recording three spots for Ed Sullivan, the circus moved to Washington, where the Beatles were to perform their first US concert at the Coliseum. I watched the show from the back of the auditorium standing alongside Brian. In front of us a policeman put a bullet in each ear to muffle the noise when the band took the stage. A photographer snapped the three of us and, when I got back to Heathrow a week later, Jan produced a copy of *Newsweek* and I was surprised to see the picture on its cover. I knew that would not do me any favours with the powerful American agents from GAC who by now had become Eppie's jealous protectors and had themselves posed for formal photographs with him. Ah well.

The Washington gig and two concerts at the Carnegie Hall in New York fulfilled, the Beatles' next stop was Miami. At the reception desk of the Deauville Hotel, the road managers Neil Aspinall and Mal Evans (who some years later was shot dead by the LAPD) and I were obliged to wait while two old ladies argued with a desk clerk over the room rate of $60 a night. Finally, after checking in, we found ourselves sharing a lift with them. I turned to Mal and Neil and said, 'Isn't that amazing? Rooms with an ocean view for $15 a night. What a bargain.'

I heard one of the women turn to the other and hiss, 'Did you hear what he said? Let's go back down and sort that clerk out.'

Neil shook his head in disbelief. 'You're behaving more like Henri Henriod every day,' he said (the Beatles and their roadies knew Henri well).

Was I? It certainly made me realise that I had changed, but

was it for the better? 'Come on,' I said to lighten the mood, 'let's have some fun' and I set about hiring a Cadillac convertible for the three of us to drive down to Miami South Beach. Alas, the electric roof got stuck halfway through its raise-and-drop cycle and we drove the entire afternoon with it protruding six feet above the car. But what the hell: this had to be better than hanging round our respective Torquay and Liverpool council estates hoping for a ride on the ice-cream van.

Six weeks after we all returned from the US, on 21 March 1964 – 20 years and one day after her birth – Jan and I were married at St Paul's Church, Arbourthorne, Sheffield. It was the first day of spring and she looked stunning in her wedding dress and carrying a simple bouquet of her favourite flowers – freesias. Maurice and Berenice arrived late in the white Rolls bringing Norman Newell, the highly successful (and very camp) record producer and songwriter who temporarily brought proceedings to a halt by falling flat on his face at the entrance to the church. Brian Epstein was to have been my best man but a week before the wedding the *Sheffield Star* ran a story on its front page under the headline, 'BEATLES' CHIEF BRIAN EPSTEIN WILL ATTEND CITY WEDDING'. Fearing that his presence would cause a mini outbreak of Beatlemania, Brian had pulled out at the last minute and my brother Phil stepped into the breach. Among the telegrams he read out at the reception for 40 friends and family at a local hotel was one from Brian and another from the Beatles. Jan and I were extremely happy but, with straight-laced, working-class Sheffield coming into contact with Swinging London (not to mention my mother, who wore an expression resembling a volcano about to erupt), there was bound to be a culture clash. There were no formal speeches but at one point Norman stood up and declared, 'Well, she got him before I did.' At this I heard one guest, wearing his cloth cap at the table, say, 'Our Jan's not marrying a poof, is she?' No, I assured him, she wasn't.

We spent the first evening of our honeymoon at the Aerial Hotel close to Heathrow Airport from where we were flying the next day to Ibiza. That night Brian telephoned the hotel, full of apologies 'for disturbing Mr and Mrs Hutchins on their first night as man and wife' but he wanted to place some stories about the Beatles' plans before I departed. It was an omen and not a good one.

Once in Ibiza, I was far from being the ideal bridegroom. Almost from the moment we touched down in the Balearics, I was straining at the leash to get back to London, acutely aware of the excitement I was missing back home. Ibiza in the early 1960s was not the lotus-eating destination it is today, and March was certainly not the month to go there. Each morning I would call reception and ask to be put through to the airport in a bid to get us on the next flight home. Each time I was put through to a man who would tell me the earliest available was on the date we were due to fly back anyway. Our hotel was run by two brothers and it took me some time to realise that, every time I called down to the desk, one brother was putting me through to the other rather than the airport. They were determined that the Hutchins should see out their booking. Looking back, I realise how utterly selfish of me this was. In those early years of marriage I spent little time at home, explaining to anyone who would listen that I was 'busy'. Alas, the truth is it was often more fun to be 'somewhere else'.

Back in London, Jan and I settled down to married life in a bedsit in Cranley Place, South Kensington, while we waited for a flat in Kew to become available. She got a job at the

Automobile Association's headquarters in Leicester Square as I became more and more involved in the music scene. We formed a close friendship with Mickie Most – the independent record producer responsible for hits by the Animals, the Nashville Teens, Donovan and Herman's Hermits – and his wife Chrissie. While Jan and I lived in a bedsit, Mickie was on his way to being a multi-millionaire with a Rolls-Royce in the garage and a 12-berth motor yacht moored on the Thames. Once we all travelled in the Roller to Torquay where the boat had been sent ahead. In view as we turned on to the sea front were the splendid Torbay hotel where we were staying (and where I had once served coffee), the Palm Court (where I'd flogged ice creams from a kiosk)... and the spot where Jan and I had first met. Magic.

Such excursions with the Mosts were a lot less traumatic than that of the boat's maiden voyage under Mickie's ownership. Despite his wealth, Mickie tended to do things on the cheap and he had hired a rather inept captain for his vessel. Along with Peter Grant (whom I still regarded with some suspicion), we set off from Sunbury-on-Thames intending to travel to the pirate radio ship Radio Caroline, anchored in the North Sea. The first day went smoothly enough as we sailed down the Thames to Charing Cross pier where we moored for the night. The following day we reached the Thames estuary, but it was late and the weather (this was winter) was bad and getting rapidly worse. At one point we were approached by a police launch and, using a loudhailer, an officer asked us where we were going. When Mickie replied that we were on our way to the radio ship, the policeman pointed to a tarpaulin bundle on their deck and said, 'There's two bodies under there which we've just hauled out of the sea. They weren't very good sailors either. We suggest you wait until conditions improve.'

It sounded like good advice and we found a sheltered spot to drop anchor for the night. But when Mickie's low-budget skipper let out the anchor, it was only to discover that he had failed to attach the non-business end to the boat, with the result that both anchor and chain were lost. Tied up alongside Southend Pier, we spent an uncomfortable night being tossed around in a boat that crashed so loudly against the pillars that we thought it was going to break up. Filled with fear, we talked about our past lives over mugs of cocoa. It gave Peter and I chance to discuss the night he'd kidnapped me for Don Arden and become good friends. The following day we sailed back up the Thames, mission abandoned but feeling like heroes who had been to sea for months.

Come August it was back to the States for the Beatles' first full-scale US tour. This meant a first-time visit to the west coast – Elvisland, John called it – for all of us. Shortly after arriving in San Francisco, Brian was handed a Western Union cable:

TO BRIAN EPSTEIN AND THE BEATLES STOP ON behalf of ELVIS AND MYSELF WELCOME TO THE USA STOP SINCERE GOOD WISHES FOR A SUCCESSFUL TOUR AND A WONDERFUL TRIP AND TO ALL YOUR ENGAGEMENTS STOP IF THERE IS ANY WAY I CAN BE OF SERVICE TO YOU AS A FRIEND DO NOT HESITATE TO CALL ON ME ALTHOUGH THERE IS NOT MUCH I CAN DO AS HAVE BEEN LAID UP WITH A BACK AILMENT STOP BUT MY EFFORTS MAY BE OF SOME HELP IF NEED BE STOP *GIVE MY BEST TO CHRIS HUTCHINS* AND IF YOU HAVE TIME GIVE ME A CALL WHEN YOU COME TO TOWN STOP SINCERELY THE COLONEL

I was flattered to have been remembered in the Elvis camp's first communication with the Beatles but sensed that they were vaguely put out that I should have been mentioned. The cable clearly meant a lot to them and clearly they didn't appreciate having to share the glory of it with a journalist and discarded it. Someone must have retrieved it from the bin, however, because sometime later it turned up in a Sotheby's auction of Beatles memorabilia. It was bought by the Hard Rock Cafe owner Isaac Tigrett (later to marry Ringo's first wife, Maureen) and is now displayed on a wall of the Hard Rock in Piccadilly, London.

From San Francisco the entourage moved to Las Vegas. There the band spent much of their time confined to the Sands Hotel, besieged by their fans. The worst time was mid-afternoon, when everyone was up and about but with nothing to do and nowhere to go. Every so often, someone would get past the cops outside and the security at the door by name-dropping. Once a bespectacled girl appeared in the doorway of their suite and announced, 'Hi, guys, I'm Donald O'Connor's daughter.' (O'Connor was a song and dance man who'd starred in some of Hollywood's most successful musicals.)

When John responded by saying, 'I'm sorry, love, I really am,' I knew he was up to something bad.

Confused, the girl asked, 'What do you mean, you're sorry?'

'Just heard it on the radio, about your dad's death.'

At this, she broke into hysterics and had to be sedated and taken away in an ambulance.

John was unrepentant. 'Soft cow, why the hell did she think we'd care who her father was? It's always, 'I'm the mayor's wife' or 'my brother knows the President'. Well, I'm a Beatle but I don't go round bragging about it.'

John – the man I tagged 'the Beatle that bit' – had by far the harshest tongue of all four but the viciousness of his reaction on this occasion can be partly explained by the cabin fever brought on by the relentless pursuit of their followers. One of the few occasions he did succeed in shaking off the fans long enough to get out on his own was the day we made an early-hours trip to the Desert Inn. The Inn was then home to the eccentric oil billionaire Howard Hughes. John had long been fascinated with Hughes, who had bought the hotel to live in after being refused permission to rent a floor. With the help of Irving – 'Oiving with an O' – Kandell (the Greek American who had the programme concession for the tour), I got John kitted out in a doorman's uniform, complete with braided cap, and we borrowed a caterer's van to drive him down the Strip from the Sands' trade exit. There was never any chance of him getting inside Hughes's lair but it seemed to be enough for John to be nearby. He stood at the roadside looking up at the hotel for several minutes, lost in his own private reverie, while Irving and I waited patiently in the van. It was ironic: here was John, a man trapped, as it were, in a bubble by his fame looking up at a man who could have all the freedom in the world but had chosen to be its most famous recluse.

In one of my regular calls to Maurice in London, I carelessly mentioned that Paul had had a fling with a girl at the previous venue. He did me no favours by writing in the *NME*'s Alley Cat gossip column, 'How sad: Paul McCartney left his tart in San Francisco.' The atmosphere froze when McCartney and I next came face-to-face. Having had a minor role in his getting together with Jane Asher that night at my flat, I may also have made a small contribution to their subsequent break-up. We had always got on well and had spent hours during the 13-hour flight to California playing cards. Now, it appeared, I had had my last warm conversation with the Beatle I'd dubbed 'the charmer'.

Next stop was Los Angeles and it was here that I hoped to finally meet the Colonel in person. I called him on the night of arrival and he promised to send a car to the Beverly Hillcrest Hotel to pick me up the next morning. He was as good as his word. At ten o'clock sharp a station wagon with the Colonel's assistant Tom Diskin at the wheel pulled up and I was driven via the famous Rodeo Drive to Parker's first-floor apartment in Westwood. And there was the man himself – stretched out on the orthopaedic bed of the 'hospital room' to which he had been confined for weeks by the back injury he had referred to in his telegram.

Here then was the man who, when I had first made contact with him, asked if my call was paid, taking care of business while a nurse fussed around him. He was a big man, who had put on considerable weight since the photographs I had seen of him taken in the days when he was touring the carnivals with his travelling Wild West show, *The Colonel's Exhibit*. Then he had cut a dash with his droopy moustache and full head of hair, but the man I saw before me had lost his handsome looks along with most of his hair.

He waved me to the bedside while he concluded a deal for the sale of half a million framed portraits of Elvis. Then he put down the phone and gave me a broad smile before proffering his hand to shake mine. This was the moment I discovered that Tom Parker had a way of inspecting you with unblinking eyes and I prayed that he could not detect evidence of the toll drink and drugs were beginning to take on me. Having always been a non-drinker, I had taken to the Beatles' favourite potion – brandy and coke to wash the Dexies down – and I still had to take Mandrax (Mandies) at night if I was to get any sleep. It was not good.

'How are you?' he said. 'How are the Beatles? Elvis wanted to meet 'em but he arranged ages ago to spend this break between filming in Memphis. He and the boys left a week ago.' He added some colourful detail about Elvis and his boys travelling to Tennessee in their bus, drinking coke and eating sandwiches on the way like Cliff Richard in *Summer Holiday*, but somehow I didn't believe him. The message I got was that Elvis had got out of town before a meteor called the Beatles hit it.

Before I could probe the matter further, a small, elderly woman appeared at the other side of the bed. 'Meet Mrs Parker,' said the Colonel. So this was Marie, the older woman Parker had encountered in Tampa, Florida in 1935 when she was manning the cigar stand at a carnival to feed herself and her ten-year-old son. I would have liked to ask her about their wedding since no evidence of a marriage had ever been found, but she did not share her husband's gregarious nature and, after asking him if he needed anything, vanished as suddenly as she had appeared.

'Hell, I'm going out,' he told the nurse who offered no resistance. 'I haven't been out of this place in two months. Come, I'll take you down to the office.'

Tom Diskin, waiting in an outer room, was ordered to fetch the car while the Colonel dressed. Before we left I phoned Brian, who invited the Colonel and I to have lunch with him at his hotel afterwards. That agreed, we left for Paramount Studios, with Parker marvelling at 'getting de-caged'.

The Parker suite at Paramount was a lesson in tackiness. The walls were covered in posters and photographs and an illuminated sign over the door plugged his latest film. But plugged it to whom? Practically no one was allowed in here except those on the pay roll or the movie-making payees themselves. Laid out on a table in a side room were six table lamps styled as Western wagons, six cowboy belts complete with holsters – four in plain leather, one in silver with rhinestones and the other in gold rhinestone – and six complete sets of all the Presley albums. 'These are for the Beatles, Brian and you,' he said. Picking up the silver rhinestone belt, he said, 'This one's yours. The guy who made all Roy Rogers's gear handmade this stuff specially for us to give to you guys.'

I examined the belt: it had been inscribed 'From Elvis and the Colonel'. I still have it and often wonder if John, Paul, George and Ringo kept theirs. This was the generous side of Thomas Andrew Parker.

The walls of his inner office were covered with photographs of well-known people from politicians to movie stars, many of them with Elvis and the Colonel. He pointed at one wall and announced, 'All these fellas have passed on. When someone dies, I move their picture here. I call it my dead wall.'

On his desk were four framed photographs of him and in each one he had his arm around an American president. No one could accuse this one-time carnival and circus hustler of failing to make his mark on America.

'Now let's go meet Mr Epstein,' he said. 'Maybe he'll get his picture on one of my walls.'

Meeting in the splendid foyer of the Beverly Hills Hotel, the two managers of the world's biggest rock stars made an incongruous duo. Despite the heat, Brian was, as ever, immaculately dressed in a suit, shirt and tie. If the Colonel, in ill-fitting sports shirt and slacks, was uncomfortable in these surroundings, he didn't show it. In the dining room over lunch he told the former English public schoolboy, 'I don't dress fancy but I guess we've got a lot in common otherwise.'

Having said that, he then engaged in a needle match with his rival over the matter of security. 'You don't have to protect the Beatles as we protected Elvis because with them there is no jealousy,' he began.

Brian swallowed nervously. Surely the American was aware that a few miles up the road the largest contingent of police ever assembled in connection with a showbusiness event was standing between the Beatles and thousands of girls who would have given their right arms, or whatever, for a few minutes in the company of any one of the four.

'Your problem is to protect the small fans from getting crushed. We never had them so little.' Now he was rubbing salt in the wound. 'When Elvis toured, angry boyfriends would throw missiles at him on stage. We never had to send the police to get them though – the girls always got 'em first.' Brian sought to change the subject by expressing surprise that the Colonel had never taken on any other artist. The answer rankled: 'Elvis has required every moment of my time and I think he would have suffered if I had signed anyone else... but I admire you for doing it.' It was a slap, rather like the telegram stars ritually sent each other on opening nights in Las Vegas: 'WITH TALENT WHO NEEDS LUCK? SO GOOD LUCK TONIGHT.'

Brian seemed relieved when the meal came to a speedy conclusion, at which Parker said, 'Now I have presents for you and the boys. Shall I deliver them in person?'

'Er, yes,' Brian responded. 'Why don't you go up to the house tomorrow? Chris has the address and I'm sure he'll go with you.'

The following afternoon I took Elvis's manager to the house on St Pierre Drive where the Beatles were staying. To my surprise, he had dressed up for the occasion. 'I put on a tie specially for these guys,' he said, as the car made its way through the Bel Air estate, making frequent stops for the LAPD to check our credentials – a note Brian had hastily scribbled with the code word 'cellar' contained in it. He needn't have bothered. John, Paul, George and Ringo had just finished lunch when we arrived at the house and the remains of their meal were still on the table when they invited Parker to join them round it. To my surprise Brian was there – by now casually dressed. John was still in his swimming trunks.

Looking increasingly uncomfortable in collar and tie, the Colonel began, 'Elvis phoned this morning to say he was sorry he couldn't be here but you're welcome to visit him at Graceland if you're in the area.'

Now it was Brian's turn to play top dog. 'I don't think our schedule will permit, Colonel. The boys are terribly busy.'

'Sorry about that,' added charmer Paul, as if to soften the blow.

Then, like a mid-summer Santa Claus, the Colonel began to distribute his presents from five large paper sacks. The albums, the table lamps and, of course, those belts from the man who made belts, holsters and saddles for the man who rode Trigger. Ringo, ever the entertainer, went into the house and re-emerged minutes later wearing his belt and a Stetson borrowed from the chef. Someone had produced a handful of toy guns and, as I wrote in the *NME* at the time:

> "Bang bang' said Paul on one note [sic] as he aimed his gun at the Colonel. Ringo ran around the table waving his shooting irons. John pointed his gun at his own head and said 'Bang.' George said: 'I wish we had real guns.' John just looked at him...'

It seemed absurdly childish at the time but it was the first thing that came into my mind on that awful morning I heard that John had been shot dead in New York and it sent a chill down my spine.

By now Jan had arrived in LA for a short holiday during a break in the tour. We were to have precious little time together and so she was not best pleased when the Colonel arrived at the Hillcrest each morning to whisk me off with him to the office where he insisted on teaching me about 'the Colonel's school of management'. Just like a student having private tutoring, he had me sit across the desk from him as he conducted his business. I listened to his phone calls and sat in on his meetings, gaining a valuable insight into the philosophy behind the way he operated. To give a journalist such an opportunity might seem strange for such a secretive man but for once he had an audience he felt he could trust – and an opportunity to show off.

The most important thing I learned that week was the importance of keeping the artist out of the reach of the press. In those days, journalists could, from time to time, get to Sinatra and Dylan but Parker would not let anyone near Presley. The result was that the star remained an enigma. The harder it was to get to him, the more journalists and fans tried. This had practical advantages for his manager too. If anyone wanted to do business with Elvis, they had to go via the Colonel.

He stressed the importance of being paid for any marketing done 'on your back'. For example, when he discovered that Elvis's record company, RCA, was promoting albums by other artists on an Elvis album sleeve he demanded (and got) $50,000 for the advertising space. 'Ever buy a new car and find that the dealership has put a sticker on the back window proclaiming where you got it from?' he asked in this context.

'Then tell 'em you'll carry their ad for $500 a month or have 'em remove it.'

He taught me how to court what might seem like negative publicity. For example, it was him – not, as legend has it, the TV network – who insisted that Elvis be filmed only from the waist up for his *Ed Sullivan Show* debut 'for the sake of public decency'. The subsequent publicity over the sexual potency of Elvis's gyrating pelvis proved it to have been a masterstroke. 'Light a fire and then be seen pretending to put it out,' he told me, 'and exploit every dime's worth of your client's value. When I first went on the road with Elvis I saw that only the girls bought 'I love Elvis' badges, so I had 'I hate Elvis' badges made for the boys and our badge sales doubled overnight.'

Inevitably, I was duped at one point myself. On the first day, we had lunch with his staff around a table in his office. When I had finished, he asked, 'How did you enjoy your desert rat?' I felt physically sick. Years later he admitted it had been quail. 'But I snowed you, didn't I?' he said. The Snowmen's League was a Parker creation and he was its potentate. 'You snow people and then melt away before they can find you.' It sounded as though conned would be a better word than snowed. 'It has a very exclusive membership,' he went on, 'including some former presidents.' He then pinned on me a gold-coloured medal engraved around the edge with the words 'COL TOM PARKER SNOW AWARD' and a snowman embossed on it and had my name typed on a card attached. I still have that, too.

He loved an audience when he was joshing with me so, when I asked him if it was true that Elvis paid him a 50 per cent commission, he called Tom Diskin into the room and asked me to repeat the question. Then he answered, 'You've got it wrong, my friend. You screwed up again. I pay *him* 50 per cent of everything we earn. I am dedicated to my work for my client. See this ring here?' he said, pointing to a ring on his signet finger engraved with the letters 'TCB'. 'Mr Presley gave me this ring. The letters stand for Taking Care of Business.' It seemed churlish to mention at this point that I heard Elvis gave all his friends a similar ring but engraved with 'TLC' for Tender Loving Care.

Parker was constantly boasting about the deals he had pulled off for 'Mr Presley'. But the most impressive episode that I witnessed involved him turning one away. A delegation of businessmen from New York, interested in signing Elvis up to endorse a range of their products, were waiting in the outer office when Tom Diskin came in to tell the Colonel that 'an old carnie hustler' had turned up and was asking to see him. Parker peered through the doorway, recognised the man and invited him in. The man said he had 500 balloons left from his latest tour and was willing to let the Colonel have them for $50. Parker appeared to think about it long and hard before making a counterbid of $20 and the two began to haggle. Diskin came in to say the New York contingent was growing impatient but Parker was not about to stop. The argument over the value of the balloons continued until Diskin interrupted again to say the visitors were now quite angry about being kept waiting. The Colonel instructed him to invite them into his office and they watched with amazement as he completed his deal for the balloons, eventually agreeing to pay $35. As the carnie hustler walked out, a broad smile on his face, the New Yorkers demanded to know why he had kept them waiting in order to negotiate a $35 deal when they had travelled thousands of miles to discuss contracts worth millions. 'I wanted to show you how I work,' the Colonel replied. 'I could have given him $50 from my back pocket but it would have looked like a handout. This way, the guy has gone away with some pride.' By now the high-handed approach of the men from the Big Apple had alienated Parker and he told them he didn't want to do business with them. When they said they would deal with Elvis direct, he said with weary confidence, 'OK, go find him.' Naturally, they never did.

After the city slickers had left, the Colonel had second thoughts about allowing me to witness the incident. 'Don't you write or tell anybody about that,' he said. 'People may hesitate to come and do business with me if they think the press are going to be there. You could say, though, that I told you the story.' I took the restriction to apply only to his lifetime.

Despite the time the Colonel had 'stolen' from our holiday, Jan liked what she saw and heard from him during a brief encounter. So we went to Bullocks on Wilshire Avenue to buy him a gift – a small silver vice which we had engraved 'The Colonel's only vice' (how naive that turned out to be). He had it on his desk in Las Vegas the last time I saw him alive.

Soon I was back on the road with the Beatles. A few days after the entourage left LA we were in Atlantic City and I received a message at the hotel to 'phone the Colonel'. I placed the call and he did something totally uncharacteristic: he gave me Elvis's phone number in Memphis and said, 'Have the Beatles call him.' What was going on, I wondered.

'What's going on?' was John's reaction too.

'Well, I'll speak to him,' Paul said, turning to me, 'if you'll get him on the line.'

This seemed too good to be true. I had Elvis Presley's telephone number and was about to call him. What would Mickey Witherington say?

At Graceland, 'Diamond' Joe Esposito, Elvis's tour manager by profession but more importantly his confidant, picked up the phone. 'We've been expecting your call,' he said. 'You got the Beatles there?' I told him I had Paul McCartney standing by to talk to Elvis, but could I have a word with him first? 'Sure' was the casual response. And then he was on the line: Elvis Presley, the man who held sway over more young people in the world than any other. 'You guys having fun?' was his opening line. 'It makes me kinda itch to get on a stage again.' I couldn't believe it: he was offering soundbites before I'd even asked a question. And so he went on, although whether he had got himself high for his first communication with the men who were threatening to steal his crown, I shall probably never know. He sounded taken aback when I asked him if he had any Beatles records. 'Man, I got every record they ever made. I'm looking at a copy of 'Hard Day's Night' right now and I've hired a copy of the film which we're going to show up here at the house tonight. That's how I pass most of my evenings – watching pictures privately… We have a lot of fun down here. Pity you all couldn't have made it down.'

And with that I passed the phone to Paul, who took up where I left off. 'I want to tell you that we all think it's a drag that we can't get down to Memphis to see you,' he began.

This was beginning to sound like a public-relations exercise, but having been set up by a journalist I suppose that's exactly what it was. The other three sat in silence as Elvis told Paul he'd bought a bass guitar to learn some of the Beatles' riffs and was getting calluses on his hand as a result. Paul told Elvis the Beatles had no intention of invading his territory – Hollywood – because they were happy to make films in Britain. There was more banter about managers and album sleeves before they promised to meet up some time in the future.

Putting the phone down, Paul told his fellow musicians, 'He's just like one of the lads.'

To which John responded, 'Well, that's a fuckin' disappointment.'

Back in Britain, Jan and I moved into our flat opposite Kew Gardens in Richmond, Surrey. For a while, things were relatively normal as we got on with our lives and separate jobs in London. Normal, that is, if you don't count socialising with some of the world's biggest stars and that often included dining and nightclubbing with John, Paul, George and Ringo. That part of it Jan definitely did not enjoy and, when I made an appearance on the live peak-hour BBC TV show, *Juke Box Jury*, she told me when I got home that she'd been watching ITV and had missed *JBJ*. It was a way of telling me that she was not impressed by the showbusiness side of my life and I was ultimately grateful to her for that.

There were a few people that she enjoyed meeting. One of my fellow *Juke Box Jury* panellists was the American star Roy Orbison, whose first hit 'Only the Lonely' I had played over and over on the juke box in a Torquay coffee bar and whose subsequent hit 'Pretty Woman' was to inspire a major Hollywood movie. I joined Roy for dinner the following week and Jan came too. She liked his wife Claudette (who was to die tragically in a motorcycle accident) and the four of us met up occasionally while the Orbisons took a flat in Victoria and lived in Britain for a while with their son Roy Dewayne.

I took Roy and Claudette to Twickenham Film Studios to watch the Beatles making their first movie. John was filming in the bath on the set when our little group arrived. 'Hey, Orbison,' he called out, 'bet you don't get six baths a day.'

'No,' replied the droll American, 'but I guess *I* don't need 'em.' It was a taste of the humour I was to enjoy during our association in later years.

If ever I envied the four Beatles their incredible popularity and rapidly growing riches, then it was brought home to me that there were times when John at least yearned for the normal domestic routine that was my life. 'You can go out walking with Jan and live a regular life. I bloody can't. We live in goldfish bowls and it looks as though it's going to be that way for ever,' he once complained. So when I got a cheery call from him one Saturday morning, inviting Jan and me down to the house he'd just bought at Weybridge in Surrey, I was prepared for a few surprises. We set out that afternoon. The location of the house was a surprise for a start – St George's Hill is very much in the 'stockbroker belt', although those who inhabit it like to think they live in the country.

Surprise number two was John's garb. He was wearing a green corduroy suit – not at all the uniform of a rock star but, he explained, 'It's what people round here seem to wear and I suppose I ought to make an effort to fit in.' From one goldfish bowl to another, I thought. The next surprise was his fascination for the domestic arrangements. He proudly showed off the kitchen he'd had installed. It was *very* St George's Hill with a cooker set in an island in the centre of the room under a giant extractor hood and would have made a talked-about feature for *Ideal Home*. 'And what d'ya think of that dining suite?' he asked. 'Those chairs are 300 years old. I thought it'd be a laugh for people to eat off that old table sitting on those old chairs.'

I made all the right admiring noises but it wasn't very rock 'n' roll and I didn't expect a rebel like John to take such an interest in home-making. I thought that in reality he was uncomfortable really but pretending to like it for the sake of his wife Cynthia.

This was not a rock 'n' roll occasion. I've read most of the 'heavy' interviews that John gave to such publications as

Rolling Stone and *Playboy*, but this was just the plain ordinary man talking about domestic life – getting his record player fixed because it was 'burned out', buying a Rolls-Royce although he had no inclination to learn to drive ('Paul's got this new Aston Martin in dark blue with black leather interior – says he touched 140 going up to Liverpool in it the other day'), wondering what he could buy George Harrison for Christmas and showing off Julian's bedroom which he'd painted red himself.

I thought of the red bedroom that night as we sat around nite lights set in red tumblers at the Ad Lib, a penthouse club off Leicester Square, drinking Mateus Rose with the composer Lionel Bart and the singer Alma Cogan (a mother figure with whom John was to fall in love). I had driven John, Cyn and Jan into town in the Jaguar bought with the proceeds of a Beatles column I ghosted for the American magazine *16*. John seemed oblivious as they played the Beatles hits, but he got up and danced with Cyn to Len Barry's ubiquitous hit of the day, '1-2-3'. Then he came back to the table and, without any clue that it was coming, launched into the following strange exchange:

'How did your dad die?' he asked.

'He topped himself.'

'Wish mine would.'

His father Freddie Lennon, who had walked out on John and his mother when he was a small boy, had emerged from the woodwork and was proving to be something of a pest. The acid Beatle was back again – not the man proudly showing off his kitchen or the decor of his son's bedroom.

Chapter Four

THE MAN IN THE CORNER IS ELVIS

I did not see Colonel Parker again until August 1965 when I arrived in Los Angeles with the Beatles on their second full-length US tour. Then he and I drifted into the same routine as we had had the previous summer. He would call at the hotel each morning – always wearing a short-sleeve beach shirt, slacks and a white panama hat and clutching a cane topped with a silver elephant's head – and, with Tom Diskin at the wheel of the station wagon, he would take me to his office at Paramount Studios. By now I was growing impatient and nagged him incessantly. 'When can I meet Elvis?' I'd ask over and over again, and each time he would reply wearily, 'How many times have I gotta tell you? Mr Presley don't talk to the press. No exceptions.'

Then one day we were walking to lunch at the studio restaurant complex when he said he had to make a slight detour to drop off some papers. Like all studios, the Paramount lot is a curious amalgam of vast sound stages, office buildings and idiosyncratic houses where writers and directors work and stars rest between shoots. We stopped at one of these and the Colonel motioned me to take a seat as he went to see someone upstairs. As I had stepped out of brilliant sunshine into a dimly lit room, it took me a few moments to get accustomed to the gloom. When I did, I became aware that I was not alone and almost immediately I realised that the figure sitting just a few feet away from me was... Elvis Presley. I was, after all, an exception.

Ever the courteous man, Elvis, wearing a green bolero shirt with puffed sleeves and tight black slacks and shiny black boots studded in silver, stood up to shake hands. Given the scale of the build-up to this moment, it was probably inevitable that I would fluff my lines and I suspect that most of what I came out with was drivel, but I remember well his opening gambit. 'You're the guy travelling with the Beatles I talked to on the phone last year. I hear you want me to meet 'em.' So nervous at the prospect of him saying 'no', I simply nodded my reply. 'What are they like? What's Lennon like?' Clearly curious about the four who had taken the world by such storm, he said he had had his girlfriend drive by their rented house to assess the situation. 'She said there were a heck of a lot of fans outside,' he added. I wasn't sure whether he thought that was good or bad.

'What you really want is a story for your newspaper,' he said, breaking into a broad grin. Then he was serious again, wanting to know more about John. 'I hear he's a fag. Is that right?'

'No,' I replied, explaining that the story emanated from an incident I witnessed when John stepped outside his motel room during a stop on the previous tour and asked the cop standing guard if he could get him some fags. 'He meant cigarettes,' I told Elvis. 'That's what we call them in England.'

He shook his head. 'English sure is a weird language.'

We talked about this, that and nothing for several more minutes. He seemed very tall and very thin, and his hair was dyed very black. But the shock of the meeting had dimmed my powers of concentration.

Then, as suddenly as he had vanished up the stairs, the Colonel came back down them and, without a word to Elvis, said to me, 'Come on, let's go get that lunch.' As we walked outside, I was keen to thank him for setting up such a memorable meeting but he was having none of it. Staring straight ahead, his teeth clenched on a cigar, he said woodenly, 'Mr Presley? I didn't see no Mr Presley.' It must have been hard for him to break his life-long rule of keeping Elvis and journalists apart and he was clearly not keen to even admit that he had done so.

There were more insights into his character when we reached the restaurant complex. Lunching rights on a Hollywood studio lot are so Byzantine and arbitrary that they make the British class system look elementary and democratic. At Paramount you passed through a cafeteria, then through a dining room which had waitress service but fairly functional decor. Finally – if you were a producer, a director, a star or Colonel Parker – you slid into the opulence of a splendid oak-panelled restaurant.

As we made our way through the self-service area, I was greeted by Suzanna Leigh, an English actress who was playing the female lead in the film Elvis was then making, *Paradise, Hawaiian Style*. She had paid me only scant attention at a gathering the previous evening, but Suzanna was no slouch when faced with a potential opportunity and, seeing me with the Colonel, she seemed to have swiftly revised her estimation of my usefulness. 'Hi there!' she called out. But, as I paused to respond to her cheery greeting, the

Colonel kept on walking, so, after making my excuses to the actress, I ran to catch up with him.

'Who was that?' he asked.

'Who was that?' I said, mystified by his ignorance. 'That's Elvis's co-star in the movie, isn't it?' Without so much as a glance in my direction he said, 'Well, you see where she's eatin'.'

I had my second meeting with Elvis that same afternoon. The Colonel took me to the sound stage where he was filming to have my photograph taken with him. And waiting with Elvis when we got there was... Suzanna Leigh, who the Colonel had included in the picture, explaining to me later, 'Well, you made such a fuss over her at lunchtime. Besides, if that photograph gets published in the English papers as I suspect it will, it might do her some good.' Beneath his remark I detected a sense of guilt about how he had behaved towards her in the restaurant. So even Colonel Parker had a conscience.

Now it was his turn to make a request. 'Elvis says he'd like to meet the Beatles. Can you set up a meeting between me and Brian?' You bet I could.

Once again the three of us had lunch at the Beverly Hills Hotel, but this time Parker was boxed into a corner. Elvis had said he wanted to meet the Beatles so the Colonel had no bargaining power. Nevertheless, he continued to fence over the summit's location. Brian argued that, since the Beatles were now the hottest act in the world, Elvis should go to them. The Colonel was having none of that. It was all done very politely over the salmon mousse, for both men were acutely aware that what was being proposed was a piece of music history. It was Parker, perhaps unsurprisingly, who came up with the winning line: 'Mr Epstein [he never once called him Brian to his face], if we were in your country you would be the hosts but this is our country so we will be the hosts.' Brian graciously conceded the point, and I went with him to tell the band we were going to call on Elvis at his home three days later.

On the evening of Friday, 27 August, the bar of the Beverly Hillcrest was swarming with journalists desperate to find something to write about the Beatles. I was drinking alone (and this time it was plain Coca-Cola), knowing that within a couple of hours I was going to witness one of the great moments in rock history but determined to keep the scoop to myself. My shrewdest competitor was Don Short, a reporter from the *Daily Mirror*. Porky, as Don was known, was a chubby, prematurely balding man with a great sense of fun. He detached himself from a group further down the bar and came to join me.

'I've spoken to Brian,' he said conspiratorially. 'Something's going on. He wouldn't tell me what. It's Elvis, isn't it? Elvis meeting the Beatles?'

'Brian's in New York,' I said. 'Anyway, why ask me? If I knew anything like that, I wouldn't be sitting here, would I?'

But Porky refused to be put off and eventually I admitted that the meeting was to take place that night and that I was going to be there.

'Just give me the address,' he said. 'I'll make my own way and take my chances.'

I levered myself off the bar stool, took out my pen, scribbled an address on the back of my bar bill and handed it to him. 'Pick up the tab,' I said. 'If anyone asks, I've gone to the movies.'

The meeting had been fixed for 10pm at Elvis's rented mansion on Perugia Way. The arrangement was that Tom Diskin, the Colonel and I would meet Brian – who was flying in from New York – at the airport. We would then drive to Benedict Canyon to collect the Beatles and their roadies Neil Aspinall and Mal Evans. It soon became clear that the Colonel was determined to milk as much drama from the situation as possible and, after collecting Brian, we switched cars on Sunset Boulevard, exchanging the station wagon for a white stretch limo. Once we got to Benedict Canyon, we changed cars again. This time we piled into a black limousine with one of Elvis's Memphis mafia at the wheel. The Beatles followed in another limo driven by their amiable British chauffeur, Alf Bicknell. The Colonel seemed keen to shake off any unauthorised pursuers but, as the entourage had a police escort at all times, quite what the limo-switching achieved remains a mystery. As we turned on to Sunset Boulevard, heading towards Beverly Hills, police cars blocked the traffic in order to give the convoy a head start on any pursuing pack and shortly before ten o'clock we pulled into the driveway of Elvis's house.

The ten of us filed through a door off the entrance hall that led into a sunken sitting room. Elvis and Priscilla were sitting in the centre of a horseshoe-shaped couch, he in a red shirt and black jerkin with a sweeping wing collar, and she, a petite young woman, in a figure-hugging sequinned mini-dress and with hair dyed as black as Elvis's. We were all very impressed. To us, this was the epitome of high glamour.

I reckon both sides were probably nervous, but even though he was on home ground Elvis seemed the most twitchy man in the room. The meeting was highly contrived for a start. The only thing Elvis and the Beatles had in common was their status as global pop idols. They came from different countries and had very different backgrounds. Elvis was a former tank sergeant who was a strong supporter of the Vietnam War, while the Beatles were art-school types who, equally vehemently, opposed it. Without my pushing, I realised, the five might never have met. Later I conceded that might have been better for all concerned.

In what I can only assume was an attempt to break the ice, John put on an Inspector Clouseau accent and said, 'Oh, zere you are.'

At this, Elvis looked confused but smiled hesitantly as he shook hands with the Beatle he had been most curious about. After everyone had been introduced – a lengthy process as Elvis had eight sidekicks of his own in attendance – the legend returned to the couch, where he sat with John and Paul on one side and George and Ringo on the other. What followed was two hours of extremely stilted chat. The ground rules for the meeting dictated no cameras on either side and I was banned from producing the notebook in my pocket but I made what notes I could by making regular visits to the loo and feverishly writing down everything I could remember. These visits became so obviously frequent that at one point Elvis remarked, 'Somethin' wrong with your bladder?'

Initially, there wasn't much dialogue to report. When the track playing on the juke box came to an end there was an uncomfortable silence. It was clear this was not going to be a meeting of minds. Then they did what musicians do best – they took refuge in music. Electric guitars were produced for Elvis, John and George and a white piano for Paul. Elvis apologised to Ringo for the absence of a drum kit but he was happy to shoot pool with a detachment of the Memphis mafia.

And I had something to one day tell my grandchildren and, of course, a great scoop for the *NME*. Porky Short never did get anywhere near the house on Perugia Way, due in no small part to the fact that the address I had written on the back of my drinks bill was that of a strip club in downtown Hollywood, which I'd read off a card left by the bar payphone. Fortunately, Porky saw the funny side and later told me he had enjoyed several drinks at the house of ill-repute while I sat in Elvis's den with five of the most famous people in the world.

Having effected this titanic – if anti-climactic – introduction, the rest of my time in LA was fairly uneventful – apart, that is, for a visit chez Beatles by Jayne Mansfield. Paul, George and Ringo had gone to the Whisky-A-Go-Go on the night the bustiest star in Hollywood came calling, so she was left to the tender mercies of John Lennon and myself. The first thing she said after walking in with a boyfriend was 'Only two Beatles left around here?' The arrival of yet another interloper was always calculated to irritate John, but, by confusing me for a member of the band, she had made things even worse for herself.

She asked for a cocktail and I went into the kitchen to make her one, pouring slugs of gin, vodka and whatever liqueurs were to hand before topping the abominable concoction up with red wine. John, who had followed me into the kitchen, had an even worse idea. Seizing the goblet from my hands, he poured a third of the contents down the sink, unzipped his flies and urinated into the glass, exclaiming, 'Here's a little liquid Lennon for the lady.' When we took it out to Jayne she drank it without any obvious displeasure. John's dark side satisfied, the evening might have gone smoothly if the boyfriend hadn't thrown down some Tarot cards and predicted an awful end for 'somebody in the room'. That was enough for John: he ordered them out.

With Jayne out of the way, John suggested we join the others at the Whisky-A-Go-Go. After struggling through the crowd outside the club, we forced our way in and found their table. The place was heaving and everyone was trying to get close enough to catch a glimpse of the Beatles but, even before our drinks had arrived, John and I heard a now familiar voice: 'Hi, fancy seeing you guys here.' It was Ms Mansfield again. This time she had a photographer with her and, ever the great self-publicist, was determined to get a picture of herself with the Beatles. But the photographer's snapping irritated George and he threw his scotch and coke over him. In the melee that followed, John pulled Jayne towards him and broke the news that he'd peed in her drink. We didn't stay long enough to take in her reaction.

The Beatles' West Coast dates complete, they headed back to New York for their greatest ever concert, a 55,600-seat sell-out engagement at Shea Stadium. Andrew Oldham, Mick Jagger and Keith Richards planned to sail up the Hudson to the stadium on the *Princess*, a yacht belonging to their American business manager, tycoon Allen Klein. Andrew invited me and the American singer Brian Hyland to join them. At the outset, we all had photographs taken by a teenage girl who flirted outrageously with the Stones. A bit of a groupie, one couldn't help but think. The observation turned out to be correct. The girl's name was Linda Eastman, a self-confessed admirer of pop stars. Indeed, she went on to marry one – Paul McCartney.

Once under way, I called the Beatles on the ship-to-shore telephone and each of the Stones present – Brian Jones wasn't there – took it in turns to have a chat with George Harrison. We learned later that a couple of thousand other vessels within radio range listened in to the call and it was even picked up by a local radio station and broadcast. Then, as we lazed in the hot August sunshine, I took what Oldham pointed out to me was a rare chance to interview Jagger. 'I don't envy the Beatles,' he began. 'Look how much freedom we've got and they're locked up in their hotel bedrooms without even being able to go out for a drive, let alone do something like this.'

But, if I ever had any fears that Jagger was going soft, they were soon allayed when I overheard him ask Klein how they could expel Brian Jones from the band. 'He's just not one of us,' Mick was saying. 'He thinks he's the leader and he's not even one of us. He's a pain in the arse and we want him out.' (Four years later, Mick got his way. Early in June 1969, Brian was expelled from the Stones.)

Once moored at Flushing Bay, we made the short trip to the stadium via the artists' entrance. 'It's the famous Stones,' John told an irate cop who'd failed to recognise the next big thing. 'They're the same as the Beatles, only wilder.' I could tell by the big grin which crossed his face that Mick liked that.

Back in London, my enthusiasm for working at the *NME* was on the wane. I wanted to be a record producer and make lots of money like Mickie Most. I had already produced a few records on the quiet, including one for Lonnie Donegan, which would have enraged Maurice if he'd ever found out – you couldn't be on both sides of the fence, he would say. When I finally summoned up the courage to tell him I was going to leave the paper, his reaction came as a surprise. Instead of being angry, as AG Angel had been when I quit the *Mid Devon Times*, he was both understanding and helpful as only a mentor (yes, he had long since joined the growing list) could be.

Maurice advised me to go into public relations rather than record production, on the basis that I had virtually no experience of the technical side of the music business but knew an awful lot about the promotional side of it. He even offered to help me to procure some clients. I could see the wisdom of his argument but I was only interested if I could put the specialist knowledge I had acquired to good use. 'I'll do as you suggest,' I said, 'if I can get one very special client...'

Chapter Five

ME AND MR JONES

Armed with all I had learned from Colonel Parker, I went in search of my own Elvis. It didn't take long to find him. Tom Jones had everything: a great voice, the sort of sexual magnetism that made otherwise sensible women want to remove their knickers and throw them at him, and a worldwide hit already under his belt. But he was desperately in need of an image-maker. He came across in the media more like the hod-carrier he used to be than the star he was swiftly becoming. He was photographed for magazines wearing an apron and doing the washing-up alongside his wife Linda in the kitchen of their modest house in Manygate Lane, Shepperton. I knew what the Colonel would have said about that.

His manager was a fellow Welshman, Gordon Mills, who had given up his job as a bus driver to come to London to join the Morton Fraser Harmonica Gang. He was a talented composer – he had, after all, written Tom's first smash hit, 'It's Not Unusual' – and he had a supremely tough attitude to business. But he had little idea of how to project a star. Though I'd never met him, I knew he had a reputation for arrogance and I would have to tread carefully.

One morning, I called Gordon from the *NME* and said I'd heard he was looking for a publicist for Tom – a lie, as it happened, but I had to find a way to make him approach me. When he said, 'No, I'm not but why do you ask?' I apologised for bothering him and hung up. When he called back moments later, I knew he was hooked. I made him ask the question again several times before giving him his answer. I'd asked, I explained, because I was thinking of setting up a PR company and would like Tom as a client. 'I think I could do a lot to accelerate what you have already achieved with him,' I said.

He took the bait. 'Meet me at the Ivy for lunch tomorrow,' he said.

Keen to observe Mills arrive, I was early for our date the following day at the fashionable restaurant in Covent Garden. After all, this was a man I would need to work closely with, probably for years to come. I saw him step in from the street wearing a cashmere overcoat that reeked of new money. He removed it at the desk to reveal an immaculate three-piece suit, smart shirt and tie. A handsome man, he had baby-blue eyes, a fine head of wavy hair and a proud stance. This was a man who was clearly absorbed by his appearance. In that, he easily outshone the fellow he had, to my surprise, brought with him: Tom Jones. Tom wore no tie and had the air of a man who had been called from his bed too early. This was going to be interesting.

Over a lunch carefully picked from the most expensive items on an expensive menu, it was Gordon – razor sharp and never losing eye contact – who asked all the questions. Who else was I going to represent? How much would my services cost them? And – the easy one – how did I see Tom's image? The answers must have been right, for over liqueurs and cigars we struck a deal. My move into PR had been decided. Alas, it was not one that Jan was happy with.

I liked Tom Jones from the start. He was straightforward, easy-going and had a great sense of humour. He liked what I had to say about Colonel Parker's handling of Presley and seemed flattered that I felt he could be an equally big superstar. I also noticed that he seemed a little nervous of his manager – but then so was Elvis of his. Maurice generously let me out of my contract with the *NME* and, as a bonus, procured me two more clients from his friend, the agent and impresario Harold Davison. They were the Small Faces (previously known as The Faces when Rod Stewart was with them) and the singing duo Paul and Barry Ryan, who were Harold's stepsons.

But Tom Jones had to have priority. My first step was to cancel every interview Gordon had set up for him – and there were plenty since he was now riding high in the charts with 'The Green Green Grass of Home' – and to make journalists aware that meetings with him would be at a premium in future. Although his voice was far superior to Presley's, he was neither as tall nor as handsome. What's more, he had had a botched nose job. If anyone needed a photographer who had a grasp of light and shade, it was Tom. In an effort to keep things in the family, all his photographs were taken by Grace, the sister of Gordon's wife, Jo. They were nice enough snaps but they did nothing to enhance their subject, so I brought in the man I regarded as the world's best star photographer, Terry O'Neill.

Terry has an uncanny ability to bring out in his subjects what others call dignity, but which I saw as fear. I came to realise that, while Terry was one of the most charming men I've ever met, he also carried an aura of tension that made even his most famous sitters vaguely uneasy. They could sense that he was not a man to be messed with. The result was that all his portraits – whether of Tom, Elizabeth Taylor, Paul Newman or Faye Dunaway – had a distinctive style. I had met him first when he came to photograph Tom for the *Daily Sketch*. All three of us hit it off from the start and Terry was to be a close friend for the next 25 years.

As part of the early campaign, I started planting stories with a bit of spin in them. Newspapers were told that, following his chart success (by now 'The Green Green Grass of Home' had given him his second no 1), Tom had become Britain's highest-paid star. The effect was immediate. His agent Colin Berlin said that club owners anxious to book him were offering double what they had paid before. When Gordon and Colin secured a modest fee for him to sing at the Flamingo Hotel in Las Vegas, I called a press conference and announced that he was getting a million dollars for the engagement even though the true sum was a fraction of that. The contract he was holding in the photographs that appeared in all the following day's papers was actually an agreement for the Moody Blues to appear at the California Ballroom in Dunstable for £120. I had no qualms about pulling such strokes at that time. Everyone was in collusion. More sceptical journalists might have asked to see the contract but they knew that their editors liked a nice round figure in a headline and, if that was what we were claiming, they weren't about to scrutinise it too closely.

Gordon and Tom both seemed pleased with the early success of the campaign and the fact that we were all kids from the provinces who were now making waves in the capital gave us something in common. I knew I had been accepted socially by the two of them when I was invited to join their weekly curry night at an Indian restaurant in

Hammersmith (provided I took my turn to pay, of course). Soon I had graduated to Tom's playmate, something that did not go down too well at home – clubbing with a pop star was taking precedence over my marriage and I failed to spot the damage it was doing. We would begin our nights out with cocktails at Trader Vic's in the basement of the Hilton on Park Lane before moving on to the Westbury Hotel for dinner. Then it was on to Tramp, the nightclub operated in St James's by Johnny Gold. Knowing he would have had too much to drink to drive home, Tom would usually take the precaution of checking into the Westbury over dinner and return later to stay the night. At that stage, I would go home but, since we seldom left the club until the cleaners' lights went on, I'd often not return much before dawn.

With our first child on the way, Jan was not best pleased by my increasingly nocturnal lifestyle. And it wasn't only the nights. On Sundays, when he was playing concerts in far-flung resorts like Blackpool and Great Yarmouth, Tom would pick me up from home in his Mercedes sports to go with him. He was invariably late and he only knew one speed to travel at – the fastest the car would go. But we laughed a lot on those journeys; a deep throaty laugh went with his fabulous sense of humour. I considered him a good and considerate pal. Although a member of his band, the Squires, was later to accuse him of being 'mean' for selling him his second-hand suits, I did not find him so. Knowing how much I enjoyed the open-top Mercedes, he never thought twice about regularly lending me the car. We would go away together for boozing breaks at the Bibury Court, a hotel in the Cotswolds which I had found specially for such occasions. When I bought and was developing Bryn Bach, a beautiful house in north Wales, he would travel there with me and, as a former bricklayer ('and the bricks loved it'), give his views on the construction. Bob Tizzard, the builder, hated it when Tom was critical of his work but got his own back when he and his daughter Jill thrashed Tom and his son Mark at late-night darts sessions at the White Lion Hotel in Bala, where we stayed while work on Bryn Bach went ahead. Once, after an early-morning visit to the building site some miles away, I returned to Bala's high street to see a queue in the street outside the hotel. It snaked its way up the staircase to Tom's room where the bleary-eyed singer, clad only in a bathrobe, was signing autographs in his doorway.

In those days he was insecure about his entry into a social order he had not been born to and would politely ask about the way to behave in certain places and situations. On reflection it was odd that a kid from a Torquay council estate was demonstrating social graces to a man with all the security of knowing that he had been brought up in a house his parents owned.

Once when Tom had been away from home for three nights, he looked at me nervously across the table at Tramp and said, 'I'm going to be in hot water this time, Chrissy. Any suggestions?' We'd be best off fleeing the country, I said. So, armed with our house keys, Tom's road manager Chris Ellis was dispatched under cover of dark to our homes to collect our passports. Another of Tom's favourite photographers was out with us that night and he agreed to accompany us to wherever we ended up going to shoot pictures for the next tour programme – a perfect excuse for being absent without leave for a few days.

Accompanied by a Playboy Bunny Girl who had attached herself to the group, we set off well before the sun rose for Heathrow with the intention of getting on the first available plane – wherever it was going. That turned out to be a flight to Switzerland and, after pausing only to notify Tom's record company there of his impending arrival, we boarded. Hung over from 72 hours of hard drinking, we had resolved to detox over the next 24, but the stewardess produced a bottle of champagne with the compliments of the airline and we finished that off over breakfast. When the plane landed, the welcoming man from the record company insisted on taking us for a lavish meal in Geneva and then it was a couple of bottles of wine on the train taking us most of the way to Zermatt, the chosen location for Tom's photo-shoot.

By now it was beginning to dawn on me that drinking at this level was taking its toll on my health. Not only was I throwing up on a regular basis but also my emotions were all over the place. I couldn't work out why I was feeling down at a time when I should have been elated (I have learned the hard way that alcohol is a depressant). I had a loving family, a fast-growing and financially secure business and was flying first class all over the world, staying at the best hotels and dining in the finest restaurants. It was to make no sense for the best part of two decades. Never once did Jan say, 'I told you this would happen,' although she was frequently entitled to.

When we arrived in Zermatt, still in London-nightclub attire, the realisation quickly dawned that we were not dressed for a Swiss ski resort in the middle of winter. So the following morning we walked into the nearest skiwear shop to get kitted out with anoraks, padded trousers, bobble hats and fake-fur snow boots. Then, still feeling the effect of the previous days of drinking, we set about the job in hand and trudged off to the nearest mountaintop. During the general larking about, I fell over and got snow in my most prized possession, an 18-carat-gold Piaget watch. I was determined to get it mended, so we all trooped off to a jeweller in town and looked on as the watchmaker removed the face of the watch and, with one intake of breath, put his lips to the

internal works to draw out the moisture. At that point I
turned to Tom and said, 'Look, he's a clock sucker.' Suddenly
the guilt, shame and remorse disappeared. Tom went into
hysterics and collapsed on to the floor where he lay laughing
uncontrollably. I had become court jester too.

No sooner was one problem solved than another emerged.
That night the paparazzi, having heard that Tom Jones was in
town with a Bunny Girl, arrived in force from Rome. 'What
are we gonna do now?' Tom asked, gazing from his hotel
window at the photographers gathered outside. The solution
was simple: Zermatt could only be reached by train so we
would slip out of the back door and catch the last train down
to Visp, leaving our pursuers stranded. 'And where do we go
from there?' was his next question.

'Obviously Rome,' I said. 'If they're all stuck up here,
you're not likely to get bothered there.'

Bidding farewell to the Bunny Girl at Geneva Airport, we
flew to Rome in the midst of a terrifying thunderstorm and
checked into the Excelsior Hotel. I was beginning to flag but
Tom was on a roll and keen to go out. The concierge
recommended the 21 Club for dinner but was a little taken
aback when we were back in the lobby ten minutes later, still
in ski jackets and fur boots, to demand transportation to the
21. Once inside the club, we realised that, when Roman
society goes to the 21, it dresses up for the occasion. We were
scruffy to put it mildly. Seated at a long table in the centre of
the opulent dining room was a party hosted by Michael
Caine, splendidly attired in a white dinner suit complete with
dress shirt and bow tie. His guests were equally well turned
out, the ladies all wearing evening dresses. Clearly appalled at
our appearance, but reluctant to turn away an international
star, the maitre d' showed us to a dimly lit corner table out of
sight of the main party.

Caine, however, had spotted Tom and came over to chat.

'Where do they hide the women in this town?' Tom asked.

Caine paused, pointed to his elegant suit and, in his inimitable manner, said, 'Tom, it took me half an hour to get dressed up like this. Later on it's going to take me 15 minutes to get me out of all this gear and [nodding in the direction of his companion] another 15 minutes to get her out of hers. I take the view that the least the women can do for all that is to come and find *us*.'

Tom, being Tom, wanted to move on to a less demanding venue – the kind of sordid place one seeks out after the umpteenth drink. So the next problem was how to avoid him being photographed by the three or four members of the Rome pap pack who were not stranded in Zermatt but standing outside the doorway of the sleazy joint we had ended up in. At that point the photographer who was with us said he would have a word with the snappers outside and make sure that no pictures appeared in the papers. A few minutes later, he came back and told Tom to make a dash to a waiting taxi. But, as Tom hurried to the cab, the paps clicked away, and I couldn't work out why our photographer friend had allowed this to happen. It was only when we were safely ensconced in the cab that he explained: as he had chatted to them about their equipment, he had fiddled with their lenses so that any shots they took would be out of focus. Sure enough, no photographs of Tom's departure from the world of lowlife ever appeared.

Jan has always said that 11 September 1968 was the happiest day of her life. It was the day our daughter Joanne was born in Kingston Hospital. The birth came a little earlier than expected and I was in Newcastle with a client, John Walker of the Walker Brothers, when Jan called to say she was on her way to the maternity ward. Alas, I didn't make it back in time. Nevertheless, I maintain that nothing can prepare a father for the emotional impact of seeing his child for the first time – even when that father is unhealthily obsessed with his career!

Seeing this joyful bundle and watching the blissful state Jan was in, I resolved to spend more time in the bosom of my family, so I was at home in the Kew flat when, 15 months later to the day, Daniel was born. It's probably an apocryphal story but I was supposedly in the next room watching a favourite television programme when the midwife popped her head around the door to say, 'You have a son – you can see him now.' I – allegedly – asked to be allowed to watch the remaining 60 seconds or so of *The Avengers*.

Within a year of its foundation, CHI – Chris Hutchins Information, the image-making operation I built around Tom Jones – had grown into the most high-profile showbusiness PR operation in the UK. I had used the word 'Information' rather than 'Publicity' because I wanted the name to suggest to journalists that we were offering something they wanted as opposed to something the clients needed. As the roster of clients grew, Jan, Jo, Daniel and I were still living in the flat but the small hallway was often packed with journalists. They would be waiting to interview Steve Marriott (of the Small Faces) in the bedroom and Frankie Vaughan in the lounge while Val, my loyal and loving secretary from *NME* days, made tea for them in the kitchen. Clearly either the family or the business was going to have to move out.

I found offices in Mayfair and hired some of the sharpest PR men around (including Max Clifford). Our client list had expanded to include such bands as the Bee Gees – then a five-piece outfit which included the Gibb brothers, Barry and twins Robin and Maurice, the Moody Blues, the Move, Status Quo and Cream, and balladeers like Frankie, Sacha Distel, Petula Clark and Engelbert Humperdinck.

I got on well with them all, but in varying degrees. The Gibb brothers were as nervous as they were polite, but since I also represented the Robert Stigwood Organisation (their management) they got all the attention they needed and I became a regular visitor to Robin's home in Montpelier Square, Knightsbridge. Status Quo were being managed by one of their dads, a gas fitter, and the office would reek for hours of fitter's grease whenever they called in. I didn't understand the music of Cream (another Stigwood band) and others have told me since that I hid under my desk whenever they turned up, leaving them to Nick Massey who did a great job for them and ultimately for me. A pity really because these days I count Eric Clapton among my friends.

I never met a nicer man than Frankie Vaughan. We had fun whipping up a lot of publicity and I persuaded Gordon to make a record with him: 'There Must Be a Way (Which Doesn't Remind Me of You)'. It was a Top Ten hit but he was rarely able to perform it straight-faced after Jimmy Tarbuck (briefly another client) pointed out a double entendre in the meaning. Everybody loved Frank and his devotion to his wife Stella was a rare insight (in showbusiness circles) into love in its truest form.

The only one I thought twice about taking on was Petula Clark who, I was warned, could be difficult. But her husband, the French record company executive Claude Wolff, was so charming when he asked me that I relented and my forebodings turned out to be groundless. Jan, however, was less than pleased when we went to stay with the couple and Sacha in the French ski resort of Megeve and

Pet insisted Jan wore a jacket of hers which she considered the correct attire for the restaurant we were dining at one evening. Women!

Despite the colossal success he was to achieve worldwide, it was Engelbert, a tall, handsome, Indian-born singer from Leicester, who proved to be the biggest problem. As Gerry Dorsey, he was a long-standing friend of Gordon Mills, and Gordon had promised him that if he ever made it in management he would transform him from an obscure cabaret singer into an international star. When his first record flopped, Gordon decided that he needed a change of name. He plumped for Engelbert Humperdinck, after the obscure composer of *Hansel and Gretel*, probably the most memorable unmade-up name around. 'Engelbert' went on to have a massive worldwide hit with his first single, the country ballad 'Release Me', greatly exciting his record company Decca. They took a long time to catch on to the fact that their new signing and the underperforming artist called Gerry Dorsey they had let go were one and the same.

Engelbert, a personable enough chap, was married to Pat, a vivacious girl from his home town of Leicester, and they lived modestly with their children over the Times furniture store in the main street of Hammersmith. He was co-operative and willing to take advice but a problem soon emerged: Tom did not feel he should have to share his manager, PR and record producer with a rival for the crown of Top British Male Singer. 'Release Me' was a staggering success all over the world. Under Gordon's direction, Engelbert followed it up with a series of no 1 hits and almost from day one was easily outselling Tom.

The friction between the two almost led to blows during a party at Gordon's house on one occasion. In what was probably a calculated attempt to wind him up, Tom greeted him with the words 'Hi, Gerry'. Engelbert was delighted with his new identity and had no wish to be reminded of the name he associated with past failure. Gordon separated them on that occasion and kept them apart as much as he could thereafter.

My own, often blunt, sense of humour did not help the situation. Everything Tom got, Engelbert wanted too – a Rolls-Royce Silver Shadow to drive around town, a Rolls-Royce Phantom limousine with a chauffeur for longer journeys, an upmarket West End tailor and, eventually, a house on the estate at St George's Hill, Weybridge, where John Lennon lived. In his dressing room in Berlin at the start of a European tour, Enge (as he liked to be called) said to me, 'I hear Tom's got himself a bodyguard. Well, I want a bodyguard.'

'Why?' I asked. 'You've nothing to fear. You only see Tom two or three times a year.'

He was pissed off with me for days afterwards.

I thought that my celebrity charges were a bit like children. Despite their seemingly indestructible belief in their own brilliance, in my view they required nannying and constant reassurance. Few people can muster the confidence to go out and face an audience of many, many thousands and say I'm going to entertain you. But the performance invariably continues when they come off stage. As I saw it, entertainers expected the same kind of adulation in the dressing room – and often the home – that they've just had in the auditorium. And for some of them, if they don't get it, their dissatisfaction manifests itself in the form of tantrums. Employees get sacked on a whim, hotel rooms get trashed and the mildest criticism prompts a furious tirade. What I might have treated as a petty issue took on major significance. To me, it seemed as if it was a measure of their power that they could get whatever they wanted. And, in the same way, it was a measure to some of them of their weakness – or mine – if they didn't.

When Tom went to America to fulfil his engagement at the Flamingo Hotel in Las Vegas, I put the PR operation into overdrive. To back up the story about his deal being worth a million dollars, I borrowed a sizeable detachment of security guards and had him photographed being escorted to and from the stage. People are often fooled into believing that a star's status is matched by the size of his/her security entourage. J-Lo and Mariah Carey currently work this old chestnut. Watching the Jones circus pass through the casinos Sinatra-style also helped to convince the most cynical Vegas punters that a new superstar had arrived.

Using the white telephone that I had hankered after since I first saw one as a stage prop at the Torquay Pavilion, I had called Colonel Parker before leaving for the States and sought his advice on how to build media interest in Tom. In reality he had nothing to teach me about handling newspapers but he was sufficiently intrigued to send Elvis to Vegas to view Tom's act. He had – to use his own terminology – been snowed on a grand scale.

The first I knew that the flattery card had worked was when 'Diamond' Joe called me to discuss arrangements for The King's visit. Presley rarely went out in public and his arrival – amid bristling entourage – at the Flamingo for Tom's second performance of the night was the talk of Las Vegas. Photographers swarmed around the hotel and three were allowed backstage to record the moment the two stars met in Tom's dressing room. Unaffected by all the fuss, my wife and Elvis's sat together in a corner showing each other photographs of their babies, Jo and Lisa-Marie.

The publicity resulting from Elvis's attendance at the court of the new king ensured that Tom's performances were sold out every night. Promoters came from far and wide to check out the Welshman who would soon be filling football stadiums for them. Needless to say, Gordon and I also took the opportunity to inform everyone that there would soon be another superstar following in his wake: Engelbert Humperdinck.

One afternoon I got a call from Alex Shoofey, the vice president of hotel tycoon Kirk Kerkorian's fledgling Vegas empire, telling me that the Colonel was coming to town. The two men were having dinner together that night and Alex said that, if I joined them for coffee, I would learn something of great interest. I turned up to be greeted amiably by the Colonel, who made it clear that he considered me no longer a pupil but a player. Alex explained that Kerkorian was building a new hotel nearby that would have a much larger showroom than the Flamingo and a proper theatre in which they planned to put on shows from Broadway and the West End. 'Like Rex Harrison in *My Fair Lady*,' he said.

But it was the identity of the 'cabaret act' signed for the opening night of the world's biggest showroom that was meant to make me sit up. Inspired by Tom's performance, Elvis Presley had told the Colonel he wanted to make his comeback as a live performer and Parker had chosen the town where he could indulge his own addiction to gambling. What I didn't realise at the time was that, far from being men who didn't have a financial care in the world, Parker and Elvis were both desperate for the money the deal would generate. The days when an Elvis record would go straight to no 1 were over and the film deals were drying up as his movie audiences dwindled. A contract for a number of cabaret engagements was a welcome fillip to their finances, if not a lifesaver.

Parker duly wrote the terms of the agreement of this historic deal on a napkin – largely for my amusement, I suspect – signed it and handed it to Alex Shoofey. Then he turned to me and asked, 'You play craps?' I never had. 'Then come to the casino. It's time for your uncle to teach you how to be a *real* player.'

At the table he proceeded in his bullish way to dominate the table, betting $1,000 on each hand while allowing me to gamble only a few dollars at a time. But it didn't lessen the excitement of the game, coming, as it did, on the back of the secret of Elvis's stage comeback which, for the time being, I had to keep to myself. Despite the low stakes my luck was in but it took a couple of hours to accumulate a little less than $300. At that point, the Colonel ordered me to pick up my chips before leading me to the casino cage where I cashed them in. I felt a bit hard done-by when I saw the huge amount that he collected but, as he said, any profit's better than a loss.

'Now you go to bed and I'll see you tomorrow,' he ordered.

As soon as he was out of sight, however, I went back to the casino, bought some more chips and started to play again – this time without the benefit of his direction. Unsupervised, it took me just 15 minutes to lose $3,000 – a big sum to me in those days. I slept badly that night and was in the coffee shop for an early breakfast when I heard a voice say, 'You look glum this morning, Mr H.' It was Alex Shoofey.

'Not glum,' I replied, suddenly inspired, 'just pensive. I was thinking about your new hotel and wondering how you are going to convince stars like Rex Harrison to appear in it. After all, they've never heard of the Vegas International. Nobody in Europe has.'

'OK, I'll buy it,' he said, taking the seat opposite me. 'Got any bright ideas?'

My PR company, I told him, would promote the International in the UK right up to and including Elvis's opening-night performance.

'How much?' asked the shrewd operator.

'$3,000,' I said.

He wrote me a cheque later that morning. I had recovered my gambling losses and been hired to see a show I wouldn't have missed – Elvis Presley's comeback performance. All I had to do was get a couple of British journalists along to share in the fun of this great event. 'Double-snowed Colonel,' I whispered under my breath.

Back in London I added Roy Orbison to CHI's client list. His music was extremely popular and his stage appearances – always in black to match his heavily dyed hair – were a great success. Audiences often linked the dark glasses he wore to his shy, retiring nature, but he had once turned up for a gig without his normal specs and, being shortsighted, had worn his prescription sunglasses on stage. Someone had told him that it was a good gimmick and the man in black never looked back.

Like me, he had become addicted to sleeping pills and we had several long discussions about this apparent weakness. We concluded that it was because we both loved what we did for a living so much that, when the day's work had ended, life seemed anti-climactic and sleeping pills were a means of escape into oblivion. It was only later that I was to learn that this craving for oblivion had deeper and darker roots.

Apart from his love of tall, beautiful women, Roy had another obsession. He was frugal to the point of neurosis. When he flew in for a British tour and I mentioned that, as I represented all the artists on the bill, I would be going on all the dates, he said, 'Good, then I'll ride with you. It'll save me the cost of hiring a car and driver.'

The tour opened in Cardiff and after the second show we were both hungry but it was late and there didn't seem to be a restaurant open in the city. Driving out of town I spotted a fish-and-chip shop and brought back our supper wrapped in newspaper. Roy tucked in enthusiastically to the salt-and-vinegar-laden repast before asking me how much the meal had cost. Thinking that he was anxious to pay his share I told him not to worry: the meal had cost less than a pound for two. Roy was impressed. We ate fish and chips for most of the next 14 nights.

This failing was redeemed to some extent by his wry sense of humour. When we stayed at the hotel built over Central Station in Glasgow he told me over breakfast he had been kept awake all night by the noise of the trains and at one point had phoned down to reception and asked, 'What time does this hotel get to London?'

Meanwhile, Tom's career was going from strength to strength. In 1968, he was signed up by Lew (later Lord) Grade's ATV to make a television series that went on to be a hit not only in America and Britain but all over the world. Soon after Gordon had agreed the deal I got a call from Lew. He was going to announce the signing to the press and wanted to know how much I thought we should say Tom was getting for the first series.

'Let's go for a big round figure, Lew. Let's say £5 million. That'll make great headlines.'

With his shareholders in mind, I thought he would baulk at the sum, because it was considerably more than the real figure, but I was wrong. 'Chris Hutchins, you say five million? I think bigger than you, much bigger, so I'm gonna tell them it's £20 million.'

His figure was duly revealed to an astonished nation in all the following day's papers. I thought people would be sceptical but, some years later, whiling away the time in a dentist's waiting room, I opened a copy of the *Guinness Book of Records* and spotted the following entry: 'Highest TV fee ever paid to a British entertainer – £20 million to Tom Jones for his ATV/ABC series, *This Is... Tom Jones*.' Hype? The Colonel would have called it a snow job.

Working with Tom was the most enjoyable job I ever had but I wanted to be a manager and it was never going to happen with him. My chance to take control of an artist's career came when there was a split in the ranks of the Bee Gees. Robin Gibb had decided to break away from Barry and Maurice and telephoned early one morning to ask if I would handle his career. Like Cream, the Bee Gees were managed by the very able Robert Stigwood, whose group of companies, remember, was represented by CHI. Despite their blood ties, the Bee Gees, like so many groups, were a volatile bunch who were all dependent on fixes of one sort or another. Barry was known as the pot-head, Maurice as the alcoholic and Robin as the pill popper.

Robin was a sort of flawed genius. He could have been a big solo star but his focus, I thought, was damaged by his dependence on the uppers that gave him huge energy but also spawned a decadent and self-destructive sex life. He once called me at 3am, begging me to drive to his house in Montpelier Square, Knightsbridge. He sounded so desperate I thought his life must be in danger and broke the speed limit all the way into town. When I got there, it was to find that Robin was as high as a kite and his desperate need was for some company for him and his wife.

But, however eccentric, I liked Robin and he frequently came down to Richmond for long Sunday roast lunches, after which we would stroll through Kew Gardens and discuss the endless list of 'future projects' he always seemed to have at one stage of completion or another. In addition to a song dedicated to my wife, 'Janice, I Promise You This', he wrote an entire score for a musical based on Scrooge. Not that either work ever saw the light of day.

I well remember that day when Robin called and declared that he had decided to go solo and asked if I would be his manager. I thought about it for 24 hours. Taking on Robin would mean severing my lucrative contracts not only with the Bee Gees but also with Stigwood's organisation. Finally, however, I decided it was what I had always wanted – to mould and direct a star of my own. I threw caution to the wind and informed the trade press that Robin had left the Bee Gees and I was his new manager. It did not please Robert, with whom I had always had a good working relationship, but I knew he had been struggling for some time to keep them together.

A few nights later, very late, Robin turned up at my flat flushed with excitement: he was clutching a tape he had brought direct from the studio. It was a song he had written and Maurice had secretly produced. The song was called 'Saved by the Bell' and before he had played half of it I knew that this was going to be a no 1 hit and was capable of establishing his solo career. By now I was fending off legal threats from Robert but I arranged simultaneous releases for the record throughout Europe. Offers of television appearances poured in and the first one I fixed was in Germany. Obligations to my other clients prevented me going th him on that occasion so I asked Henri (Henriod – my ie friend from the NME days) to take Robin to Cologne s solo TV debut.

s not prepared for what was to happen on their Trouble brewed even as the plane landed. An enri – used to dealing with temperamental rock d to tell me that, as the aircraft taxied to the in looked out of the window and declared he wasn't getting off. 'He said there were no crush barriers and he feared for his safety as the Bee Gees were very big in Germany and their fans would crush him,' said Henri. 'I had to grab him by his collar and frogmarch him off the plane. He was almost crying.'

I knew what the problem was. Robin and I had gone over it again and again. He had never appeared on TV – or anywhere, come to that – without Barry and Maurice and he was terrified. Before he left, he told me he could do it but the reality was that without Henri's bullying he never would have.

When Robin returned to London, I met him at Heathrow and took him home with me in a bid to reassure him that he had the talent to find stardom in his own right. But it was not to be. He didn't have the confidence to cope without his brothers. So, when Robert Stigwood announced that he was taking his company public, I knew that he would need the Bee Gees back intact. Our lawyers began negotiations and Stigwood agreed to pay £10,000 for Robin's release from his contract with me. What he saw as the poaching of Robin had led to furious rows between us and, unsure of the reception I would get if I went to see him, I sent Henri to collect the money. Henri got £3,000 for his services and the remainder paid the deposit on a handsome house on Richmond Hill. My career as a manager may have been brief, but Jan, Jo and baby Dan were happy to have a new home to move into. I still live there with the memories of all these heady days.

Chapter Six

WHEN A PRIME MINISTER CALLS...

In the early hours of the morning following the General Election of June 1970, I lay in bed listening to a radio news bulletin. It was probably the matter-of-fact way in which the newsreader said that the outgoing Prime Minister Harold Wilson's police escort had left him as he reached the outskirts of Liverpool on his journey back to London that made an impact me on me, leading to yet another unusual adventure in this most bizarre of lives. Goodness only knows how I could ever have imagined it to be any of my business, but the thought of Wilson's Special Branch minders abandoning him within an hour or two of his defeat at the polls seemed incredibly cruel and I felt a compulsion to do something.

My maternal grandparents had been as pro-Conservative as you could get but when she became impoverished my mother turned into a determined Socialist. I had never cared much about either party but, more out of professional curiosity than anything else, I had joined the local branches of all three major parties in a bid to find out which was the best organised. In the back of my mind, I had always thought it would be good for business to find CHI an interesting political client. By the time Jan and I sat down to breakfast on that post-election morning, I was on a mission: I wanted Harold Wilson back in power. He needed, I decided, what in today's parlance is known as a spin-doctor. Here was a chance to take my manipulative skills to the table where sat the most powerful people in the land. Pop stars had fans but the government had an entire electorate at its feet.

That morning I began the first of many fruitless attempts to make contact with Wilson. On the assumption that a cold call to Labour Party headquarters would prove futile, I called on a variety of contacts from newspaper executives to various friendly political journalists. Weeks later I was beginning to lose heart when I remembered reading somewhere that Wilson had an unlikely friendship with the singer Kenny Lynch. I had met Kenny from time to time and called him to tell what I had in mind. Lynchy, as he is known, promised to 'have a word'.

Less than a week later, he called and said, 'Harold's interested in a meet – one night next week in his office at the Commons.' In the event, the day we agreed on coincided with the funeral of veteran backbencher Bessie Braddock and I assumed it would be cancelled, but Kenny called again to assure me that Harold would be back in time and was keen to go ahead. Then something dreadful happened.

On the afternoon of the appointed day, Jan called the office to say she was worried because our live-in nanny had gone missing while out walking with Dan. I told her to call the police and rushed home to hear the whole story. It emerged that Jan had confronted the nanny that morning about some missing clothes. The girl had then taken Dan on what was supposed to be a short walk but three hours later had still not returned. By now an incident room had been set up at Richmond police station and Jan, who was looking after Jo, was getting more anxious by the minute. My first thought was to cancel the meeting with Wilson but then I thought, if anyone can help, it's probably him.

Full of mixed feelings, I drove to Westminster, parked the car and made my way to the office of the Leader of Her Majesty's Opposition, where Kenny was waiting for me with Harold's political secretary, then plain Marcia Williams. The man himself was a few minutes late getting back from Bessie's funeral and was clearly in a foul mood. He was wearing the Gannex raincoat – as closely associated with him as Columbo's is with him – and sucking on that famous pipe. After we'd been introduced, he said, 'As a former journo, you'll understand this, Chris. I came out of the church, obviously looking glum. It was a fucking funeral, after all. The photographers were snapping away and I wanted to smile but obviously couldn't. I kept thinking the buggers will file these sour pictures away and use them next time I've got some good news to put across. You can't win with the media. But that, I s'pose, is why you're here.'

When a chance arrived to get a word in edgeways, I explained my own pressing problem – the situation at home – and said I had taken the liberty of giving the police his private office number in case they needed to contact me urgently. As soon as he heard of the drama surrounding Dan's disappearance, Harold's whole mood changed. He swung into chief executive mode, grabbing a phone to call a contact at Scotland Yard. I listened as, in that distinctive Yorkshire accent, he had the search stepped up. Then we sat looking at each other for what seemed an age before the same phone rang. A smile broke out on the face of the former Prime

Minister as he listened to the voice at the other end: a British Transport policeman had spotted Dan and the nanny on a platform at Liverpool Street Station waiting for a train to who-knows-where. Both were soon in a police car headed for Richmond. While a now joyous Jan awaited our son's safe return and the unfortunate nanny was carted off to a psychiatric hospital, Harold broke out a case of bottled beer which we drank from the neck with our feet up on the very table at which he conducted his Shadow Cabinet meetings. What an introduction.

The family crisis over, and with the beer having its glorious effect, our conversation turned to politics. Harold's successor, Edward Heath, was in all kinds of trouble over policy on the apartheid regimes in southern Africa and I suggested that Harold went there with a good photographer, and be seen to be building bridges with the blacks in the townships rather than the white men in government. He liked the idea and later wrote to me saying he wanted to pursue it but, although we did discuss it further on the phone and exchanged letters on the subject, the project came to nothing.

Unfortunately, news of our meeting had leaked. The *Daily Telegraph* carried a front-page story suggesting that Harold had called in a 'pop PR'. This was disastrous as far as I was concerned. I knew and liked Joe Haines, who had been his press secretary in Downing Street and remained his media adviser in opposition. I called Joe to clarify my position and he told me not to worry, saying he was writing to the *Telegraph* to demand a retraction. Many years later, he told me that Marcia (later to become Lady Falkender in an honours list she had a part in compiling) had lobbied for me to replace him. In fact, this was never my intention. The entertainment side of CHI's business was far too lucrative to abandon for what, for me, could never become a vocation.

I next saw Harold in 1972 when I was about to leave for America to open an office for Gordon Mills in Los Angeles. Jan and I threw a farewell party at Richmond, inviting friends, clients and neighbours and, at the last moment, it occurred to me that Harold might like to come. I contacted his office on the afternoon of the party and spoke to Marcia, who called back later and said, 'Harold says he would love to be there – and, by the way, he drinks Bell's whisky.' We had plenty of booze in all varieties but no Bell's, so I collected a bottle from the off-licence at the top of the road and gave it to Jan with strict instructions to offer it to no one but Harold.

Gordon had been nagging me for weeks to set up a meeting for him with Harold, so he was delighted at the news that the former PM was coming to the party. His wife Jo was born in Rhodesia and he wanted to discuss that country's future with the man who had negotiated with the whites' leader Ian Smith in the wake of his unilateral declaration of independence (UDI). Harold had refused to set foot on Rhodesian soil, so he and Smith had met at sea aboard HMS *Tiger*.

When Gordon arrived with Tom and Engelbert in tow, he was in especially bullish mood. 'Where is he?' were the first words he uttered as he came through the front door. I had to put up with regular enquiries from him about Harold's whereabouts but the politician was running late and did not arrive until shortly after 11pm. 'Sorry I'm late,' he said as he came in, his wife Mary following meekly behind. 'There was a division in the House over Rhodesia.'

Without waiting to be introduced, Gordon charged at him and said, 'I'm glad you mentioned Rhodesia, I want to talk to you about that. I'm Gordon Mills, by the way.'

Tom and I exchanged knowing glances and retreated to the kitchen to break out the champagne as Jan handed Harold his first half-tumbler of Bell's.

Ten minutes later, a red-faced Gordon charged into the kitchen, demanding, 'Throw him OUT!' When I asked who – convinced he must have had a row with another guest – he replied, 'Wilson! I've tried to explain to him about Rhodesia but he won't listen.' It took Tom and I several minutes to talk him down.

Some time later, when I went back into the front room I was confronted by a bizarre spectacle. While Mary Wilson was reciting poetry to a bemused Jan on the sofa, Harold was dancing in the centre of the floor. He had one arm around Marion Spence, the vivacious blonde wife of Tom's musical director Johnnie Spence, and the other around Tony Cartwright, Engelbert's Liverpudlian road manager, and the three of them were high-kicking, chorus-line style, as they sang 'Eee I addio.' It was truly a sight to behold.

Twenty minutes later I realised the source of Harold's new-found exuberance when Jan told me we were out of Bell's whisky. 'I asked you not to give it to anyone but Harold,' I said in exasperation. 'I didn't,' she said, and the awful truth dawned. Harold had downed the entire bottle in little more than an hour. By now Mary was looking increasingly disgusted by her husband's behaviour and it wasn't long before Tony Cartwright and I took one arm each and helped the giggling former (and future, as it turned out) Prime Minister down the steps to his car. He won my vote that night.

A week later, Jan, Jo, Dan and I flew to California where we had rented the actor Ben Gazzara's colonial-style home close to Hugh Hefner's 'Playboy Mansion West' in the exclusive Holmby Hills district of Los Angeles. Jan lazed by the pool while our new nanny taught Jo and Dan to swim and I drove to the office at Creative Management Associates (CMA) on Beverly Boulevard, arriving early enough each morning to park my rented Mercedes next to that of the Hollywood agency's powerful chairman, Freddie Fields. With an eye on possible film contracts for CHI, I socialised with the big guns at CMA and from time to time brought them home for dinner parties at the imposing Gazzara house.

An early interesting encounter was with a tall, fair-haired young woman who called at the office one morning claiming to be 'Engelbert Humperdinck's greatest fan'. While she was keen to meet Enge, she had a fascinating success story of her own to tell. Her name was Kim Grove and, having left her native New Zealand for London a few years earlier, she had found a job as a waitress at the Lyons Corner House close to Trafalgar Square. It was there that she first set eyes on a handsome young Italian customer named Roberto Casali.

'I chatted him up and hoped he might be that special person for me,' said Kim. 'Unfortunately, he was about to leave for Los Angeles, but he did give me an address where I could write to him. I sent him all these corny love letters and at the end of each one I drew two little figures – a girl with blonde hair like me and a boy with black hair like him. Underneath each I wrote a corny caption beginning with the words, 'Love is...'.' Unbeknown to Kim, Roberto showed the letters to a friend who worked at the *Los Angeles Times*, asking if the paper might be interested in running the drawings as a cartoon. 'I think we would' was the response. So Roberto wrote to Kim asking her to send more of the little drawings, and that's how the now world-renowned 'Love Is...' cartoon was born. Kim gave up her job as a waitress, moved to Hollywood and married Roberto, who became her manager and business partner.

By the time she called on me at CMA, the cartoon was being syndicated internationally and the one-time waitress was well on her way to becoming a millionaire. I arranged for her and Roberto to fly to Las Vegas where Engelbert charmed 'his greatest fan' and we became good friends. When they sold their Hollywood home later that year – two weeks before they were due to fly back to live in London – the Casalis came to stay with us. Kim doted on Jo and Dan – she loved children and wanted to have a large family of her own. When they left for London, we promised to keep in touch and link up when Jan and I returned.

Meanwhile, business was going well. In 1973, Tom or Engelbert were often in town, and we would dine at places such as Spago and Ma Maison, then the most fashionable restaurants around, before moving on to a bar or a club or both. And whenever Gordon decided to visit Las Vegas, we always went by private jet. This, for a boy from Empire Road, was high living indeed. One relationship, however, began to suffer. With Tom and Elvis regularly appearing in Las Vegas at the same time, the Colonel and I found ourselves rivals in a war of hype and were regularly competing to buy the best billboard sites at enormous cost to both sides. Parker's posters would announce: 'Elvis Presley is at the International', so I would have ours read: 'Tom Jones is in town...' making it appear that he was so famous the punters would find out the venue for themselves.

It was later that year at a party in Beverly Hills that I was introduced to cocaine, a drug that was to wreak havoc in my life for years. The party was thrown at the home of a model-turned-actress and I didn't give it a second thought when she said, 'Here, try some of this – it'll make you feel good.' It did make me feel good. So good, I called her the next day to ask for some more of the expensive (in more ways than one) white powder. And so it went on.

The drug had an adverse side-effect: like speed, it made

sleeping almost impossible. But I had the antidote to that – I simply stepped up my intake of sleeping pills, my real drug of choice. When I added alcohol to the mixture my behaviour became unpredictable and I would go into what I now know to be blackout – periods when I functioned but had no recollection afterwards of where I had been or what I had done. I would wake up in the morning and find myself surrounded by plates containing the remains of meals I had cooked and then discover I had also made telephone calls, many of them transatlantic, without any recollection of whom I had spoken to or what I had said. More than once Terry O'Neill would call me from another country and say, 'You were in good form last night. That was a brilliant idea you came up with. Let's do it.' And then I would have to confess that I didn't know what he was talking about. Poor Terry, how it must have confused him.

It was the occasional bouts of unreliability that alarmed me most. One of the worst was when, after a long flight from London where I had been bingeing, I arrived at the showroom in Caesars Palace on the afternoon of Tom's opening night. Already on stage rehearsing, he spotted me and called out, 'Ah, you're here at last. Where are the lines, Chrissie?' Now I used to write many of the one-liners he would deliver between songs when he was short on inspiration. Corny stuff like (at the end of a sequence of patter) 'Now I must get back to doing what I do best, but first I'm going to sing a few more songs...'

'You've already got the lines for this year,' I spluttered. 'Remember we do one lot for each year's tour? I did them in January.'

'No,' he reminded me, 'this is the second time I've appeared in Vegas this year. Can't do the same act. Now you have written some, haven't you?'

115

'Yes,' I lied.

Feeling distinctly unwell after a chemically induced sleep on the plane, I dashed to a local record store and bought a copy of an album Frank Sinatra had recorded live at the nearby Sands Hotel. It had some brilliant material written by professional writers. Sinatra started something like this: 'Good evening, ladies and gentlemen, and welcome to the Sands. It's undergone $10 million worth of renovation since we were here last – they borrowed three million from the banks and seven million from the cocktail waitresses.' I updated that for the script I prepared for Tom: 'Good evening, ladies and gentlemen. Welcome to Caesars Palace – they've spent $25 million on it since I was last here. They borrowed five million from the banks and 20 million from the cocktail waitresses.' When the purloined material was ready, I rushed it round to Tom in his dressing room. He looked pleased. 'Very good, Chrissie. You've excelled yourself this time.'

I sat with Gordon in his booth for the first performance – the one covered by the reviewers. All went well and when it ended I went backstage to receive renewed praise from Tom. No one had noticed and the gags had worked well between his usual faultless rendition of great songs.

'If you don't mind,' I said, 'I won't stay up for the second show, I'm knackered.'

'No, you get some sleep,' said Tom, who was obviously still feeling well disposed towards me.

In my room, I took some sleeping pills, climbed into bed and had started to doze when the phone rang. It was Tom's son Mark. 'Dad says will you please come down – the press are in.'

'No, Mark,' I said, 'they were in for the first house. I spoke to them all and they've gone now.'

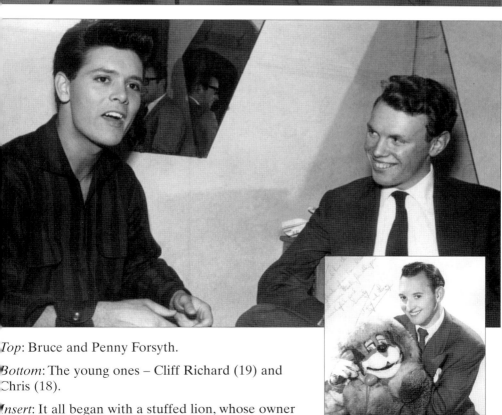

Top: Bruce and Penny Forsyth.

Bottom: The young ones – Cliff Richard (19) and
Chris (18).

Insert: It all began with a stuffed lion, whose owner
Terry Hall wrote, 'To Chris, the founder of our fan
club with sincere thanks for all your wonderful work,
sincerely, Terry and Lenny'.

Top: Winner takes all! On tour with the Beatles in 1964. Including, second from left on the top row, Don Short, the *Mirror* man, third from left Chris, far right one of the US radio DJs; middle row, George, Paul, John and Ringo and bottom row, from left, Alf Bicknell (chauffeur), Tony Barrow (PR), Mall Evans (roadie) and Neil Aspinall (then a roadie).

Bottom: Chris, Brian Highland, Andrew Loog Oldham and Keith Richards snapped by a groupie on the way to the Shea Stadium for the Beatles concert in 1965.

Elvis, Suzanna Leigh and Chris in the summer of 1965.

Top: Tom Jones and Chris in Zermatt in 1971.

Bottom: Gilbert O'Sullivan with Jo and Dan Hutchins.

Top: Priscilla Presley by her lover Terry O'Neill.

Bottom: Jo Hutchins in Princess Margaret's Mustique bed.

Inset: Roddy Llewellyn's signature in 1975, proving the relationship was underway a full two years before the Palace admitted it.

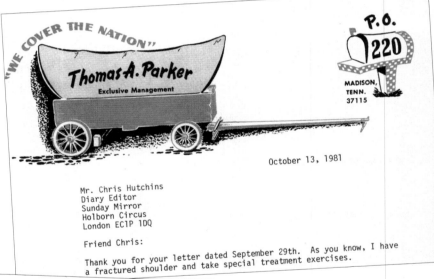

"WE COVER THE NATION"

Thomas A. Parker
Exclusive Management

P.O.
220
MADISON,
TENN.
37115

October 13, 1981

Mr. Chris Hutchins
Diary Editor
Sunday Mirror
Holborn Circus
London EC1P 1DQ

Friend Chris:

Thank you for your letter dated September 29th. As you know, I have a fractured shoulder and take special treatment exercises.

In answer to your question about the passport, that is totally bunk. First of all Elvis at all times made the final decision if he wanted to go on tours, not me. We presented the tours to him and on several occasions tours of Japan and England were talked about but we never got a final OK. I used to receive the complaints from some fans and Todd Slaughter about why Elvis did not come to England and I told them to tell Elvis to let me know when he wanted to go as I was tired of hearing from them that Elvis wanted to go but I would not let him. This was ridiculous as he could do whatever he wanted with his career. As for me not being able to go, if so, it meant nothing for we had plenty of people available on my staff to do so.

Top: In 1964, Colonel Tom Parker and Elvis gave belts to each member of the Beatles and Chris got one in silver with rhinestones.

Bottom: A letter from the Colonel to Chris in 1981.

Deerest Chris,

Many happy returns. Have a wonderful birthday. Thanks so much for your help during my recovery — you've been a good friend and an honest one. You also do help many other and for me you are a perfect (nobody's perfect but you know what I mean!) example of how this Programme works.

Thankyou again

Love

This Photo Kills.

Top: A birthday card from Elton John in 1991.

Middle: A postcard from the Beatles, doctored by the band themselves, which they signed 'The Bifokals'.

Bottom: A Beatles postcard from France addressed to 'Chrisp Hutchy'.

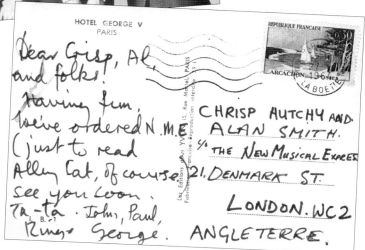

HOTEL GEORGE V
PARIS

Dear Crisp, Al, and folks! Having fun, we've ordered N.M.E (just to read Alley Cat, of course) see you soon. Ta-ta. John, Paul, Ringo George.

CHRISP HUTCHY AND.
ALAN SMITH.
% THE NEW MUSICAL EXPRESS
21. DENMARK ST.
LONDON. WC2
ANGLETERRE.

Top left: Jo Hutchins and Barry Gibb in Miami.

Top right: Gerri Hutchins in 2004.

Above: Chris Hutchins interviews Lord Mountbatten in the year he was to be assassinated, 1979.

Inset: Lord Snowdown and Chris.

'No, they've come back again – Frank Sinatra's in.'

For several moments, I didn't dare breathe. Then I pulled on my clothes and dashed downstairs, desperate to get to Tom before he went on and performed the stolen lines in front of their rightful owner. As I took a shortcut through the kitchens to the backstage area, I heard the band playing the opening bars of 'It's Not Unusual'. I was too late: by the time I'd got to the wings he was already on stage. 'Good evening, ladies and gentlemen. Welcome to Caesars Palace – they've spent $25 million on it since I was last here. They borrowed five million from the banks...' Adrenaline pumped through me, nullifying the effect of the sleeping pills. I was soaked in sweat as I listened to Tom innocently repeating the lines from *Sinatra Live at the Sands* with the man himself seated right there in the audience.

After his performance, Tom dashed, as usual, to take a long shower and reduce his body heat. I was waiting – cowering might be a better word – in the outer dressing room when Ol' Blue Eyes strode in followed by six men with squashed noses. This, I was convinced, was the end not only of my association with Tom but also of my career as a publicist. Then I looked again at Sinatra. For his part, he was looking at no one in particular. He was drunk, too drunk to have noticed much about the show he had just sat through. Perhaps I would get away with it after all. Tom emerged from the shower and exchanged pleasantries with Sinatra and his retinue, and a few minutes later the visitors began to file out. The last man to leave turned to me and said, 'Frank thought that was a great tribute.' Alas, I never did get round to owning up. Perhaps one day I will get a chance to make amends.

By the end of 1973, Jan, in her inimitable style, had made it clear to me that there would be no more California summers for her and the children. Jo and Dan had attended a playschool in Beverly Hills where their friends were the offspring of entertainers – they were especially close to the daughter and son of Cher and Dionne Warwick respectively. But she was right; it was time they settled down to an English education and a more structured lifestyle. That meant I would have to live on my own in LA for the length of future tours by Tom and Engelbert.

The Gazzara house was far too big for one person, so I moved into the Beverly Hilton Hotel. Then Tom rented a house built by Mike Nesmith of the Monkees but preferred the Santa Monica beach house belonging to Peter Lawford where President Kennedy had enjoyed sojourns with Marilyn Monroe, so he moved and I took over the Nesmith house. Terry O'Neill came to stay from time to time as he was seeing Raquel Welch, who lived nearby. She, by the way, was the most self-centred actress I ever met and I avoided Terry's company when she was with him. (I inadvertently got my revenge on her selfishness several years later when Terry invited me to join their table at San Lorenzo after spotting me sitting alone. Mistaking her for another of Terry's many girlfriends, I said, 'Oh Priscilla [Presley], how nice to see you again.'

Terry looked shocked and said, 'Chris, it's Rocky [his pet name for Raquel].' If looks could have killed...)

After less than two months, I decided the Nesmith house was too big and I was also irritated by its incredibly complicated alarm system, which would invariably go off if I got up and moved about in the middle of the night. The alarm automatically summoned police cars and an LAPD helicopter and it cost me a small fortune in false call-out fees. I duly gave up the house and moved back into the Beverly Hilton, flying home to the family whenever I had a few days to myself.

It was about this time that I reconnected with a notorious businessman I had last seen in London several years earlier. At one point, John Bloom was the Richard Branson of his day. He had come up with the inspired idea of selling washing machines direct to the public, promoting them in full-page newspaper advertisements that featured a prominent picture of himself. Sales of Rolls washing machines boomed for years but it all ended when he had an affair with an attractive employee while on a company junket to Austria. She later confessed the liaison to her husband and, during a vicious row, he murdered her. During the trial that resulted, both the defendant's QC and the judge made scathing remarks about John and, because of the salacious nature of the case, these comments were covered widely.

Given the degree to which John was identified with his product, the publicity virtually destroyed his business overnight. He languished in his flat off Park Lane, where Henri took me to meet him one summer's day. As we walked into a large living room, I was impressed to see Bloom playing complex classical music on an organ. He had his back to us, but, when he stood up to greet Henri, the organ continued to play. That, I discovered, was typical of the man. By then, he had moved into the nightclub business and I heard he had encounters with some of the less pleasant characters in the business. When one of them decided John had crossed him, he lay in wait for him one Friday evening. Knowing that, as an orthodox Jew, John would not so much as turn on a light switch after dusk on a Friday, he beat him up so badly he left the country two days later, fleeing to California.

By the time I next bumped into John he was running a Tudor-themed restaurant called AD1520 in Los Angeles. The idea was that guests sat down to a six-course banquet served by waitresses dressed as 'pinchable wenches'. The concept

CHRIS HUTCHINS

initially proved a great success and people queued to get in. But, as the courses were cut back one by one, the queues disappeared. Although John said he was acting 'in the interests of weight-conscious American waistlines', the truth is he was failing to pay his suppliers. When I went there one evening to be told the jacket potatoes were off because the vegetable supplier's bill had not been paid, I knew the place was doomed.

John subsequently moved into the soft-porn film market, storing videos in his garage. On a visit to his house in the ultra-exclusive Truesdale district of Beverly Hills, I asked him why he had an artificial lawn. He replied, 'Show me a gardener you can guarantee is not an undercover FBI man and I'll have real grass.' He was a brilliant businessman but also one of the strangest I've ever met.

My frequent shuttles across the Atlantic brought me into contact with a number of well-known people. In TWA's first-class lounge at Los Angeles International Airport. Tom Stout, the airline's amiable head of public relations, always did his best to ensure that members of what he termed his 'flying family' – of which I was one – sat next to someone interesting. One day he asked me if I knew Rod Steiger.

'Never had the pleasure,' I replied.

'Then come and meet him. He's also flying to London and I think you two will get on well.'

Tom was right. The star of *In the Heat of the Night* and I hit it off from the first cocktail and we were soon swapping anecdotes about mutual acquaintances. In particular, he had much to say about his close friend Elizabeth Taylor and that 'madness' he thought she was going through.

As the jumbo jet climbed into the sky above LA, I noticed that Steiger couldn't take his eyes off the 'Fasten Seat Belt'

120

sign. 'Can't wait for that to go off,' he said. 'I hurt my back playing tennis the other day and I want to get out of this suit. I've got a kaftan in my bag here.' When the sign was finally switched off, Steiger rose painfully to his feet and made his way to the lavatory to change. A few moments later, a fellow passenger tapped me on the shoulder and said, 'Excuse me, but we're having a little bet back here. Is the man who was sitting next to you Rod Steiger, the movie star?'

The 'movie star' and I had been exchanging some wickedly amusing stories ever since our meeting back in the lounge and I was in high spirits. 'It was, madam, but it won't be in a minute!'

'What do you mean?' asked the puzzled fan.

'Well, you see, Rod's a transvestite and when he/she comes out of the loo, he/she will be wearing a frock and will be Rowena, so please do not address him/her as Mr Steiger.'

Clearly shocked, the woman went back to her seat without a word.

'That's better,' said Rod, as he eased past me and settled himself back into his seat, his kaftan looking for all the world like a loose frock. But it didn't take long for him to suss that something was going on. Word of his 'secret proclivity' had quickly spread around the cabin. There were whispered conversations, followed by stifled giggles, and fellow passengers looked at him curiously as they passed by. As we ate dinner, Rod turned to me and said, 'There's something funny going on here. I don't know what it is but I can sense it.'

Unable to contain myself, I burst out laughing and explained the joke to him.

'You mean half the people on this plane now think I'm a woman? Oh my God, how could you do such a thing?' He looked sick but he had the grace to laugh and add, 'Just wait till I get my own back.'

He never did get his own back, although we did have dinner together several times during his stay in London. On one occasion I picked him up from his hotel to discover that he was wearing an absurd-looking hat. 'Got to wear it,' he said. 'They've shaved my head for the part in the film and I'm not going out looking completely bald.' But when the three of us (Jan enjoyed his company too) arrived at the restaurant, I told Rod that he had to remove his hat – the maitre d' would never allow him to wear it at the table. He finally gave in and sat sulking self-consciously throughout the meal.

During a winter break back in the UK, Gordon called one evening with instructions to pack. 'We're going to Los Angeles in the morning. Johnnie Spence [Tom's musical director] is coming with us. I'll tell you why when we get there.' It was not until the morning after our arrival (we had stayed up all night after a pliant record company representative brought a supply of Benzedrine for us to share) that he came clean. 'We're going up to Vegas to see your friend the Colonel. He's been in touch. I get the distinct impression he wants me to co-manage Elvis. If he does, you'll handle the publicity and Johnnie will revamp his music.'

Soon after we arrived in the gambling capital, Gordon set off alone for the summit meeting, leaving Johnny and I at the hotel to twiddle our thumbs in eager anticipation. It was two hours before Gordon returned and before he uttered a word it wasn't difficult to detect that things had not gone well. 'He's wasted my time!' he ranted. 'All he wanted was to take over Tom's concession rights selling bloody balloons and badges at the concerts. He thinks I'm missing out on a chunk of money. Oh, I'm *so* bloody furious.' Going into greater detail later, he said that Parker had even made his assistant, Tom Diskin (a former hoofer), dance on his desk to entertain their visitor. 'The man's a bloody megalomaniac,' Gordon stormed. 'I don't know why you talk to him.' Shades of the party night with Harold Wilson all over again.

In April 1974, Tom set off on a tour of South America and I went with him. Many of the regimes in the region were quite precarious at that time and, when a certain group threatened to kidnap Tom's teenage son Mark who was travelling with his father, the promoters hired armed guards to accompany him and Tom everywhere. On arrival in the Venezuelan capital, Caracas, on the last leg of the tour, tempers became frayed when Tom was jostled by the crowd as he left the plane and, in the confusion, a reporter was hit. He later identified his assailant as Tom's Welsh bodyguard, a gentle giant called Dai Perry. We succeeded in getting Dai on a plane home before they could arrest him but, after his first concert, the police placed Tom himself under house arrest. Suddenly the armed guards, who had been high-spirited companions throughout the tour, became jailers. For the next two or three days we were confined to Tom's hotel suite and the mood within was beginning to sour.

Then I had an idea: why not use my connection with Harold Wilson, who had by then begun a new term as Prime Minister? Coming to the aid of a popular star would, I knew, be the kind of act he would like to see in the papers. I dispatched a cable to No 10 explaining the position and asking Harold to come to the aid of this British celebrity hero-figure being held hostage in a South American country. My feverish excitement about the publicity it was bound to generate appears to have affected my prose style: 'Implore [help of] Her Majesty's Government in seeking release of British citizen Tom Jones, who has been refused permission to leave Venezuela because of an incident in which he had no involvement.' Nevertheless, it had part of the desired effect. Leaked by No 10, Tom's predicament made front-page news all over the world.

Coincidentally, a couple of hours after sending the wire, we received a call from a lawyer: if Tom Jones presented himself at the chambers of a local judge at six o'clock the following morning and handed over $9,000 in 'compensation' he would be released. Escorted by the guards, we left the hotel before dawn and made our way to the judge's office. Tom went in alone. He told me afterwards that the lawman was a sour individual, who took a handgun out of his belt and placed it on the table before asking, 'Have you got the money?' The cash was handed over and the judge counted it before declaring, 'There's a plane departing for Miami in 90 minutes. Be on it, Mr Jones. If for any reason you are not, you will be brought back into the city and required to go through all this again tomorrow.' With the help of a police escort, we made the flight with minutes to spare.

When the plane landed in Florida, the first editions of that day's papers were already trumpeting his release. Back in London, Harold was soon taking the credit for securing Tom's freedom but history should record that it was a $9,000 bribe rather than any diplomatic manoeuvres that brought it about.

The South American incident was not the only problem caused by Dai, a lovely but uncomplicated fellow who had been Tom's friend since boyhood. Once, when I arrived at Heathrow to meet Tom arriving back from the US, I was told by an airline official that a police car had gone out to meet the plane and they were going to question Tom about an incident which had occurred during the flight. Tom explained later that he and Linda had had a row before leaving New York, and he'd got drunk during the flight home. At one point, he was listening to music on his headphones and loudly clicking his fingers to the beat when a passenger across the aisle complained. Dai was sitting next to Tom and – ever defensive of his charge – had responded aggressively. A brawl ensued. The shouting, the pushing and the shoving attracted the attention of cabin staff and when one man in uniform came down to remonstrate with Dai, who was by far the most vocal, he got out of his seat and wrestled him to the ground. As he sat on the man in the aisle, Dai said, 'You're staying there till we land.' To which the man replied, 'If I stay here, we don't land. I'm the captain.'

Management Agency & Music (MAM), the public company Gordon had built around Tom, Engelbert and his newest discovery, the singer/songwriter Gilbert O'Sullivan, was doing well for its shareholders. But Gordon and his managing director Bill Smith were ambitious men and keen to develop new projects to expand MAM's entertainment base. They were particularly interested in the burgeoning fortunes of independent television companies which produced programmes and sold them to the US, as Lew Grade had done so successfully with *This Is... Tom Jones*. So when I proposed an international chat show, hosted by Muhammad Ali, to come from a different world 'hot spot' each week, Gordon responded enthusiastically. 'Do you think you can get him?'

'Leave it to me,' I replied.

Jimmy Tarbuck's agent, Terry Miller, gave me the name of the New York agent who arranged Ali's speaking engagements and I called him and told him what MAM would like to do with Ali. Two days later he rang me back. 'Get your ass over here,' he said, 'Ali's interested. Now you have to come and make your pitch to him.'

So in the agent's Manhattan office a few days later, I came

face to face with a man who – just like Harold Wilson – had long been one of my heroes. Tall and even more good-looking in real life than on television, the world's greatest and most charismatic boxer soon made it clear that the idea of the chat show appealed to his ego. Although he was not the kind of man you could flatter – he did enough of that for himself – he was impressed by the access I said it would give him to world leaders. 'I'd go to Tripoli and sort out Colonel Gadaffi,' I remember him saying as he started to list the international statesmen he would like on what he was now calling 'my show'.

Our initial discussions over, he offered to take me for a ride in his open-top Rolls-Royce Corniche. We drove to Harlem where I was teased mercilessly as he introduced me to the 'brothers', all the while extolling the benefits of being a Muslim. When we returned to midtown Manhattan, he parked outside the Plaza Hotel (right on the cab rank but who was going to argue with a world champ?) and asked when I thought the project could be up and running.

'Just as soon as I can get the networks to give us the go ahead,' I said. Then I had a question to ask him: 'How can I become a Muslim?'

'That's impossible,' he said, banging his fist on the steering wheel. 'You the wrong colour, man. You know that.'

Back in London, Gordon and I went to see Lew Grade about the Ali project. 'No way,' Lew shouted. 'Are you two mad? There is no way the networks would buy a programme in which a black man was seen putting the world to rights. They wouldn't stand for it.'

I went home that night to write to Ali, via his agent, and tell him the bad news. I couldn't bring myself to give him Lew's reason.

The following year, I found myself reunited with Ali on a

flight from New York to Los Angeles. He was on his way to California for a press conference to announce his forthcoming 'Rumble in the Jungle' – a match in Africa against his old adversary, Joe Frazier. After a brief chat about the aborted television project, he started spouting poetry he had written and which he insisted I copied down. During one break I asked him once again if I could become a Muslim, knowing that the rules had been changed. 'Yes you can,' he replied.

'Ah,' I said, 'the last time we talked, you said I couldn't.'

Ali's reply was profound: 'Show me a man who says today exactly what he said a year ago and I'll show you a man who's wasted 12 months of his life.'

I did, however, put the connection I had made with Ali to good use when Gilbert O'Sullivan toured America soon afterwards. Although he had scored a no 1 hit with his plaintive song 'Alone Again (Naturally)', few tickets were sold for his concerts and the tour was looking like a commercial disaster. Desperate for some publicity to generate interest in Gilbert (real name Raymond O'Sullivan) and his album *I'm A Writer Not A Fighter*, I thought of Ali when we arrived in New Jersey a day ahead of a show there. Ali was at his training camp in the nearby mountains preparing for a fight and, when I called to ask him if I could bring Gilbert up to be photographed with him, he readily agreed. Next I called Mickey Brennan, a cameraman I knew who was happy to take the pictures. Unfortunately, the limousine we hired had seen better days and the interior reeked of fuel. Gilbert – never my idea of good company – moaned throughout the three-hour journey.

When the three of us finally reached the camp, we found Ali in great form. He laid on a meal for us prepared by two female chefs he had hired. 'We picked them up on the way here,' he said, adding to Gilbert's obvious disdain, 'They came in cookin' and ended up fookin'.' When the time came for Mickey to photograph the boxer and the singer in the ring, they both went off to get changed. Ali had loaned Gilbert some trunks but when he emerged from the changing room he was also wearing a T-shirt.

'We don't box in shirts,' said the world champion.

'I'm too skinny to be photographed without one,' responded Gilbert.

At that, Ali grabbed the shirt and, in one swift movement, tore it off Gilbert and squared up to him. Mickey moved in swiftly and in little more than a minute the magical pictures had been taken. Within days they had been published, not just in America, but all over the world. Ticket sales picked up almost immediately but Gilbert never forgot his scary moments in the ring with Muhammad Ali and we were at loggerheads for the rest of the trip. In Los Angeles we were lunching at a restaurant in Beverly Hills when the protestations grew too much. I excused myself to go to the men's room, slipped out the back entrance, hailed a cab to the airport (via the Beverly Hills Hotel to collect my luggage) and flew back to London. When I called Ray the following day he said, 'Where the fuck are you?'

'Home,' I said, 'where I belong.'

By the beginning of 1975 – the start of my ninth year in the PR business – I was getting restless. It was time to move on. I had no idea what I was going to do and I was already committed to handling tours of America, Japan, South Africa and Europe. But I knew it was going to be a year in which I would see even less of my young family than before and I wanted a lifestyle that would allow me to spend more time with them. Things were not helped by the increasing scale of my drink and drug consumption. Indeed, the incident that finally made up my mind came about partly as a result of my winning a sake-drinking contest in Tokyo during a tour with Engelbert.

That night I awoke in agony. Although I didn't know it at the time, I was suffering my first attack of acute pancreatitis. The hotel summoned a doctor who injected me with morphine and made preparations for my transfer to a nearby hospital but, as we were due to fly home the next morning, I begged him to let me go. He agreed but on condition that I went back to him for another morphine shot before leaving for the airport and that I went directly to hospital as soon as I reached London. Fooled by the painkiller into believing the problem had gone away, I did not go back for the second shot. A big mistake as it turned out.

By the time a journalist sidled up to me on the jumbo jet and asked if he could sit with Engelbert for an hour to compile a 'Travelling With' piece for *Punch* magazine, the excruciating pain was beginning to return and I was more than happy to vacate my seat and sit on my own. The subsequent *Punch* piece described what happened next: 'Engelbert was talking about his hits when a worried steward interrupted to ask him if he knew whether Mr Hutchins carried any medication for whatever was causing the problems. 'No,' he said, and moved on to the subject of his fan clubs – 'the biggest in the world'.'

At that point the steward asked Engelbert to accompany him to the flight deck and the journalist went too. "We are quite concerned about your friend,' said the captain. 'This is our current position,' he added, indicating a chart laid out in front of them, 'mid-way between Tokyo and Moscow. There is nowhere we can put a 747 down to get him the help we think he needs."

At this point, according to *Punch*, Engelbert turned to the journalist and, pointing to an island off the coast of Japan, said, 'Do you know how many people I sang to there?'

I had to laugh when I read the magazine piece, but I decided it was time for a change and so I talked to Mick Green. I'd first met Mick in Devon when he was with a group called Johnny Kidd and the Pirates. Over the years he had turned himself into one of the greatest lead guitarists of his generation and our paths had crossed again when he joined Engelbert's band. He too had had his fill of the singer's behaviour and quit the band. Apart from the fact that we had both fallen out with the star, we had something else in common. In the days when we toured together, we had often talked about how badly run most record labels seemed to be; how abysmally they treated their artists. We had dreamed of setting up a label of our own and this seemed to be the time to do it. I called Mick and he was as keen as ever. Within days we had registered our label: Thunderbird Records.

I was, however, committed to CHI for the best part of the year ahead, so Thunderbird had to stay on hold for most of that time. The next few months were as eventful as ever. My diary entry for 13 February 1975 reads: 'Tom almost shot me.' In a particularly merry mood after dining with a female agent in Farrah Fawcett's company at the renowned Gelsons restaurant, I had gone to his bungalow at the Beverly Hills Hotel and, instead of knocking on the door, had kicked it, Jerry Lee Lewis-style. I thought Tom would appreciate the joke but, when he opened the door, he was holding a handgun and it was pointed at me.

'Chris, you mad bugger,' he said. 'I could have shot you.'

There was good reason for his paranoia. Foolishly I had forgotten that Tom had only recently discovered that his name was on the list of potential victims compiled by Charles Manson, the man who murdered Sharon Tate just a mile or two away. No wonder he was jumpy. Had he shot me it might have been considered poetic justice for some of the pranks I had played on Tom. When we were in Miami earlier that year I had plonked in front of him the daily pile of autograph books and scraps of paper he was required to sign for fans. In the middle of the pile I placed a blank open card on which he duly wrote 'Best wishes, Tom Jones'. Had he looked at the cover he would have seen it was a Valentine's Day card, which I duly posted to Linda back home in Britain. Only cowardice prevented me ever asking Mr or Mrs Jones how it was received.

To relieve the boredom of yet another summer in Los Angeles, I booked daily karate lessons with Mike Stone, who had been Elvis's instructor but had left Las Vegas in a hurry when Presley realised he was having an affair with Priscilla and threatened to have him shot. I took the lessons at Priscilla's house and she would prepare a light meal for us when the hour was over. I paid just $25 a time but, strange as it may seem, they needed the money. Elvis was so enraged by Priscilla's infidelity that he was refusing to maintain her. Between visits to her father in Memphis, the Presleys' daughter, Lisa Marie, would be there and occasionally she would read out to me the heartbreaking letters she was writing to her daddy and I helped her with the spelling.

By this time, Tom was one of Elvis's closest friends. Whenever they were in Las Vegas at the same time, they would take it in turns to host after-show parties on a nightly basis. Their relationship, however, had to survive the odd spat. On one occasion I was called in to help resolve a flare-up that threatened to end their friendship once and for all. I was in my room at the Beverly Hilton when I got a call from Tom in which he outlined the problem. He'd gone on stage at Caesars Palace the previous night and someone in the audience had thrown him a napkin. There was nothing unusual in this as people would throw whatever was to hand in the hope he would sign it and toss it back. But he had turned it into a joke, placing it over his face Ku Klux Klan-style before turning to the Blossoms (the black singing trio who backed him) and said, 'And you three be out of town by midnight.' Understandably, the girls took offence and after the performance walked out saying they would never work with Tom again.

Elvis was in town and that night it was his turn to party at Caesars. When Tom told him what had happened, Elvis got on the phone to Memphis and arranged for his backing trio, the Sweet Inspirations, to fly immediately to Vegas. But the following day Tom went to the Blossoms and apologised. They accepted his apology and agreed to rejoin him. Next he called Elvis and explained the situation but, by then, the Sweet Inspirations were already on their way. By the time Tom and his entourage arrived at the International for that night's get-together, the Inspirations were assembled around the grand piano in Elvis's suite. Elvis, seemingly high as a kite, said, 'Listen to this Tom,' and he played and sang, 'The first time, ever I saw your face' with the backing group singing a harmony the four of them had newly arranged. When they finished, Elvis turned to Tom and said, 'What d'ya think?' Tom had said politely, 'Very nice, very nice indeed,' to which Elvis responded, 'See, guys, I told you he'd like it. Let's do it again for him.' He went on to perform the song over and over again until Tom's eyes glazed over. Noticing his reaction, Chris Ellis crossed to where Elvis was sitting and pulled the piano stool from under him. Chris meant it as a joke but Elvis was furious and that night the Jones party left under a cloud.

The next day Chris was asleep in his room at Caesars

132

when he got a call from an oriental man who had taken over from Mike Stone as Elvis's karate instructor (or choreographer, as Tom preferred to call them). 'Elvis velly cross,' he said. 'He want you here at six o'clock sharp to aporogise on bended knee.'

Ellis's response was to say, 'Tell Elvis I'll be there if he really wants me but I'll bring a gun with me and I'll use it if I have to.' He never did go, of course, but he did report the conversation to Tom who called to relay it to me.

'What would you have done if Chris Ellis had gone over there and Elvis had given him a pasting?' I asked.

'I'd have gone over and rammed his fuckin' karate belt down his fuckin' throat, that's what,' Tom replied.

A few days later I went with Tom to Phoenix, Arizona, for the start of a one-nighter tour. He was clearly troubled about the bad blood that had been caused by the Chris Ellis incident. I talked to him about it until he finally said what I had wanted him to say all along: 'Get Elvis on the phone. I'll sort this thing out one way or another, once and for all.' I did what he asked and then left the room to allow him to have what was clearly going to be a difficult conversation in private. When he emerged some minutes later, Tom was smiling. 'Everything's sorted. We're friends again.' We all breathed a sight of relief. There was no further discussion of the matter but I knew it would not have been Tom who gave in.

This was not their only sticky patch. Since their first meeting in Hawaii in 1966, they had developed a close friendship but remained fierce rivals. While enormously complimentary about each other's talent in public, privately they could be quite bitchy. I once joined Elvis's party at Caesars Palace when Tom was on stage and heard him say to one of his retinue, 'Look, he sticks a sock down his trousers.' Similarly, when I sat in Tom's booth at the International watching Elvis performing his choreographed routine, Tom remarked, 'He looks like a big chorus girl.'

Tom was always conscious that when Elvis came to see him perform it was a big distraction for the audience. He could put up with that but it irritated him when Elvis insisted on joining him on stage on almost every occasion. Of one thing he was absolutely certain, he didn't want Elvis to sing with him: that would have spoiled his performance. So he gave orders to Chris Ellis to hide the spare microphone when Elvis was in and he never let go of the one he was holding

My second encounter with Frank Sinatra – this time he was sober and we actually had a brief conversation – came about in New York that August. Tom had been appearing at the Westchester Premier Theater some distance outside the city, and after his closing night we had both drunk more champagne than was good for us. 'Let's go find Frank,' he said, as our small party climbed into the limousine and headed for Manhattan. Locating Sinatra when he was in New York was never a problem: he ate every night at Jilly's, the restaurant owned by his friend Jilly Russo. By the time we got there, however, the place was closed but a cleaner said the Sinatra-Russo party had gone to Jimmy Weston's that night so we headed there.

The Sinatra team had taken over the entire restaurant and if it hadn't been for Tom we would never have got in. But, even though it was after 2am, Sinatra, immaculately dressed, invited us in. The conversation between the two superstars was to be an object lesson in showbusiness psychology. Frank said, 'I heard Elvis was back in the [Baptist Memorial] hospital in Memphis, so I called him and the girl on the switchboard said, 'Who's calling Mr Presley?' I said, 'Frank Sinatra' and was expecting the 'Oh yeah, and I'm the Pope's girlfriend' line but the next thing I knew I was talking to

Elvis.' Sinatra sounded as surprised as any of the millions of Presley fans might have been had they had the same experience.

Then he worked his way neatly round to a business proposition. 'I told Elvis he's gotta get well because we're all going to buy a Las Vegas Hotel and become partners. Tom – with you, me, Elvis, Liberace and Streisand owning the place and appearing there regularly, they could fire a cannon down the rest of the Strip [the gambling resort's main street] and not hit a soul.'

We left an hour later with Tom deep in thought. As we stopped to relieve ourselves at a kerb edge, Tom asked us what we thought of the Vegas idea. There were about half a dozen in the group, including his teenage son Mark. Most of us made approving noises until Mark spoke up. 'Load of bollocks, Dad,' he said. 'What do you know about running a hotel?'

'Right,' said Tom, 'that's it then.'

The matter was never raised again. That was the moment I saw Mark as a potential successor to Gordon Mills, which is exactly what he later became.

One month after this episode, on the lookout for artists to sign to Thunderbird, I arranged to hear a Canadian singer called Gino Vannelli at a Los Angeles club called the Roxy on Sunset Boulevard, on a particularly hot September night. Earlier that evening, I had taken Bruce Forsyth to the Bel Air Hotel for dinner after he had called to say that Anthea Redfern, whom he was to make his second wife, had flown back to London and he was at a loose end.

When I told Bruce about the gig at the Roxy he asked if he could come along. He was a little older than most Roxy goers and I didn't think it would be his bag but he was insistent. At the club I introduced him to some of my friends and explained to them what a big star Bruce was in England and as a result he was soon surrounded by friendly folk shaking his hand. I was, however, a little surprised when he came to me halfway through Vannelli's act and said he was going back to his hotel (he was staying at the Beverly Hills) in the company of a strikingly attractive black girl – though I had no reason to believe they had not gone for a friendly chat over a cup of coffee somewhere quieter than the noisy Roxy.

Driving to Los Angeles Airport the following morning with Terry O'Neill, a mischievous idea occurred to me. When we got to LAX I went to a payphone, called the Beverly Hills Hotel and asked for Mr Forsyth. Once connected, I did my best impression of a boy from the 'hood and said, 'Bruce Forsyth? I hear you wuz with my woman last night. I'm on my way ovuh...' And with that I hung up. At the time I liked to think he would have realised it was a wind-up and found it funny but, knowing what I know now, I suspect he was in shock for days.

On 31 October, to Gordon Mills's great annoyance, Mick Green and I launched Thunderbird Records. The project was soon consuming most of my energy, and what little remaining enthusiasm I had for the PR business was waning fast. On a trip to South Africa with Tom, Gordon and I quarrelled incessantly about Thunderbird, which – with some reason – he considered would be in direct competition to his own independent label, MAM Records. That Christmas I resolved to break with Gordon and his stable entirely and fold CHI, nine years to the day after I had founded it. Gordon phoned three times on New Year's Eve insistent that I reverse the decision and the expletives came thick and fast when I refused. No seasonal greetings were exchanged and I was soon to discover that I had made myself a powerful enemy.

Meanwhile, now that I was finally back in England for good, Jan and I began to live a more conventional domestic life. One consequence of this is that we began to see a lot of Kim (*Love Is...*) and Roberto Casali, who had moved into a house in Weybridge, and we were frequent dinner guests at each other's home.

One Sunday morning things took a dramatic turn when Roberto turned up on our doorstep looking ashen. 'I've just been to the Royal Marsden Hospital,' he said. 'They've told me I've got cancer, incurable cancer. Oh, my God. I'm on my way home to break the news to Kim.' To say Kim was devastated would be a grotesque understatement. Up to that point, her life was pretty much as she had always wanted it to be. She had a handsome husband, a growing fortune and two fine children. But more than anything Kim wanted to have more of Roberto's kids.

In the months before Roberto became completely incapacitated, she persuaded him to donate to a sperm bank. It was 17 months after his death that she gave birth to the first of three more children by him. Drawing the *Love Is...* figures that represented her and her late husband became a labour of love. Kim herself died a few years ago, but the cartoon lives on – drawn now by one of the sons Roberto fathered but never lived to see.

Chapter Seven

POP STARS NOT GANGSTERS

The invitation to meet Billy Weinberger in the Polo Lounge at the Westbury Hotel in Mayfair came as a surprise. After all, he was the boss of Caesars Palace, which still had Tom under contract. I had not seen or spoken to Gordon (or Tom) since our row on the last day of 1975 and this was early 1977. Over a dry martini, Billy explained why he had called. 'Your name came up at a meeting at the hotel the other night,' he said. 'Gordon was in Vegas to talk about Tom's next engagement and I happened to say, 'What a shame Chris Hutchins isn't around – we could have had another poster war with Colonel Parker.' Gordon wasn't too happy at the mention of your name. His exact words were 'I made Chris Hutchins and I'll break him.'

Billy's revelation did not come as a complete surprise to me, as I already suspected that Gordon had made various moves behind the scenes to impede the progress of Thunderbird. One executive at a major record company had told Mick Green that, when Gordon heard he was about to offer us a distribution deal, he called to say that if the company signed a contract with us he could say goodbye to any more records from him. Gordon's power extended beyond the labels he was directly involved with. Such was the measure of his success that many lived in the hope they could poach Tom, Engelbert or Gilbert when their existing contracts expired.

Billy's story indicated, however, that Gordon was not content to make the odd phone call but was single-mindedly out to wreck our enterprise. Now I knew why Mick and I had fared so badly: we were being sabotaged by one of the most important men in the music business. I excused myself, went to a payphone in the lobby and dialled the private line of my friend Mike Molloy, the editor of the *Daily Mirror*. Ever since I had quit MAM, Mike had been trying to persuade me to write an account of my decade as an image-maker to the stars. But I had always refused. Billy's account of his conversation with Gordon at Caesars Palace, however, changed all that. I was enraged. '*Now* I'll do it,' I told Mike.

The 14 months since my exit from the PR business had been tricky and not simply because of the thwarted ambitions of Thunderbird. I had also got caught up in the film business, partnering an old chum – now an established producer – Keith Cavelle in making a picture called *Golden Lady*. Writing the screenplay with Keith had been enjoyable but the level of risk involved in funding an independent production disturbed me and I sold him my half-share in the film before shooting began. (It turned out to be a wise move on my part. I believe I made more by selling my share to Keith than he made out of seeing the film all the way through to its release.)

With Thunderbird doomed and my brief foray into the film business at an end, I was back where I started – in the writing game. Working day and night, I completed an account of my life as a star-creating publicist in six short weeks. I can't remember which of us came up with the title, *The Family*, but Mike was delighted with the result and so was the Mirror Group chairman, Tony Miles, who personally masterminded its publication. Mirror executive Peter Thompson had day-to-day control of the series, and self-deprecatingly has credited his subsequent promotion to deputy editor as an indirect result of the series' success.

It ran in the *Mirror* for ten days under a logo of *The Family* rendered in the same typeface as the title of the mafia epic *The Godfather*, as Mike saw parallels between Gordon's autocratic style and that of Don Corleone. The series started on Saturday, 16 April 1977, with my account of the spat between Tom and Linda as they were driven from Manhattan to JFK Airport on their way home to the UK. Both had been enjoying what Tom liked to call 'a nice little drink' and Linda was bemoaning his rise to international stardom, saying they might have been happier staying in Pontypridd, the Welsh mining town where they met, grew up together and fell deeply in love. At that point Tom said something that sent Linda nuclear. This is how he told me about it later: 'I pointed to her jewellery and made some remark about how she hadn't done too badly on it. That did it. She opened the car window and started pulling her jewellery off. And throwing it out – rings, bracelets a necklace, the lot. When she tried to pretend that her diamond ring [valued at around £50,000] wouldn't come off. I started to laugh. I couldn't help it: you had to see the funny side of it.'

It wasn't long before Gordon issued his first statement about the articles. Perhaps naively, I was surprised by the vehemence of his reaction. I knew that he was a secretive man but even he had conceded that one day the inside story of his operation – admirable in so many ways – would be told. He had even talked of writing it himself. I think his anger on this occasion was down to his inability to control the situation.

The series began in earnest on the Monday, and the *Mirror* couldn't be accused of underselling its scoop. Three-quarters of the front page was devoted to highlighting *The Family*. Under the tag line, WORLD EXCLUSIVE, came the headline: 'TOM JONES AND MARJI, THE TRUTH'. This was followed by Mike Molloy's hard-selling line: 'Starts today: the most explosive showbusiness story of the decade.' Inside, the paper ran the story of Tom's relationship with the former Miss World Marji Wallace and how she had attempted suicide after he had told her to leave Las Vegas to avoid the press catching on to their liaison.

I can't be sure when Gordon decided to take legal action but, as we had made it clear at the outset that the misery was going to continue into a second week, it didn't take him long to decide to try and nip it in the bud. On the Tuesday morning, his lawyer (and previously mine), Michael Balin, went to the High Court, applied for and was granted an injunction against the *Mirror*'s publication of any further episodes. Mike Molloy, assistant editor Peter Thompson, and I were given the news over a Fleet Street lunch. The meal abandoned, we raced the few hundred yards to the court, arriving just in time to hear our QC, Robert (now Lord) Alexander, commencing an appeal before three senior judges, including the Master of the Rolls, Lord Denning. The other side had hired a heavyweight pair of QCs in Sir Peter Rawlinson (a former Attorney General) and his junior, Leon Brittan (later to become Margaret Thatcher's Home Secretary).

Their argument was that I had signed a confidentiality agreement. What they didn't seem to be aware of was that some time later I had complained bitterly to MAM's managing director, the amiable Bill Smith, that this imposed an unacceptable limitation on my activities as a writer and unless it was rescinded I would have to resign. Bill and I were close at that time – we had adjoining offices – and he went to the file cabinet containing my contract and handed me the agreement, which I tore up in front of him. When Rawlinson raised the subject of confidentiality, I turned to Peter Thompson and told him that I still had the torn-up pieces of that agreement.

'Then for goodness sake let's get them,' he said, and a driver was despatched to the Mirror building where the pieces were sitting in a hold-all I kept under Peter's desk. This was duly handed to Robert Alexander (later to become chairman of NatWest) who triumphantly passed it up to their lordships. From that moment the other side's case crumbled and it became clear that the judges were minded to allow the appeal when Lord Denning asked Robert at what time the *Mirror* would need to know the result if it was to publish that night. The judgment, when it came, was comprehensively in our favour – indeed, Lord Denning told Peter Rawlinson, 'If American law were to be interpreted as you wish us to interpret English law, Nixon might still be President.'

The following morning Tony Miles asked me to go on the influential television current affairs programme *Newsnight*. 'I know I promised you that we wouldn't ask you to do any promotion for this series,' he said, 'but the fuss has reached such epic proportions I have promised the producer that you will do a live interview tonight.'

Protesting vigorously, I pointed out that I had barely slept for three nights as Mike, Peter and I would go out to dinner each evening and then on to the nightclub Tramp, where we waited for the first editions to be delivered. That left very little time for sleep before we reunited early each morning to work on the following day's pages. But Tony was adamant and I caved in.

In an effort to make me feel more comfortable about it, Mike said I could take an early-evening nap in the office of his deputy, Derek Jameson, who was in Manchester, and promised to wake me in time to be driven to the BBC studios. At 6pm, I duly went into Derek's office, took several of my pills and went to sleep. Alas, less than half an hour later, Derek – who had returned unexpectedly from the north – marched in and said, 'What's all this about? Wake up, Hutchins, we're going to the Stab [the Stab In The Back, then the *Mirror*'s local] to celebrate the success of the series.' By then circulation reports showed that *The Family* had put 180,000 copies a day on to the *Mirror*'s circulation.

So to the Stab we went. At about 9.30pm Joyce Hopkirk (the Woman's Editor who had been charged with getting me to the BBC on time) came into the pub in a panic. She had gone to Derek's office to wake me and drive me to the BBC and of course I wasn't there. 'Come on, we're late,' she said and we headed for her car. Once at the BBC I was shown into a darkened studio and given a chair opposite the presenter John Timpson. 'Relax, Mr Hutchins,' he said. 'We're the only live item in the programme tonight and we're the last on, so just relax.' I did better than that, I went to sleep. The next thing I knew, Timpson was shaking my knee violently and saying, 'Mr Hutchins, Mr Hutchins, wake up, we're on air,' and someone in the background was counting: 'Five... four... three...'

Timpson's first question was: 'Mr Hutchins, how do you think the wives of the people in your story are feeling tonight?'

I responded with a question of my own. 'Do you mean about their husbands' behaviour or the fact that it's been chronicled?'

The reply took him by surprise and set the tone for a relatively amiable ten-minute conversation.

In the cab on the way home, the driver looked at me in his rear-view mirror and said, 'You're that guy I've just seen on television. Aren't you scared about what those people you've written about might do?'

'No,' I said. 'They're pop stars not gangsters.'

'Yeah, you're right,' he said. 'Now, if it was Frank Sinatra, that would be different.'

I swallowed hard, only too aware that the following day's *Mirror* was already rolling off the presses with my stories about Sinatra.

Despite our court victory, the comments of the judges, my feisty performance on *Newsnight* and the *Mirror*'s circulation leap, I felt bad about writing the series in a fit of pique on hearing Gordon's adverse comments from the Vegas casino boss. As I had put it together, I had convinced myself that I was writing an entertaining story about a life travelling the world with a group of highly talented scallywags. But, as the bitterness between the parties intensified, I began to realise that I had started a chain reaction that I was powerless to control.

The stress generated by the controversy got to me. The *Mirror*'s switchboard reported receiving death threats aimed at me. I felt I needed a very long sleep and went to see my doctor, Gordon Kells, a man who had a reputation in the celebrity world as the man who would helpfully hand out pills. He rented a surgery on Harley Street in a house owned by another doctor, Paul McLaughlin, who also ran a close-protection service for predominantly wealthy Arab clients. Both were present that Friday afternoon as Gordon sedated me. The first – rather generous – dose failed to put me to sleep, however, partly because of the drug tolerance I had developed and partly because I was in a manic frame of mind. Kells looked at McLaughlin and said, 'I can't believe this. That should have put a horse out. Shall I give him more?'

Paul was a bit wary of increasing the dose but Gordon went ahead anyway. The next thing I knew it was lunchtime on Sunday. I woke up in Paul's top-floor flat, desperately hungry and thirsty because I had not been put on a drip feed. Sitting opposite me was a man I didn't recognise and on the table in front of him was a gun.

When he saw that I had come round, he said, 'I've been hired to guard you.' He then fetched me a curry from a nearby take-away and then set out his protection plan. We should, he said, keep on the move. That night, we left London for an obscure hotel in Portsmouth. The following morning the *Mirror*'s chief lawyer, Hugh Corrie, called to say he needed me in London to sign a statement. We may have seen off the injunction but now a libel action threatened. My bodyguard vetoed any move back to London, but Hugh was equally adamant that the document be signed that day. The pair of them eventually agreed that we should meet halfway – in a greasy spoon cafe behind a filling station at Hindhead. Hugh, a tall, elegant, old-school type, says he has dined out on the story ever since. I can still hear him telling people in his best Edward Fox manner, 'I was sitting there having a cup of tea with Chris when this fellow takes a gun out of his pocket and plonks it on the table.'

My bodyguard stayed with me, night and day, for two weeks. But we never really bonded. Apart from the fact he had a severe case of BO, I would irritate him by constantly trying to give him the slip. On one occasion, he lost me for almost 24 hours after I slipped out of a back entrance of the Wig and Pen club opposite the very law courts where the battle had commenced. The only reason I kept him on – and I was footing the bill – was because Mike Molloy thought it would be prudent and so did the good doctors Paul and Gordon. After a fortnight, however, I reckoned any threat had petered out. I never did see him again but later heard that he had died in a shoot-out while guarding an Arab client in the Gulf. I took the precaution of renting Paul's Harley Street flat for six months. But Jan never visited me there and, while I made occasional visits to the family home in Richmond, the whole affair put colossal stress on our marriage.

It was only after Gordon Mills's death in 1986 that I was made aware of the depth of his anger towards me at that time. I got a call from a hardman in Newcastle, who Gordon had used to sort out 'problems' that he preferred not to give to his lawyers. 'You wouldn't have known this at the time,' he said, 'but, when Mills lost the court action to stop your series running in the *Mirror*, he called me and said he wanted a contract taken out on you. I talked him out of it but, at the time, he just didn't want you to be around any more.'

I often wondered if Gordon's fury was embedded in the knowledge of a conversation I once had with Tom after he had been booked to headline *Sunday Night at the London Palladium*. He was white hot at the time and understandably not best pleased to learn that Gordon had agreed he should share the last segment of Britain's biggest TV show – after the second commercial break – with a comedian. Big American stars were always given that segment to themselves and here was Tom being afforded just ten minutes of it. He and I were discussing the situation during an alcohol-fuelled night out at the Penthouse club in Mayfair and I suggested that for his last number he insist on a rostrum being constructed out from the stage into the audience – rather like the one Elvis danced out on in the finale of the film *Loving You*.

We were taking a leak in the club loo when Tom said, 'Gordon would never go for that either, but listen, if I split from him, would you take over?'

I said I would if he would phone me and ask me again the next day when we were both sober. Tom's call came around three the following afternoon. 'Nice little drink we had last night, wasn't it, Chrissy?' And, needless, to say, there was no mention of the dramatic proposal he had put to me as we stood at adjoining urinals in the early hours. In the cold light of day we both knew that, in the face of such a mutiny, Gordon's anger would be unbearable. Thinking back to that time, I actually felt sorry for Gordon, who, despite his attempts to sabotage my business, had shown himself to be charming, funny and highly intelligent. Like me, he never escaped the shadow of a scheming and manipulative mother. From a poor background in south Wales, he had made great efforts to improve himself not only materially but also intellectually. He was not only better looking than any of his stable of performers, but he also had far better taste and was much better read. His downfall stemmed from an inability to curb his explosive temper when he failed to get his own way. He liked to say that his maxim was 'familiarity breeds contempt', but at the end of the day he enjoyed a deeper measure of familiarity with those around him than he cared to admit.

Four months after the row over *The Family*, I was one of the first journalists to discover that The King was dead. I had kept in close touch with Elvis Presley's camp since getting to know them in my *NME* days and, on Tuesday, 16 August 1977, I received a call from one of my contacts at Graceland, his home in Memphis.

'You'll be hearing this soon,' he said, 'but since you're a

148

friend I thought I'd let you know personally. Elvis is dead. I can't talk now but I'll try to call again later.'

It was 9.50pm and I knew that the *Mirror* would be preparing to print its first edition. I called Peter Thompson who set about clearing the front page and several inside pages for the second and subsequent editions while I started typing frantically at home. The news of Elvis's death broke on the wires about half an hour later but my call from Graceland had given the paper a valuable head start.

A month later, I had a long telephone conversation with Colonel Parker, who tried to explain why he had behaved so badly at Elvis's funeral. He had turned up in a Hawaiian shirt, refused to be one of the pallbearers and never showed any sign of emotion. 'If I shed a tear after Elvis died, nobody saw it,' he told me. 'If some people had as much as seen my eyes glaze, they would have been busy trying to get their hands in our pockets and I couldn't have had that, no sir.' For all his shortcomings, Gordon Mills could never have been so cold and hard.

Chapter Eight

ROYALS BEHAVING ODDLY

B y now I had had my fill of sharing life with the world's
leading rock 'n' rollers. I wanted a new challenge and
there seemed no more interesting territory to explore than
that occupied by the Royal Family. In the spring of 1978,
London society was rife with rumours that Princess Margaret
was having an affair with a landscape gardener called Roddy
Llewellyn. While there had been many references to their
relationship in the press, it had been conducted almost
exclusively at the Princess's house on the Grenadine island of
Mustique. Access to Mustique was strictly controlled by the
island's own police force. Nobody could land by plane or
boat without prior permission and that was effectively
limited to residents and their friends. It was to all intents and
purposes a private fiefdom.

Fully aware, however, that even the richest inhabitants of
such an island were usually prepared to rent out their villas
when they were not in residence, I decided to try a bit of
enterprise. After all, this was an opportunity to get an

inside track on the Queen's sister's activities. The company that had the best reputation for procuring holiday lets in the Caribbean was a Mayfair-based one called VIP Travel. Aware that I would get nowhere if I told them I was a journalist, I introduced myself as a Welsh landowner (which was a bit of a liberty given that Bryn Bach, the house I had bought in north Wales, occupied less than three acres). The travel agent heard my request to rent a house on Mustique called Les Jolies Eaux without blinking an eye. When he called back, however, he sounded highly excited: 'Do you *know* who that house belongs to? It's Princess Margaret!'

But this proved no impediment to me renting it. Providing I could get a cheque for £1,480 via VIP Travel to Kensington Palace by five o'clock that afternoon, it was mine for a fortnight. I was later obliged to switch the booking from January – when, Jan pointed out, the children would be at school – to March and even then the Princess had to agree to give up two days of her own vacation because the holidays clashed. She did. Margaret was clearly keen not to imperil what was a financially attractive deal, even by royal standards.

When the day of departure finally arrived, Jan, Jo, Dan and I took a scheduled flight to Barbados, where a light aircraft had been chartered for the 45-minute onward journey to the forbidden airstrip on Mustique. The first thing that struck me when we arrived at Les Jolies Eaux was that there were two pairs of identical gates that led on to a single driveway. I learned later that after the Princess had sold half her plot to her cousin, Patrick (the Earl of) Lichfield, she had insisted he erect his own set of gates, even though both would open up on to the same track. No one but the Princess was allowed to use her gates. It was the first of many examples of her eccentric behaviour that I was to learn about during the trip.

The house itself was attractive enough but in my rock 'n' roll days I had stayed in better. It was a three-bedroom bungalow without a swimming pool. There was no TV or radio – Margaret brought her own radio/cassette player and took it with her each time she left – and the only form of entertainment available was a 1,000-piece jigsaw of Windsor Castle. What's more, we were to discover that the cook couldn't cook and the maid ruined more than one of Jan's dresses because she didn't know how to use the washing machine. Due to a water shortage on the island, the bath water ran brown. But at least Jan and I slept comfortably that night in the Princess's king-size bed.

The next morning, the first in a succession of my well-heeled neighbours turned up to check out the new arrivals. It was Lord Lichfield. He stood at the door clutching the proverbial empty sugar bowl and actually asking whether we could provide him with some to tide him over until the shop opened. It was about as lame a cover story as he could have come up with for what I interpreted as a spying mission ordered by his cousin. I poured him a glass of champagne and we chatted for an hour about everything except Roddy Llewellyn. Others were to be more communicative on that subject.

In the fortnight that followed, I was told all about the terrible rows the lovers had over the dinner table, how jealous the Princess would get if Llewellyn chatted to a younger, more attractive woman, and how he was required to follow her from the beach carrying a pail of sea water so he could rinse her feet before she stepped into her jeep. We also heard that Margaret had not endeared herself to many of the residents by her insistence on royal protocol being observed, even on the beach. 'Have you ever tried to curtsey in a bathing costume?' one American woman asked me. But one of the most fascinating things I discovered was Llewellyn's signatures in the guestbook. The first was dated 1974, two years before Buckingham Palace had admitted that Margaret's marriage to Lord Snowdon was in trouble.

I got my scoop but I have to say the rest of the family would rather have gone to our regular spot on Corfu. Mustique may be an attractive tropical island, and Les Jolies Eaux even had its own beach, but Jan did not enjoy the incessant socialising and Jo and Dan moaned – justifiably – that there was no one to play with on the private beach.

The story of my time in Mustique brought about an introduction to Jane Reid – then the editor of *Woman's Own* and more recently Rupert Murdoch's spokeswoman – and she began commissioning me to write for her on a regular basis. She encouraged me to work on other royal stories and, in the autumn of 1978, asked me to arrange an interview with Earl Mountbatten of Burma, the last Viceroy of India, Supreme Commander South East Asia during the war, and, perhaps most significantly, a member of the Royal Family. It was an assignment that was to have interesting consequences. I contacted his secretary at Broadlands, the family's Hampshire stately home, and was told that his lordship would be pleased to see me but not until the following May. Ever the wily businessman, he wanted the article published to coincide with the opening of Broadlands to a paying public.

A couple of months later I took a call from a particularly well-placed royal informant, who told me that, if I was to travel to the Bahamas the following day and install myself at the Windermere Island Club on Eleuthera, I would be perfectly placed to observe the Prince of Wales enjoying a holiday with some interesting female companions. I was packed and off like a shot: Prince Charles's love life (or lack of one) was always a subject of interest.

Once on Windermere – separated from the main island only by a bridge – I settled in and let it be known that I might be interested in renting a house for two or three months to write a novel. Within hours I received a call from David Hicks, one of Lord Mountbatten's two sons-in-law. He had a fine house, which would soon be vacant for a time. Would I be interested in viewing it? How could I refuse! As he showed me round the house, Hicks enthused about its ideal and secure situation – 'just the kind of place for a writer to work undisturbed and surrounded by great comfort'. When the time came to view the library, however, I was in for something of a shock. As we entered the room, I became aware of a tall, elderly man seated in an armchair on the far side. Hicks said, 'Meet my father-in-law, Lord Mountbatten. Dickie, this is Chris Hutchins.'

The introduction filled me with horror. Knowing that this was a trip likely to produce copy which would not meet with royal approval and only too aware that I had an upcoming official date with the former First Sea Lord, I said just enough to be courteous but not enough to be memorable. I did not want 'Uncle Dickie' to remember me come May.

Back at the Club, a man who introduced himself as Paul Officer, the Royal Protection policeman charged with Prince Charles's personal protection, approached me in the lobby. 'I notice from the register, Mr Hutchins, that you are a writer. Not one of those wretched journalists I have had to turn back at the bridge? His Royal Highness likes his privacy on these trips.'

Our conversation turned to other things and I invited Inspector Officer to join me for dinner that evening. Over the meal and some rather fine wine, with little or no prodding from me, he opened up about his royal charge. Soon the anecdotes were flowing thick and fast. 'We were in Australia on one occasion,' he said, 'and driving across a most remote section of the outback when HRH spotted some men working on the road. It was hundreds of miles from anywhere and he told the driver to stop the car. Before I could do anything about it, he was out and chatting to the men who obviously recognised him but weren't quite sure how to behave. 'How long are you out here for?' he asked them. 'Oh weeks, months' came the reply. 'What about your wives?' he asked but the royal pronunciation of 'wives' sounded to the Aussie workmen more like 'waves'. The men looked at each other nonplussed until one said to the others, 'I think he wants us to wave.' And with that they pulled themselves to attention and waved at HRH for all they were worth. He was terribly embarrassed, got back in the car and didn't say anything for an hour.'

I liked Paul and we had dinner together for the next several evenings. The days, however, were dull. Charles's female companions were family – including the Mountbatten granddaughters-in-law, one of whom has since become a close companion of Prince Philip. I watched from the beach as Charles went windsurfing for hours each afternoon. But the evenings with Paul were riveting. Once, after I had complained of a sore throat, he brought some homeopathic remedy to our table. 'HRH suggests you try this,' he said. So the Prince was aware of my presence on the island, even if his uncle Dickie (hopefully) wasn't.

On the penultimate night of my stay, I told Paul the royal remedy had done the trick and asked if I might thank my benefactor personally. 'I can't introduce you,' he said. 'But, if you happen to be on the beach around 6am tomorrow at a point just half a mile east of the club, he will be jogging by.'

The following morning I was up at five and stumbled in the dark to the spot Paul had indicated. Once in situ I promptly fell asleep only to be awoken by feet running across the sand towards me. It was the Prince. He ran about 20 yards past me and then halted.

This is it, I thought, I've been set up. Here I am with all these cameras and a tape recorder and they are going to arrest me – or worse.

The Prince sat on the beach for what can only have been ten minutes or so, although it seemed liked an hour. Was Paul lurking in the undergrowth somewhere nearby? Was I going to be shot if I approached the heir to the throne? I had my chance and decided to let it go. Charles got back on his feet and ran past me without so much as a cheery 'Hello', let alone 'How's your throat?' Back at the Club I packed and made my way to the airport. I still had plenty to write about.

My official encounter with Dickie Mountbatten came the following May. On the appointed date I drove to Broadlands with the eminent photographer David Steen and we spent the day with his lordship. It turned out to be the last interview he was ever to give – just six weeks later he was assassinated by the IRA during a family fishing trip off the coast of County Mayo.

It soon became clear that our day-long chat was to be more of a history lesson than an interview. Mountbatten explained that his great-grandmother and godmother was Queen Victoria and his mother's youngest sister was the late Tsarina of Russia. At one point he showed us the Japanese Surrender Sword. 'When those people are defeated they are utterly defeated,' he explained. 'Field Marshal Count Terauchi could have handed me his service sword but he felt he hadn't punished himself enough. So he sent to Tokyo for this most priceless of weapons. Its blade was forged in 1292. [General] MacArthur said, 'You'd better give it back – it's part of their history.' 'Not bloody likely,' I said. 'Think of all the men who died on the Burma–Siam road thanks to him.' Actually there were two swords – the other, a shorter one, had a very valuable and attractive scabbard. When I got back I offered both to the King but he chose the one that looked better and said I could keep the 1292 sword. So forget the one on display at Windsor Castle. This is the real thing.'

Then, just as David Steen prepared to photograph him holding the treasured relic, he did a most unexpected thing. With the agility of a man a quarter of his age, he hooked his left foot behind my legs and sent me crashing to the floor. There he held the point of the historic sword at my throat. Has he gone mad? I thought. The same thought must have crossed David's mind, but, before either of us had a chance to speak, the old warlord looked down at me, narrowed his eyes and said, 'Thought I'd forgotten Windermere, did you?' He had gone all day without mentioning it but his mind was as sharp as the blade at my throat. He held me there for several more humiliating moments before withdrawing the sword with a chuckle. He clearly savoured his moment of revenge.

Once I was back on my feet, he posed for the best picture of the day and then ordered tea. When he showed us out an hour or so later, he watched as David and I climbed into the car I had borrowed from Jan while my own was being serviced.

'What make of car is that?' bellowed Lord Mountbatten from the doorway of Broadlands.

'It's a Honda,' I said.

'And where is that made?' he demanded.

'Er, in Japan, sir,' I replied.

He turned on his heels and disappeared inside without even saying goodbye.

In driving a car made by the 'enemy' I had clearly committed an offence far more serious than intruding on his nephew's peaceful holiday and I thought I would never see the old boy again. But a few days later I received an invitation from him to return to Broadlands for a garden party to mark the opening of his stately home. 'And this time you can meet the Prince of Wales in the proper manner,' I was told. That Saturday afternoon Earl Mountbatten did indeed introduce me to his nephew: 'This is Chris Hutchins,' he said. 'Don't speak to him, he drives a Japanese car.' The irony of the situation was clearly not lost on Charles. He winked.

My visit to Windermere had been part of a magazine commission to write about royal holiday homes. The next part of that assignment took me to Iceland, where I had to locate a lodge in a remote area in the north east of the island that belonged to Lord Anthony Tryon and his wife Dale, or Kanga as she was better known, a woman who was to play a major part in my life some years later. The Tryons went there every summer to fish and were joined each year by Prince Charles. I found the lodge and was peering in through the windows when a sudden storm came up. It was late in the afternoon and the clouds quickly blocked out what little light there had been. Only the previous day, I had been warned by a taxi driver in Reykjavik about the hazards of Icelandic weather. His son's car had broken down when he had been travelling from the south to the north of the island and when it was discovered the following day, the young man was frozen to death at the wheel.

In the circumstances, I decided the wisest thing to do was to spend the night at the Tryons' lodge, even though that meant breaking in. Having forced the lock, I went in and inspected the place with the aid of the torch I had taken with me. The beds were unmade but there was a pile of used linen in a laundry basket, which I wrapped around myself for warmth. In an effort to stay awake, I read by torchlight the magazines left by the previous occupants. Appropriately enough, they were *Horse & Hound*, *The Flyfishers' Journal* and *Shooting Times*.

When I got back to my hotel in a nearby town the following day, I telephoned the local priest, Father Haukur Augustsson, and confessed my sin of trespass. After briefly chastising me, Father Augustsson agreed to join me for lunch and told me just the kind of stories I needed to hear, including a description of the one occasion the Tryons had invited him to dinner with Prince Charles. He recalled that he had been required to wait some time for his meal even though the food was cooked and ready. 'Apparently the Prince was still waging battle with a salmon and they said we couldn't possibly start without him,' he said. 'It was a matter of protocol. I said, 'But the food's getting cold and this is Iceland, not Buckingham Palace.'

When Charles finally did turn up at the dinner table, Father Augustsson was pleasantly surprised by his charm, having been less than enchanted by his irascible father on an earlier occasion. Apparently, Prince Philip had been there on a bird-watching holiday and, when he re-emerged from the trees surrounding a lake to discover that his taxi was still there, with no one at the wheel but the keys still in the ignition, he had driven himself back to his accommodation, leaving the driver stranded. 'I tell that story to the children I teach at the school as a lesson in ensuring that my pupils always have respect for themselves and others when the Arctic night descends,' Father Augustsson told me. Having heard the Reykjavik taxi driver's story, I didn't need to be reminded how easily one could die of exposure in Iceland.

Finally, the priest told me a little about his hostess. 'I remember Mr [sic] Tryon's wife well,' he recalled. 'She was a very jolly lady with a very interesting face and figure.' And then he added tellingly, 'The Prince seemed to have a lot of fun in her company.'

Not long afterwards, at the very lodge I had broken into, Prince Charles was brought the news of the assassination of Lord Mountbatten.

Chapter Nine

THE FORSYTH SAGA

Most of us have been in that sad situation where a married couple, who we both know and like decide, to go their separate ways and the question invariably is: Whose side do we take? In the case of Bruce and Penny Forsyth that question was answered for me by the nature of my profession. I was offered an interview with Penny and it was her side of the story I was going to listen to. It turned out to be a harrowing account that would inevitably mean the end of my friendship with Bruce.

Driving down to her home in Kent, I reflected on my first meeting with the couple. To a schoolboy they had, as I have described, what seemed to be the most idyllic relationship it was possible for two people to have. Now I was deeply curious to know what had gone wrong, what had been the root cause of the destruction of their marriage. After all, this was a couple whose lifestyle I'd once hoped to emulate.

From the moment we met (for the first time in many years), Penny wasted no time and spared no detail in telling me what I so desperately wanted to know. Despite my experience of adulterous behaviour, I sat wide-eyed as she told of Bruce's late nights out with other women, saying, 'I always knew when Bruce had another girl. He wouldn't make love to me. He didn't want to be untrue to them.' Could this be the same loving couple I had sat with on Babbacombe Downs sharing sandwiches?

Alas, there was worse to come. The bubbly ex-dancer told me how she once planned to stab her philandering husband with a carving knife when constant calls from his then girlfriend Anthea Redfern ruined their last family Christmas together.

'I said to myself there's only one way to end this and that's to kill him,' she said. Thankfully, family friend Sean Connery was on hand on that occasion and grabbed the would-be murder weapon from her grasp, calling her 'a silly arse'. Bruce, of course, had gone on to leave Penny and marry Anthea. But Penny said that, when one of his daughters confronted him about the alleged marriage, he denied it even though he and Anthea were by then man and wife.

In talking as frankly as she did, Penny was being bold. The last time she had spoken to a newspaper, she said, Bruce had called and screamed at her, 'You bitch, you cow! How dare you talk about my private life?' Was this the man who had once told this editor of the *Monthly Mirror* that he and his pretty wife were partners for life – on stage and off?

My role as midwife to Penny's revelations made Bruce an enemy for life. Although I had never invited him to my house for dinner, I had been a guest at his. That was certainly never going to be repeated.

I apparently reignited the feud some years later when I started writing about him in a newspaper gossip column. I once penned a story about how the girls on the perfume counter at Harrods would smirk at Bruce's hairpiece when he bowed his head to smell samples they placed on the hand of his third wife, Wilnelia. Apparently, this upset him even more than Penny going public about his behaviour during their marriage. I have long accepted the sad fact that comedians can dish it out but can rarely take it.

About a year later, I met another wronged wife, Lady Oona Chaplin. In a way she was a substitute for my main quarry, her late husband, Sir Charles Chaplin. I had been intrigued by Charlie ever since his music publisher, Cyril Simons of Leeds Music, had told me a story that illustrated both how difficult the great comedian had become in later life and yet how enormously talented he was right up to the end.

Chaplin had summoned Cyril to his home near Vevey in Switzerland to play him a song he had just written. After reading the lyrics and listening to the melody, Cyril's heart sank. The song was a ballad and, with Beatlemania at its height, Cyril knew it would be hard to find a reputable singer willing to record it, let alone make it a hit. His fears were confirmed when he touted it around the London music scene. No artist wanted to know. When he explained this to Chaplin, the great man sighed and said, 'Call my friend Al Jolson, he'll do it.' Cyril tried to tell him that Jolson was dead, but Chaplin said, 'Nonsense.' In the end, Cyril was forced to call his parent company's office in Los Angeles and persuade someone there to send a photographer to Forest Lawns Cemetery and take a picture of Jolson's tomb. When the photograph had been couriered to Cyril in London, he set out yet again for Switzerland to show Charlie the proof of Jolson's death. This elaborate operation made little impression on Chaplin; his only response was a mumbled 'More's the pity'. Furthermore, he remained insistent that Cyril find someone else to record his song. In the end, Cyril approached Petula Clark who, though English, lived in France with her French husband and sang most of her hits in French. According to Cyril, when she tried to sing Chaplin's composition in her adopted language she broke up laughing.

After a great deal of effort on Cyril's part, the song was eventually recorded by Harry Secombe and, just as his version went into production, Clark called to say that she had now sung it in English and was keen to record it too. (The fact that she had heard Secombe was prepared to put his name to it probably helped.) Chaplin's genius proved triumphant. When they were released, both versions of his plaintive balled – 'Love (This is my Song)' – broke the rules and went to the top of the charts.

I never did succeed in getting to meet this enigmatic and eccentric man but when he died I was keen to glean whatever secrets I could from his widow. I was also interested in how a wife coped with a man who, while he was clearly a genius, was also a renowned bully and womaniser. All attempts to telephone the reclusive Lady Chaplin were unsuccessful. Even when I called at her house in the hills above Montreux, she refused to see me, although her Scottish housekeeper, Edith Mackenzie – who had previously been nanny to all the Chaplin children – invited me in for a meal while Oona remained in her bedroom above.

My luck changed when Oona arrived in London for a stay at the Savoy. She had had a glass or two of champagne and chatted amicably but said she was far too shy to be interviewed and, in any case, was returning to Switzerland the next day. Only when I offered to follow her did she relent. A week later Oona and I faced each other across the dining table where Charlie had sat to write much of his later work. Over a meal prepared by Mrs Mackenzie, she relayed the harrowing story of married life to the greatest comic of his day. Theirs had been an unusual match from the start. As a young man, Chaplin had paedophilic tendencies. He was forced to marry his first wife in Mexico when he got her pregnant at the age of 13. Sadness etched on her face, Oona (daughter of the playwright Eugene O'Neill) told how he seduced her when she was 14 and how she promised to marry him on her 15th birthday.

As the conversation flowed, so – yet again – did the wine and she talked – as only one with alcohol-related problems can to another – about the origins of her own addiction to booze. 'I don't know why I'm telling you this,' she began. 'I've only ever explained it to Walter Matthau and his wife. Towards the end, Charlie became incontinent. He tried to beat it by going to the lavatory at least once every two hours. He was too mean, too frail or perhaps just too proud to hire a through-the-night nurse to get him there so he'd wake me up. Getting up several times during the night did nothing for my sleeping problems so I kept a tumbler of whisky on my bedside table and took a good swig every time I got Charlie back into bed. And, hey presto! – I still wake up at all hours and I still get back to sleep the same way.'

Her problems did not end with Charlie's death. Soon afterwards, his body was stolen from its burial spot in the nearby churchyard. The corpse had only recently been recovered and I asked Oona if she had ever been tempted to pay the kidnappers' ransom demand of one million Swiss francs. 'No,' she laughed. 'Charlie was so mean that if he thought I'd parted with his good money for a dead body – even his own – he'd have gone through the roof.' After the police had returned his body, Oona had had him reburied, this time under four feet of concrete.

Widowed at a relatively early age, Lady Chaplin was still a

slim, good-looking woman and attracted some surprising suitors. She was discreet in discussing her love life but she did intimate that there was a strange friendship with David Bowie, who lived locally, and that Hollywood's arch-Lothario Warren Beatty also developed a crush on her.

We had started at noon and it was six in the evening when I closed my notebook and switched off the tape recorder.

'What? No political questions?' she asked, seemingly relieved.

'No,' I said. 'I'm not interested in Charlie's politics.'

She was relieved but curious. 'But you're a political writer, aren't you Christopher Hitchens?'

'No,' I said, 'I'm Christopher *Hutchins*.'

She laughed yet again, and we opened another bottle of wine.

The next day I drove to Gstaad to hook up with the actress Lynne Frederick, with whom I was on good terms. Alas, I had left her telephone number in London so, after booking into the Palace Hotel, I strolled to the Olden, Gstaad's answer to San Lorenzo. Yane, the head barman, knew everyone and if anyone could tell me how to find Lynne it was he, but he politely declined my request until I had bought him (and myself) several large brandies. When I finally got through to Lynne I was in George Best mode and she was in deadly earnest: 'No, Chris, you can't come up. I know why you're here. You know *he*'s here, don't you?' As it happens, I didn't have the faintest idea who or what Lynne was talking about until I drove back into London and saw the *Evening Standard* placards proclaiming that she was to marry David Frost. She told me later that he was virtually proposing on bended knee when I telephoned.

David and I came across each other several times over the years and, a few months after his wedding to Lynne, we met for lunch at Verrey's in Regent Street. I was already at the table when he walked in with big smile and said, 'Thanks for sending Lynne that panda – it must have cost you a fortune.'

'What panda?' I asked.

'You know, that great big one with the 'I love you' card round its neck.'

I explained that, whoever it came from, it wasn't me and he sat and fumed throughout lunch. Lynne seemingly had an admirer he didn't know about.

When Jane Reid left *Woman's Own* to work for Rupert Murdoch, the new editor, Wendy Henry, continued to put work my way. Early on, she sent me to Paris to interview a sexy young film star. This girl's latest project had a relatively big budget and was to be launched with a champagne press reception in one of the city's better hotels. By the time I arrived, I was quite tired and my interviewee spotted me slipping a purple heart into my mouth. She walked over and said, 'I saw you were popping a pill. Can I have a couple because I'm very tired?' There was a problem: I kept my uppers in the left key-pocket of my jacket and my downers (sleeping pills) in the right. Unfortunately, when I reached into the left one I discovered it was empty. I should have admitted I had run out but I could not bear to disappoint her, so I handed her a couple of pills from the right pocket. Why did I do this? It seemed like fun at the time.

The result was predictable. Within a few minutes she was falling about. She had taken both tablets at once and was quickly becoming sedated. Her manager and a bodyguard had to carry her up to bed. When I arrived in her suite to interview her the following day, she shook her finger at me, smiled and said, 'You're very naughty.' As anyone who uses drugs knows, it's all a bit of a game.

Wendy's next commission was less glamorous. She sent me

to Blackpool to cover the Conservative Party conference. On the way there I travelled in a first-class compartment with a family of snooty Tories. The head of the family had just been awarded a peerage and in smug tones they spent the entire journey discussing what his title should be. I found it all quite odious. Since I had gone at short notice, all the decent hotels in the town were full but a helpful taxi driver found me a modest bed-and-breakfast with a 'Vacant' sign in the window. After the excruciating experience with 'his lordship' and his brood on the journey, I was pleased to be back in the company of ordinary people.

The landlady was quick to point out that there was a bar in the basement. It turned out to be a wonderfully kitsch affair complete with tropical fish tank, coloured lights and flying ducks on the wall. As I sat nursing a drink, I heard a middle-aged woman ask her friend in a broad northern accent, 'Where's your father?'

'I don't know,' came the reply. 'He said he was going to look around the shops.'

At that point, the door opened and an elderly man appeared. With his legs splayed, arms outstretched and fists clenched, he looked at the two women and cried, 'Ba-bam!'

They were clearly unimpressed by his display of a new purchase and one said, 'Father! New trousers, at your age? You'll never get the use out of 'em.'

What a view on life this job provided.

Jan and I decided to take Jo and Dan to the Algarve for the summer holidays but I made the mistake of mentioning it to Terry O'Neill. He decided that southern Portugal was just the place where he and his latest love (previous ones included Raquel Welch and Priscilla Presley, remember), Faye Dunaway, should go for their vacation. Not that I didn't enjoy Terry's company – quite the reverse. Having fun with a mate on a working trip to Barbados was all very fine, but our overboard behaviour when we got together was hardly conducive to a happy family holiday. On the very first night we got together the six of us went to a restaurant in Albufeira. As the wine flowed, our spirits soared and my wife and the Oscar-winning actress looked on in despair as Terry and I sang rock 'n' roll songs at the top of our voices. Then he went from table to table in the packed restaurant declaring, 'My friend over there does Little Richard, Jerry Lee, Elvis or Gene Vincent. What d'ya wanna hear?' Only when we had performed several duets in the middle of the floor did Jan and Faye manage to get us out of the place.

Faye, in particular, was furious. 'It's only because you're a big movie star,' I teased.

'Here I'm just a holidaymaker like you,' she retorted.

'Oh, where's your sense of humour?' I responded, opening the boot of the car. 'Why don't you get in here?'

To my astonishment Ms Dunaway smiled, nodded and climbed into what she called 'the trunk', saying something about the company might be better in there. The boot closed and with the rest of us comfortably in our seats, I drove to the estate on the edge of a golf course where we had rented nearby villas. I doubt I missed a single pothole on the way. When she climbed back out of the boot, Faye's temporary smile had gone. She was probably bruised and (understandably) was not to speak to me again for the rest of the holiday. The night of mischief was not over for Terry and me, however. We placed a call to the home of Tony Miles and told the Mirror Group chairman we had come across an amazing story. Although he had been asleep, Tony – ever the newspaperman – was hooked.

'Tell me, tell me,' he demanded.

'Well...' Terry began. And with that he hung up, leaving one of the most powerful journalists in Britain wondering what he had missed out on due to a 'broken connection'.

It was not a memorable holiday, nor am I proud of our loutish behaviour, but this is the way things happened in those heady days.

Chapter Ten

ONE YELLOW WATCH

It was a call from Tony Miles in May 1981 that spawned the controversial gossip column I was to produce for three different national newspapers over the next 11 years. He wanted me to write a column for the *Sunday Mirror* that would be 'bold and intrusive' and 'get under people's skin'. My first concern was how the paper's editor, Bob Edwards, would react to the news that his chairman had hired me as a columnist. 'Bob will love it – when I tell him about it,' said Tony. That did not augur well. Tony had been editor of the *Daily Mirror* until a few years earlier but was still uncomfortable in the role of hands-off chairman. He agreed that we should meet with Bob for a lunch at the Reform Club in St James's before taking things any further.

'Here's the deal,' said Tony, who had by now told Bob what he had proposed. 'The column's going to be called *Confidential*. I've asked Bob to give you a lot of leeway and all the support you need.'

How do you refuse an offer like that? I started within a fortnight.

Tony's aggressive approach appealed to me because by now I had adopted a mantra: 'Comfort the disturbed and disturb the comfortable.' As a publicist who had turned back to journalism, I knew all the tricks the other side played. Having spent years sanitising the images of my clients, I had, towards the end, grown to despise the process. After a while it really had got increasingly difficult to sleep at night. I would lie awake thinking, This isn't fun any more. I'm actually telling lies for a living. The more fiction you create, the more you get paid in the PR business and I had finally reached the conclusion that that was immoral. I had been deceiving the public and now was the time to reverse the process. When it comes to gossip-writing I have always shared the view that Lord Justice Lawton took in his judgment over *The Family*: 'It seems these pop stars present one side of their profile to the public and enjoy it but do not like it when the warts are shown... If you don't like the glare, stay out of the limelight.'

A good gossip column exists to cut through manufactured auras and tell you what famous people are really like. It focuses exclusively on celebrities, whether they achieve fame through talent, accident of birth or simply by becoming exceedingly rich. Everyone in the public eye seeks to manicure his or her image to some extent. It had been my job to make my clients almost godlike, people who would be worshipped by their fans and admirers. When I represented Tom Jones, I largely succeeded in presenting him as a sex god who managed to remain faithful to his wife. But I eventually reached the conclusion that it did not do celebrities any good to be told they were something they could never be. Even the Queen has her troubles. Indeed, the Royal Family almost collapsed under the strain of attempting to live up to an impossibly straight-laced image. The Duke of Edinburgh gets ratty, Tom Jones gets lusty, the Blairs get greedy. These are perfectly human traits and a gossip column is there to peel back the layers. I often felt quite sick when, as a conventional reporter, I was required to go along with hype that I could see through. The story that the wonderful Lord so-and-so has just celebrated his marriage to the lovely Letitia by giving his workers a Christmas bonus has no place in a decent gossip column. It's never that simple. The high and mighty are as flawed as the rest of us: they've just been better at covering it up.

I have lost count of the number of times I have been harangued at dinner parties about my willingness to expose affairs. My answer is always the same: if people become high profile, they can't expect wonderful publicity about how well they are doing in other fields while concealing the fact that they have failed at something like marriage. The pop singer will give any number of interviews about the inspiration behind a no 1 love song, the politician will talk long and convincingly about his commitment to family values, and the aristocrat will bore for Britain about the grandeur of his lineage. But, when it comes to the issue of lying to their wives about their affair with a waitress, they will scream 'Intrusion!'

Now, this is a perfectly natural way to behave. No one likes discussing aspects of behaviour of which they are ashamed, but I believe that a journalist is letting down the reader if he doesn't tell the whole truth to the best of his ability. It is actually dishonest not to present a rounded picture. People talk of privacy laws. Much of what I was to publish in *Confidential* would never have seen the light of day in France, where they already have one. But such legislation amounts to the Establishment protecting itself. If, for example, we elect someone to high office, it is important that we know what he or she is like. Some say we don't have to look at the man so much as his policies. But how can we rely on him to deliver his policies if even his wife can't trust him? That is not to say that a philandering politician is inevitably an unreliable leader but it seems to me that the question of whether he has the right stuff is a judgement the electorate should make, not a cabal of self-serving legislators.

In short, celebrities cannot have it both ways. When you court publicity you dance with the Devil. Pop stars' agents cannot expect to tip off photographers that a client will be arriving at a nightclub looking great at a certain time but then expect the paparazzi not to remain there and take more pictures a few hours later when that same individual leaves looking drunk and bedraggled. Yet it happens time and time again.

Confidential quickly established itself as the most scurrilous gossip column on Fleet Street and as a result I got many interesting phone calls and letters from contacts and readers. But one note that landed on my desk in October 1982 was particularly intriguing. While there was no letterhead, the writer gave her address as Buckingham Palace and, rather like a pop fan, asked for a signed photograph of me. That sort of thing doesn't happen to journos, so suspecting it was a spoof by someone I knew in the Palace press office, I called the phone number given in the letter and asked for the appropriate extension. When a young woman answered the phone, I asked impatiently if she was Michelle Riles, my mystery correspondent.

'Yes,' she said, 'who's that?'

Feeling a little embarrassed that I'd clearly got through to a bona fide reader and not an embittered press officer taking the piss, I apologised for my tone and asked her if she would like to go out for lunch. I would be less than honest if I did not admit it had instantly occurred to me that a below-stairs Palace source might prove useful at some time in the future, but I had not bargained for what this one had to impart.

A few days later, I sat enthralled at a table at Menage A Trois in Beauchamp Place as I listened to one of the most incredible stories I've ever been told by anyone outside the inner circles of the Establishment. Over two hours, Michelle poured out her story of life at the Palace. She told me about the Queen's frequent rows with her sister Princess Margaret, how Prince Charles and Princess Diana's bedroom would often be a wreck the morning after one of their ill-tempered bust-ups, and how the motherly Queen would help her to make the Princes' beds, laying out cuddly toys as if she resented them growing up.

But, most amazing of all, she told me how she came to sleep with Prince Edward.

It was the ultimate in upstairs–downstairs relationships. Michelle – who, at 20, was three years Edward's senior – was a Liverpool girl who had moved to Skegness to work at the local Butlin's holiday camp. She had got her job at the Palace after applying for the post of a maidservant at Sandringham that had been advertised in *The Lady*. When she applied, the interview was held at Buckingham Palace and that, indeed, was where the vacancy turned out to be. What she didn't tell her interviewer was that she was pregnant. When the job offer came, she went home to have an abortion.

In the taxi on the way back to the office, my mind was buzzing with the thought that one of the Queen's lowliest servants (her jobs included taking Her Majesty's corgis into the Palace gardens to relieve themselves) was being bedded by her youngest son. It was the biggest royal story for years and it deserved to be told, if only to counteract other untrue speculation about Prince Edward. The idea that she had seduced or been seduced by a senior member of the Royal Family was fantastic.

A few days later, Michelle and I met again to go over the details of what she had imparted. Over the following weeks and months we kept in touch and we met frequently. As a by-product, she told me of the effect various goings-on at the Palace had on her. One Saturday night, for example, she had to cancel a pressing engagement because Prince Andrew was throwing a birthday party for Koo Stark – long after the world had been led to believe their relationship was over – and a full staff of servants was required to wait on them. To disprove the disinformation that had been circulated, we had a number of photographers on hand to picture the arriving guests.

Publishing the scoop of the decade – *Michelle's Story: The Prince and the Palace Maid* – proved a mite more problematic. The undeniable facts were that she and Edward had shared three nights of passion while staying at Balmoral during the summer of 1981. Aware of the sensitivities involved, I prepared the story with great care. Unable to visit Michelle at the Palace personally, I asked a female friend to go to see her, take photographs and make notes about her lifestyle. Michelle also handed over copies of several letters she had sent Edward since their brief affair. She had laboriously written each of them out twice – once in a practice scrawl and then in her 'best writing' to send to the Prince, whom she called 'Eddie-babes'. Unfortunately, he had been canny enough not to reply to any of them beyond sending her a hand-drawn map of a suggested walk in nearby woods. Michelle allowed me to copy the relevant extracts from her diary. A sceptic might say that none of this amounts to forensic evidence of her relationship with the Prince but all I can say in answer to that is that I never doubted her for a moment. After years in this game, I had learned to spot a liar and I quickly realised that this particular young woman was constitutionally incapable of lying about anything.

By May 1983, Michelle's memoirs were ready for publication. I had been careful to discuss it with only one editor but someone in his office committed what – in newspaper terms – amounts to treason and tipped off the Palace. The Palace immediately called in the Queen's solicitors Farrer and Co to threaten litigation. Royal aides were in confident mood at the time following their success in blocking revelations by another royal servant, Kieran Kenny, about Andrew's relationship with Stark. Farrers made much of the fact that Michelle had signed the Official Secrets Act and they had no difficulty in persuading the Attorney General to prevent publication of her story in any form. In my view, the decision was nothing short of ludicrous. People such as Harold Wilson, his political secretary 'Lady' Marcia Falkender and the retired Metropolitan Police chief Sir David McNee had also signed the Official Secrets Act, and all of them had recently produced books of memoirs in which they revealed facts that were supposed to be state secrets without a word of protest from the Attorney General. Even the trusted Palace PR man Michael Shea has since blown the whistle with a book and doubtless Alastair Campbell will eventually join that line.

In Michelle's case, of course, there were no state secrets to protect – she dusted, made beds, took the Queen's corgis into the Palace gardens whenever they needed to pee and had a roll in the hay with her youngest son. But the people who guard the Royal Family's dirty laundry were furious that a humble housemaid might reveal what a prince was like in bed. I couldn't help but wonder what protection Michelle would have had if Edward had ever decided to write his own memoirs and recalled the occasions on which he laid the maid from below stairs.

Confidential brought me into contact with a wide variety of people, including the QC who had unsuccessfully sought the injunction against the *Mirror* publishing *The Family*, Sir Peter Rawlinson (now Lord Rawlinson). Just before Christmas, I heard from a friend that his wife Elaine was selling sexy nighties from their home. When I telephoned her, Lady Rawlinson said she had just bought her first consignment of 200 nightgowns from Florence. 'They are wonderful: silks, satins and laces,' she said.

'Are they, er, sensual?' I asked.

'Oh, most definitely,' she replied. 'Some of my customers are wearing them as evening dresses, although the one I have and like best definitely could not be worn outside the bedroom.' Then Lady R asked if I had yet bought my wife a Christmas present and, when I said I hadn't, she suggested that one of her nighties would make the perfect gift for Jan.

I arranged to meet her ladyship a couple of hours later at Simpson's on the Strand, where she was to have lunch with her husband. We rendezvoused in the bar, where I found her clutching a large bag containing samples of her merchandise. The inevitable glasses of champagne were soon being poured and, to the amusement of onlookers, she began displaying her wares. When it was obvious that only one garment remained in the bag, she said that at £100 it was 'very expensive – and very revealing'. I said, 'That sounds ideal but for that much money I'd have to see it. Don't be nervous, show it to me.' At that precise moment I noticed Lord Rawlinson enter the bar. His wife, however, did not and stood to hold the near-transparent negligee to her chest just as his lordship caught sight of her. That might or might not explain why he failed to come and join us but disappeared from view.

Jan did get the nightie but never wore it. I don't think she was amused by the escapade. It was Mustique all over again.

One of the biggest rows the column caused was that between one of Britain's foremost aristocrats and his heir. The late Marquis of Bath was clearly short of cash, because he was surreptitiously taking paintings from Longleat, the ancestral home, to a discreet London art gallery. Under the terms of the family trust, the pictures were classified as heirlooms and he was legally barred from selling them. The Marquis's scheme was to have the paintings photographed and the images steamed on to canvas before disposing of the original works for much-needed funds. The copies would then be re-hung at Longleat and his son and heir, Lord (Alexander) Weymouth, would be none the wiser. Unfortunately for his (elder) lordship, I had a mole at the gallery who tipped me off about the scam. She called on one occasion to say he had just been in with four valuable hunting scenes by Alken. Since it would have been virtually impossible to get confirmation of the deal from either the Marquis or the gallery, I called Alexander. We frequently drank together at Stringfellow's and were on good terms.

'Alexander,' I said, 'have you got four pictures of horses by Alken?'

'Yes,' he said.

'No, you haven't.'

'Yes, I have.'

'No, you haven't.'

Alexander – by now very cross – said, 'Look, I know I've got them. In fact I know exactly where they are. They are hung over the bookcases in the Bishop Ken Library.'

'Sorry, Alexander, they're not.'

'Nonsense,' he said irritably. 'I'll go there right now and check.'

I hung on while he marched off to establish that his paintings were still in situ.

He was soon back. 'They are most definitely there,' he said triumphantly.

'Copies, maybe, Alexander, but most definitely not the originals.'

By now he was on the verge of going ballistic.

'Look at them more closely,' I said, 'and you'll see that they are copies.'

The old boy had deliberately picked a position where the paintings were difficult to inspect at close quarters and Alexander had to climb a ladder to examine them. When he did, he immediately spotted they were prints. He went on to confront his father, who was subsequently forced to buy back the originals. Alexander never forgot what he considered a favour and we remain on good terms to this day. When I called him to clarify a few details for this book, his memory of the incident was still vivid. 'Yes, I remember very, very well how you brought this matter to my attention and how we got back the pictures after my father had flogged them,' he said. 'The originals are, of course, still safely at Longleat. I've moved them to the Clocktower Suite in the old stable block with the rest of what I call my father's misdoings, including his collection of Hitleriana. We've still got the fakes he had made, too.'

One of the most memorable lunches I had while I was on the *Sunday Mirror* was with the legendary TV newsreader, Reginald Bosanquet, universally known as Reggie. Like most of the nation I was glued to the screen each night he read the

News At Ten to see if he would get through it because he was invariably drunk.

For our lunch I took him to Green's in St James's, a restaurant especially popular with politicians and writers. When he turned up at one o'clock he was already quite pissed and I realised that it could be an embarrassing experience. Because he was so well known we were given a centre-stage table, so to speak. Alas, that only made things worse. When I asked Reggie what he would like to drink, it was clear he had no intention of slowing down. 'Champagne, old boy,' he said, 'to start with.'

For his main course he ordered partridge and a bottle of port to wash it down. Before long he became very loud and was talking about women in sexually explicit detail. I tried to change the subject and told him that I used to have a room in the Chelsea flat where he was living and that's where Paul McCartney met Jane Asher. Alas, such trivia was not enough to distract him so I pointed out that Michael Heseltine (then a member of Margaret Thatcher's Cabinet) was seated at a table nearby.

'Michael?' he said, standing up. 'Where?'

Reggie was a huge man, broad as well as tall, and he soon spotted Heseltine, who was lunching with a very attractive blonde girl who may have been one of his daughters. Reggie had been eating the partridge with his bare hands, which is not particularly improper, but without bothering to wipe them he picked up his glass of champagne and headed over to Heseltine's table. There he extended his greasy palm and Heseltine was obliged to shake it although he was clearly mortified by the encounter. They talked for two or three minutes and then, leaving his greasy glass of champagne as 'a gift', Reggie returned to our table.

By now he was so drunk I was finding it hard to keep the

conversation going and, still in search of a diverting topic, I said, 'I read somewhere the other day that Heseltine is dyslexic.' This clearly amused him. 'Really?' he said. 'Here, give me a pen and a piece of paper.' On a page torn from my notebook he wrote, 'Maggie rules, KO?' and weaved back over to Heseltine with it. The Minister laughed politely but I'd had enough, called for the bill, paid it and was bidding Reggie a fast farewell. But he was having none of it. 'Oh no, you're going nowhere without me, Hutchins! We're off to my club for a drink now.' He followed me out and I quickened my pace to try and lose him but with little success. By now in desperation, I began to run down the street but Reggie pursued me calling at the top of his voice, 'Come on, Hutchins! What you need is a good drink.'

Out of the corner of my eye I spotted an art gallery with a sign which read 'Press bell for admission.' I doubt I have ever pressed a bell harder than I did that one. Once the door was opened I rushed in and, as it closed behind me, told the nonplussed assistant, 'Whatever you do, don't let that man in.' My last memory of Reggie was of him hammering on the glass-panelled door, shouting, 'Come on, Hutchins, we're going for a proper drink. It's all right, it's my turn to pay.' It was an alarming experience. I have met many intimidating and unpredictable people over the years but there was something unique about Reggie in the sense that he knew no barriers. That night I watched him read the news in what can only be described as his usual manner: slurred.

An episode that came close in terms of distressing company occurred almost 20 years earlier when Andrew Oldham took me to lunch at a Soho steak house to meet Phil Spector. Andrew was riding high as manager and producer of the Rolling Stones. He worshipped Spector, who had already gained iconic status as a producer thanks to his invention of the 'wall of sound' technique. Lunch started off conventionally enough. I asked the sort of questions a music journalist would ask and Spector responded perfectly normally. Then his behaviour suddenly changed.

He surveyed other diners – none of whom he had ever met – and decided who he did and didn't like. Having done that, he picked up chips from his plate and started tossing them at those who failed to meet with his approval. Finally, after he had thrown his steak at one man, his victim got up, crossed to our table and began to remonstrate with him. Spector flipped. 'Get out of my sight!' he screamed. 'I'm gonna kill you! I swear I'm gonna kill you.' The renowned music man was so clearly unhinged at this moment that the man promptly retreated. With hindsight, Spector had obviously been high on something. I found the whole business quite disturbing but Andrew just laughed. He seemed to think it was wonderful.

No wonder Jan was never keen for me to bring my contacts home. Was I now growing just a little too like them?

Bearing in mind Tony Miles's exhortation to be 'bold and intrusive', one Sunday *Confidential* broke one of the longest-standing conventions in showbusiness and revealed the identity of a forthcoming subject of *This is Your Life* – the broadcaster and one-time crooner Jimmy Young. In those days, the Thames TV show was hosted by Eamon Andrews and had huge viewing figures. The day after our story appeared – in the form of an untitled paragraph just eight lines long – Thames staged a press conference at which a furious Andrews railed against me and said that as a result of the disclosure the Young programme had had to be abandoned.

Goaded into action, the following Sunday I ran a print version of Jimmy's *This is Your Life* – a rather more scurrilous review than would ever have appeared on the sanitised TV show. Among other things, I revealed that he was 62 at the time – not 58 as everyone believed – and named the two ex-wives that Andrews would never have dared to mention. Needless to say, Mrs Thatcher's favourite interviewer was extremely upset.

Six months later Jan and I took the children on holiday to Portugal. The previous year we had become friends with the former TV announcer Peter West, who now ran a bar at his palatial home in the Algarve. As I sat talking to Peter, I felt Jan kicking me under the table. I ignored her and finally she scribbled a note and passed it to me. It said, 'The man at the bar is Eamon Andrews.' I had not spoken to him since the Jimmy Young debacle and now the former Irish boxing champion was sitting less than five yards away, glaring at me. This was clearly a feud that had to be resolved so I stood up and beckoned him to follow me into the garden. Short, sharp words were exchanged and, after I had promised faithfully never to ruin one of his shows again, we shook hands. Peace restored, we went back in and had a drink together.

Confidential did not, however, only make me enemies. One of the nicest friendships of my whole life was with the late Speaker of the Commons, George Thomas (later to become Lord Tonypandy). We first met when he and I (in my capacity as a gossip columnist) were invited to guest on Carol Thatcher's LBC radio show on the same evening. After my spot, I went back to the green room to see Jan deep in conversation with the amiable Welshman, although she didn't have a clue who he was. Before he left he said, 'I must have you two round to Speaker's House for dinner one night.' Sure enough, some days later the promised invitation arrived. But it was not to a private dinner for the three of us – George never married – but to a state banquet for 150 guests. I called his secretary to say that, with the greatest respect, we were not keen on formal functions, and would prefer to visit on another occasion when we could enjoy a long chat with the man himself. George called back shortly afterwards and invited us to just such a cosy evening the following week.

On the appointed night, we arrived at Speaker's House to be met by Speaker Thomas, resplendent in the ancient costume (including breeches) he was required to wear on formal occasions. After a roast beef dinner, he took us on a conducted tour of his splendid residence with its huge formal banqueting hall, magnificent art collection and library of antiquarian books. He proved to be as entertaining as he was likeable and during the trek he kept us amused with tales of his childhood. He told us he had been christened Thomas George Thomas but had dropped the first Thomas when other children at school started calling him Tommy Twice. The tour completed, it was back to his sitting room to lay into the port and trade stories. He was the greatest raconteur I had ever met. 'I regularly have the Queen Mother here for dinner,' he said. 'She sits where you two are sitting now and tells me wonderful stories about what's going on at the Palace and with her family. And I tell her what some of the mad buggers here are up to. We have a jolly good laugh.' On the way out, as I thanked him for dinner, he gave me some fatherly advice: 'Now keep in touch but meanwhile here's a bit of advice for you: never make a promise you don't intend to keep... or a threat you can't carry out.'

I had found another mentor.

After that first night we met a number of times but telephoned each other far more often. In the process he became one of my highest-placed sources. He would ring me and say, 'Here's something you might like for your column,' but always followed that with: 'It didn't come from me, mind.'

George had one rival to the title of *Confidential*'s highest-placed source. After writing a mischievous and highly distasteful item about Lady 'Kanga' Tryon being in 'two minds' about accepting the presidency of a national organisation for schizophrenics, she called to scold me. In the course of this chastisement, she asked whether I knew anyone who suffered from the illness. To add to my shame I told her that my sister was a chronic sufferer. Instead of the tirade I had expected to follow this admission, Kanga said, 'Oh, the poor love. Let's you and I have lunch and see if I can be of any help.' We met at San Lorenzo and became instant friends. At that point Prince Charles's former lover also became my most potent royal source and our lives became inextricably intertwined.

One Saturday in January 1983, after a particularly tough week on the *Sunday Mirror* during which I had produced a front-page splash and a couple of features as well as *Confidential*, Bob Edwards summoned me to the editor's office. There he explained, as delicately as only this true gentleman of Fleet Street could, that he considered I was suffering from exhaustion and he had made arrangements for me to be checked out in a private hospital. That evening, one of the company chauffeurs drove me down to The Paddocks, a discreet medical centre located in a scenic part of Buckinghamshire close to Chequers, the Prime Minister's country home.

I was sedated on arrival and awoke late the following morning to find Patrick O'Connor, a retired air vice marshal and now a private Harley Street practitioner who had served me well in the past, seated at my bedside. My surroundings looked more like a country hotel than a hospital, and Paddy's opening remark was as comforting as ever. 'Bob [Edwards] and I thought you deserved a little rest and some good food in a place where we can carry out some tests and find out what's messing you up.' Then came the tough part. 'There's some good news and some bad. We've taken blood samples while you've been asleep and there's not much wrong with you that a period of abstinence will not put right. The bad news is you drink too much. You're an alcoholic, Chris. You'll have to give up the drink.'

I was outraged. How dare he call me that? Didn't drinking go with the territory in my line of work? And weren't alcoholics people who slept under railway arches and wore soiled clothes? I lived the high life and was insulted by Paddy's diagnosis. When he eventually left the room I got dressed, walked out through the main entrance, marched straight to the nearest pub and ordered a large gin and tonic.

'You in The Paddocks?' asked the landlord casually as I paid for the drink.

'Er, no,' I said, 'just visiting a friend there.'

'And will that be your friend's identity tag you're wearing on your wrist?' he asked, pointing at the plastic identity strap on my extended arm.

Any reasonable man would have known at that moment that the game was up. But not me. Ignoring Paddy's warnings I went home and – just as he had warned they would if I did not abstain – things got worse. Some weeks later, after a drinking contest with a colleague in the *Mirror*'s local, the Stab In The Back (he had an unfair advantage – he hadn't swallowed half a dozen sleeping tablets before we started), I found myself being admitted to St Bart's Hospital.

Through a haze of white noise I heard two nurses checking in my clothes and possessions. Finally they came to my pride and joy, my magnificent 18-carat-gold Piaget watch of which I was so proud that I had the left sleeves of my handmade shirts cut two inches shorter than the right in order to best display it. Alas, this most precious piece of Swiss precision did not impress the nurse making the inventory. In flat tones, she called to the girl writing the list: '... and one yellow watch'. That episode wasn't enough to persuade me to stop drinking but for a while I did cut down.

In April 1985, I was sent to Italy to cover a royal tour by Prince Charles and Princess Diana. When I arrived at the hotel in Florence, I was told that Charles's press secretary, Michael Shea, wanted to see me in the bar. It was clear he had been drinking and at that time I was off it. I had never met the Queen's official spokesman before so his opening gambit came as a bit of a shock: 'Let's get one thing straight, Hutchins. They [Charles and Diana] don't like your fucking paper, they don't like what you fucking write and they especially don't fucking like you.'

Clearly, it was not going to be an easy assignment. Nevertheless, when the journalists drew lots to decide who would accompany the royal couple on their visit to the renowned Uffizi art gallery the next day, my number came out of the hat and there was nothing Shea could do about it. Diana, in particular, looked decidedly uneasy about my presence at their sides. Charles merely nodded in my direction (perhaps he remembered Windermere) and scowled, but I prefer to think that this was his mood of the moment: I knew from the Palace maid that his marriage was already in deep trouble.

On 25 October of that year, Bob Edwards left the company. It was a bitter man who sipped champagne that night in the boardroom on the ninth floor of the *Mirror*'s building at

Holborn Circus. And with good reason. It was Bob who had brought in the notorious Robert Maxwell to buy the company from Reed International after they got to know each other as near-neighbours in Oxfordshire. Reed had initially been unwilling to talk to Maxwell because he had been branded unfit to run a public company after an investigation by inspectors appointed by the Department of Trade and Industry some years earlier. But Bob had helped and, in the absence of any other serious bidders, the sale had gone through. Within months of Maxwell taking over, however, Bob was gone.

Bob had introduced me to Maxwell soon after he took over. Despite his gargantuan proportions, he came across as an extremely affable man and, although it was only teatime on the day we met, he was already taking slugs of whisky from a large tumbler. To my surprise, he gave me a substantial pay hike on the spot. I can only assume he wanted me to go back to the office full of praise for the new proprietor. Keen to justify his confidence, when I came across him in the lift a week or two later, I offered him some suggestions about how the paper might be improved. 'Come and see me at lunchtime,' he said. His PA, Jean Baddeley, phoned three times that morning to put back our appointment half an hour each time and finally to cancel it altogether. But, as a consolation, Maxwell called me later in person and said, 'You're a bright fellow, I'm going to give you a rise.' In the space of a fortnight, my salary had gone up by 50 per cent without so much as a request from me.

Maxwell went on to run the Mirror Group right up to his mysterious death at sea in 1991. It was only after his drowning that the judgement of the DTI inspectors was shown to have been uncannily sound. It emerged that he had looted the Group's pension fund for years and gambled it not only on a succession of overpriced acquisitions but also on the tables of London casinos, where he would lose as much as £250,000 in a single night.

One eternal truth that writing the column taught me is that comics can't always take a joke. A war with Max Bygraves that lasted for more than two years began with a small *Confidential* item about his son Anthony giving up on his attempts to emulate his father's success as a stand-up comedian. My item ended with the line:

> *'It is said that, after he appeared in summer season at a Channel Island resort, residents were asked who they would prefer to return – Anthony Bygraves or the German Army of occupation. I would not be so cruel as to reveal the overwhelming result of the poll.'*

The very next day Bygraves sent the first in a series of letters addressed both to me and the editor of the *Sunday Mirror*. Complaining that I had ruined his extended festive season by having a crack at his son, he pointed out how well Anthony had done as a songwriter and producer of shows. In his letter to the editor, he threw in some personal remarks: 'The last time I saw that twit Hutchins, he couldn't focus, and for the first ten minutes called me Frankie – this from a man I used to pay £3 to do sleeve notes on record albums.'

Peter Thompson – who had succeeded Bob Edwards as the editor – and I laughed but if we thought that was the end of the matter we were much mistaken. The flow of letters and cards I got became increasingly abusive and usually started 'Dear Shitface'.

I may have contributed to the escalation of hostilities by

replying to one of his rants with a specially composed 'pro-forma' response from my secretary: 'Chris Hutchins has asked me to thank you for your letter. You will appreciate that he gets a lot of mail from readers like yourself and doesn't always get the opportunity to answer them personally but he does appreciate your interest in his column.' In response to that one, Bygraves wrote to Peter saying that he would move to Spain, on condition that 'Chris Hutchins came along but he'd have to swim back and I hope he'd be able to cut himself out of the sack.'

Our correspondence took a more humorous turn when he sent me a postcard from Australia. It read: ''Ere, Shitface, make yourself useful. Back in Bournemouth my dog's gone missing. See if any of your readers can find it. It's only got one ear, one eye and half a tail but it answers to the name of Lucky.'

Then one day I picked up a colleague's phone in the office one day to hear the instantly recognisable voice of Max himself. I explained that the person he wanted wasn't there and he asked, 'Who's that speaking?'

'Chris Hutchins,' I said – somewhat hesitantly, I have to admit.

'Hello, Chris,' he said with bizarre warmth. 'How are you? I was only thinking about you the other day.'

We went on to have a perfectly friendly conversation during which our war of words went unmentioned. I never received another communication on the subject from him and when we met at one of Maurice Kinn's showbusiness dinners he was affability itself.

After five years of baiting the Establishment and winding up celebrities at the *Sunday Mirror*, I fell out with Peter Thompson. That week the papers had made much of the news that the Duchess of Kent had complained to British Rail

CHRIS HUTCHINS

about the noise of a couple making love in the compartment next to hers as she travelled from Norfolk to London, On the Sunday, I wrote a satirical paragraph aimed at the Duchess saying, 'My wife and I wish to apologise for any embarrassment caused to her during the train journey we shared recently from King's Lynn.' Peter thought it was in bad taste and ordered me to take it out but I sneakily left it in.

Nothing was said until we were coming out of the morning news conference on the following Tuesday. Peter's deputy, John Parker, said, 'I want a word with you in my office.' There, he proceeded to give me a bollocking, clearly on Peter's behalf. I was furious, told him where they could stuff the *Sunday Mirror* and marched across the road to the Stab. From the payphone at one end of the bar I asked a friend to put the word around that I was on the market. Whatever my friend did, it was effective. Within half an hour the payphone had rung three times, with calls for me from Kelvin MacKenzie, editor of the *Sun*, Nick Lloyd, who was about to take on the editorship of the *Daily Express*, and David Montgomery, who had succeeded Nick as editor of the *News of the World*. I subsequently had meetings with all three and accepted an offer from Nick to take *Confidential* to the *Express* when he took over six weeks later. We agreed that the column would appear daily but, by the time my start date arrived, Nick had changed his mind and decided to keep the *William Hickey* column during the week. *Confidential* appeared only on Saturdays and I was to write other stories for the paper on weekdays.

Soon after my arrival, Nick sent me to Antigua to cover the wedding of the wealthy entrepreneur Peter de Savary. It was an extremely jolly affair and I would have relished a few more days on the island but Richard Young, the photographer who was working with me, insisted that we set

194

off for New York (where we were to cover the opening of Peter Stringfellow's new club) the following day. Our flight took us via Puerto Rico and when it landed there I made a customary check-in call to the newsdesk. 'You and Richard are in Puerto Rico?' they said. 'Then stay there. There's been a big fire at a luxury apartment block and at least a dozen millionaires are dead.'

Richard and I hired a taxi and headed for the scene of the fire. As we approached the police cordon erected around the building, I realised they were checking ID and I didn't have a press card on me. 'Just wave your Stringfellow's membership card,' said Richard. 'They won't know the difference.' He was right.

When we entered the lobby, we were confronted by rows of bodies covered by blankets. After we had had our fill of the gory scene and given that the fire was still raging on the upper floors, Richard said he wanted to get an aerial shot from the balcony of an apartment building across the street. We took a lift to the top floor and knocked on the door of the penthouse. The maid answered and explained that the owners were away but, after pressing a $10 bill in her hand, we were shown to the balcony. As Richard got his shots, I idly examined the framed photographs on the wall. After a few moments I realised with a jolt that they were of Bruce Forsyth and his third wife Wilnelia. This apartment was their Caribbean holiday home. I hate to think what Bruce would have thought of me – a sworn enemy since I had run those highly embarrassing interviews with his ex-wife Penny – having such access to his private quarters. I resisted the temptation to leave a 'Hutchins Woz Here' note.

In August 1986, I picked up the phone on my desk at the *Express* to hear the booming voice of Richard Stott, now editor of the *Daily Mirror*: 'Your mate's snuffed it – will you write a piece for us?' This was the manner in which I learned of Gordon Mills' death. We had not seen each other since the publication of *The Family* ten years earlier but I was greatly saddened to hear of his passing. He had been diagnosed with cancer at a point when it was too late to treat it successfully and died within a week of it being detected. There was no question of me attending the funeral but I noticed that, while Tom shed tears at the graveside, neither Engelbert Humperdinck – the 'best friend' who had parted company with him some years earlier – nor Gilbert O'Sullivan bothered to turn up.

Meanwhile, I was beginning to discover that I had led something of a charmed life on the *Express*. Through what I branded editorial timidity but what he would consider to be his sensitivity to the slightly more refined tastes of the *Express*'s Middle-England readership, Nick vetoed stories that would have been considered instant classics at my former paper. One such was the tale of Max Bygraves' illegitimate son. I had succeeded in obtaining not only a picture of the boy, but also a copy of the legal agreement Max had made with his mother at the time of the birth. Nick didn't want to run it in the *Express* and suggested I call David Montgomery at the *News of the World* and pass it on to him. David duly splashed on it and ran two or three more pages inside the paper.

This episode brought me back into David's consciousness and led to a meeting that was to change the course of my career yet again. The Tuesday after the Bygraves story ran, David asked me to meet him in the Coal Hole pub on the Strand. Over halves of lager – he was never a high liver – he told me that Rupert Murdoch was getting increasingly concerned about Elton John's legal action against the *Sun*.

Earlier that year, the paper had run a front-page story accusing Elton – falsely, as it turned out – of hiring rent boys, plying them with cocaine and engaging in drug-fuelled orgies. Kelvin MacKenzie was refusing to settle the action even though Murdoch wanted him to and David had offered to mediate, without Kelvin's knowledge, on the proprietor's behalf. Unfortunately, David knew neither Elton nor his manager John Reid – and that's where I came in. Using my contacts in the music business, David asked, could I help?

It did not take long to get John Reid's number and I duly called, leaving a message saying I wanted to talk to him about the Elton case on behalf of News International. He did not return the call for three days and, when he did, he was blunt and to the point: 'There'll be a car outside your office building at six o'clock. Be in it.' A Bentley picked me up at the appointed time and an hour later we pulled up at a pair of imposing electronic gates. John was obviously a very successful and prosperous man but I was unprepared for the grandeur of Lockwell House, his sprawling mansion (once home to Sir Donald Campbell and *Bluebird*) set in 15 acres of Hertfordshire countryside close to Rickmansworth. His driver Gary Hampshire led me through the splendid entrance hall and into a drawing room filled with photographs of John and Elton (his ex-lover) in the company of a number of world-famous figures.

After a few moments John Reid appeared. What struck me immediately was that, while he was a small man, he had enormous presence. He was also very angry. We shook hands but that was as far as the pleasantries went. For the next three hours he berated me about the evils of the *Sun* as if I were the paper's editor or the author of the piece. Did I realise how seriously the story had affected Elton's career? he demanded, before making it clear that his client would not settle for less than £1 million in damages, a front-page apology and all his legal costs. If his intention was to ensure that I transmitted a sense of his fury to Murdoch via David then he certainly achieved his objective. It was after ten o'clock when he led me to the door. As he was showing me out, I noticed a picture of Elvis Presley on the wall and casually mentioned that I knew him and his manager.

'You know Colonel Parker?' he said, his interest suddenly aroused. 'Then come back in. Stay for dinner.' John looked up to men like Parker, even though his achievements with Elton had easily eclipsed the Colonel's success with Presley. We spoke about Elvis and the Colonel until two or three in the morning. A close bond had been forged.

We had several more meetings before I got him together with David over lunch at a restaurant close to John's office in Kensington. Although John had mellowed by then, David got the same message I had been given at the first meeting: Elton insisted on £1 million in damages, all his costs and a front-page apology. There was to be no compromise. In the end, our negotiations came to nothing as the *Sun*'s case crumbled and Kelvin was forced to concede everything John had demanded on his artist's behalf. But by now I had a new best friend. We lunched frequently and visited each other's home. John also began to invite me to his parties and it was at one of these that I met Elton for the first time. He thanked me for my efforts and subsequently began inviting me to his own parties. Jan and I spent Boxing Day of that year at his house in Holland Park.

The case had also brought David and I closer together and, one Monday in 1987, he asked me to meet him for drinks at the Howard Hotel.

'Do you want your own daily column?' he asked.

My response was less than gracious. 'Unless you're taking over at the *Sun*, you haven't got a daily paper, so why are you asking me?'

That's when he disclosed that he had raised finance in the City to buy *Today*. The national daily started by the regional newspaper proprietor Eddy Shah had helped to revolutionise Fleet Street. It did so not by breaking circulation records but by launching in full colour, using printers who had signed up to contracts that included none of the restrictive practices then endemic in the industry. By the mid-1980s, however, *Today* had been bought by Tiny Rowland, was selling fewer than half a million copies a day and was haemorrhaging cash. David's rescue plan involved the paper targeting the emergent generation of yuppie property owners who were then surfing a boom and, after convincing a number of merchant banks of the soundness of this approach, he had succeeded in raising a war chest of £25 million.

Unfortunately, when word got out that *Today* was in play, both Rupert Murdoch and Robert Maxwell entered the lists. After a number of thrusts and counter-thrusts by the various bidders, Murdoch emerged the victor – gazumping his own editor in the process. I believe David thought that Murdoch bought the paper to keep him on board and when *Today* was added to the News International stable he was rewarded with not just the editorship but also the role of chief executive. On the Thursday that Murdoch closed the deal, David called me with the news. 'I'm starting there tomorrow,' he said. 'Join me for breakfast.'

'Breakfast' turned out to be instant coffee in a plastic cup, and it was over that lukewarm Nescafe that we discussed terms. David wanted me to join the paper as a member of staff rather than on a freelance contract, a move I had resisted everywhere I had worked since the *NME*. In return, I demanded a substantial salary. 'In that case,' he said, 'you'll have to do the full-page column six days a week.' I started that weekend. Thanks to the row about Nick Lloyd's change of mind over how frequently *Confidential* would appear, I had never signed a contract with the *Express* and was in a position to walk out at a moment's notice. Nick was not very happy about my abrupt departure but his reaction was nothing compared to Jan's. She was furious when she heard that I had taken on what amounted to a 100-hour week including all the party-going involved.

That weekend I turned up at *Today* on the Sunday morning without a story in my head except the revelation that the broadcaster Terry Wogan wore a wig. I had to find a dozen more stories before 6pm and then go out and gather more for the following day. The stress of churning out a daily diary column and dealing with the flack it engendered accelerated my drinking. Every day, more party invitations were added to the office diary and it was always tempting to drop off at one or two on the way home, ostensibly to pick up gossip but also, I must admit, to 'top up'.

One evening in April 1988, I was among those Mohamed Al Fayed invited to a party at Harrods. I didn't even bother to read the invitation and made my way to Brompton Road without knowing what the occasion was. Alf – as I referred to Mohamed in the column – was on good form when I arrived, playfully giving me a glass of champagne for each hand and then squeezing a copy of the book that was being launched that night under my arm. When I had a chance to look at it, I saw that it was all about Prince Edward's disastrous royal TV show, *It's a Knockout*. It was only then that I realised that the Prince was Al Fayed's guest of honour. I had no desire to come face to face with him: he had become the prime victim of our daily look at where the royals were eating out. *Confidential* would point out where they ate, what they ate and – most tellingly – who paid the bill, often, in Edward's case, with embarrassing results.

When a waiter approached with a tray filled with glasses of champagne, I relieved him of the lot and found a secluded corner where I could sit down and enjoy its contents. There I considered myself safe from any avenging royals but some minutes later I spotted the boyish Edward bounding in my direction, hand outstretched.

'Ah, Mr Hutchins,' I remember him saying. 'We meet at last.'

I remember my response too: 'Go away, I'm pissed.'

He looked startled but decided to try again.

'I just wanted to ask you where you get the information from. You know, about where we are eating and who with and...'

'Fuck off, I'm pissed,' I said.

The Queen's youngest son looked shocked but he still would not take the hint. Over his shoulder I saw one of my colleagues approaching, one who would have been aware that I was reaching my troublesome peak.

'Oh, Chris, who's bothering you now?' she asked.

At that moment, Prince Edward turned in her direction, his face red with anger.

'Oh, Your Royal Highness,' she began in the most deferential tones she could muster.

'I've told him to fuck off, that I'm pissed, but he won't go away,' I said.

By now one of the Prince's minders had arrived to steer Edward to safer waters and, glancing only once over his shoulder in my direction, he began signing copies of the book. Though I don't remember it, that must have given me an idea because three days later I received a polite note from Edward thanking me for sending him a signed (by me) copy of his own book, saying he would treasure it. I don't even remember posting it.

This is not a tale I am proud of. There was no reason for me to pick on Edward in the way that I did. He just happened to cross my path when my drinking was spiralling out of control. Days later, David Montgomery had his chauffeur drive me to the Charter Clinic in Chelsea to detox. After being sedated for 24 hours I was taken to my first session of group therapy. I sat through the meeting in a daze, slowly coming to terms with the fact that I was in a drying-out clinic rather than a conventional hospital. As I reflected on my situation afterwards I decided the solution was simple: I would stop drinking. That conclusion reached, I packed my bags and, ignoring the protests of the doctors, checked myself out. Jan was shocked when I turned up at home and when I arrived for work the next day even David allowed himself a raised eyebrow, but I told them both the same thing: the answer was simple: abstinence.

Three days after I had resumed work at *Today*, David invited me to join him for dinner at a nearby Chinese restaurant and when he ordered a beer I said I'd have one too. Within a week I was back in the Charter. This time I stayed for four weeks. During that time I became a regular attendee at meetings of Alcoholics Anonymous. By the time I left I had succeeded in breaking my cycle of drinking and did not touch another drop for more than eight years.

By now *Confidential* was well established and had gained a reputation for being, er, fearless. One of the by-products of this was that people with a guilty secret were often unwilling to return our calls. This meant we sometimes had to resort to unorthodox methods to get hold of our targets. One day my ace reporter James Steen – who went on to become editor of *Punch* – was having trouble getting through to a senior executive at Channel 4 who we knew to be having an affair. We hatched a plot. I would pretend to be a celebrity in order to lure the man to the phone. I do a passable impression of John Cleese and called the television executive posing as him. The ruse worked perfectly. The man took my call on the basis that he was about to speak to the famous comedy actor and the moment he came on I handed the receiver to James, who said cheerily, 'Hey there. It's John Cleese... from *Today*.'

The secretary at Channel 4 wasn't the only person to be taken in by my Cleese impersonation, however. Posing as Cleese, I'd once called a colleague, Sandra Parsons, whose write-up of a telephone interview with him had run that day. She had opened her article with Cleese's criticisms of our switchboard operators – they had either been rude or kept him waiting – and so I began by saying to Sandra, 'Switchboard much improved,' and went on to warmly congratulate her on a 'wonderful' piece. I watched from the other side of the office as she blushed with pleasure and stammered her thanks. The *Confidential* desk had a good laugh about the whole thing and I assumed that word would reach Sandra that she'd been duped. I never thought to tell her myself.

Unfortunately, because Cleese rarely gave interviews and would often walk out of those he did grant, the fact that Sandra had not only spoken to him but also had apparently been congratulated afterwards, brought the incident to the attention of an author called Jonathan Margolis who was writing a biography of Cleese. He then interviewed Sandra – who was still convinced she had been speaking to the man himself – and wrote up the incident for his book. The awful truth only dawned on Sandra when James bumped into her at the *Daily Mail* some time later and mentioned that the time I had hoaxed her still made him smile. She immediately picked up the phone and called Margolis to explain what had happened. I later heard that by then the book was so close to being printed that all the publisher could do was make a clumsy cut that left a whole page with only one line of text on it.

One of the people in the public eye that David Montgomery was always keen for me to keep watch on was the best-selling novelist and, at that time, successful politician, Jeffrey Archer. I had first met Archer after joining the *Express*. Nick Lloyd had urged me to get to know those of his friends he thought might prove good sources and so I had invited Archer for dinner at Green's. The meal was memorable in the sense that Archer turned out to be incredibly patronising, addressing me as if he was a schoolmaster and I was his pupil. In the circumstances, it was impossible for him not to pick up the bill when we left, even though it was ostensibly my shout. I was quite pleased about that.

Some time later, when David was still editor of the *News of the World*, he had run a sensational story about how Archer – then deputy chairman of the Conservative Party – had arranged to pay-off a prostitute called Monica Coghlan. Coincidentally, the day after the story broke, David and I were due to lunch together. Because of the turmoil the story created, I assumed that David – paradoxically a very private man in his own life – would cancel. However, he not only wanted to honour the arrangement but also asked to be taken somewhere as high profile as possible. He saw the assault on Archer as his finest hour as an editor and, for perhaps the first time in his life, craved some of the celebrity he had bestowed on others for so long. I chose Langan's in Mayfair – in those days the place to see and be seen.

Unfortunately, the *Daily Star* goofed in following up the story by substantially re-running it without any evidence. Archer sued the more vulnerable publication, won and – in order to avoid a costly libel action – Murdoch ordered the *News of the World* to back down too. David chafed at the injustice of it all. Indeed, the Archer case became his *cause célébre*. It would not be an exaggeration to say that it consumed him for years. As a result, when I was on *Today* I was under standing orders to pass on to David anything I heard about Archer. One day I bumped into Michael Stacpoole, the man who had met Coghlan at Victoria Station and handed over a hold-all containing £8,000 of Archer's cash. He told me he had a lot more to tell about the affair. When I mentioned this to David, he was very excited.

'We must get him somewhere quiet to talk,' he said. 'Can we do it at your house?'

I agreed and, much to Jan's consternation, David arranged a team of surveillance experts to install hidden microphones in our living room. The plan was for me to meet Stacpoole, buy him dinner and then invite him back to the house where David would join us for coffee. Unfortunately, he was already unbelievably drunk when he arrived at the restaurant. I did what I could to sober him up but by the time we got to the house he was still hopelessly intoxicated. David arrived around 11pm and, after giving us coffee, Jan left us alone. David grilled Stacpoole for two or three hours. But, even though the entire exchange was on tape, David and I concluded that it would be clear to any listener that he was drunk and that his information was unreliable and therefore unusable. After seeing both men out, I went up to bed. Jan was still awake.

'I never want that horrible man in my house again,' she said.

'He was just drunk,' I protested.

'I didn't mean that one,' she replied.

David Montgomery could have that effect on people. Jan considered him cold and callous and resented the stress that he was putting me under. I liked him a lot.

Celebrity-bashing meant that making enemies became an occupational hazard and I never knew when I would bump into one of my victims on the party circuit. I thought I was fairly safe when James and I turned up at a party to launch an exhibition of photographs by a former *Mirror* colleague, Mike Moloney. We had only just arrived when I felt someone grab my arm. It was Bruce Forsyth, and he soon made it clear that in his eyes I was public enemy number one. I had no desire to ruin Mike's night so I did my best to make light of his behaviour, saying, 'Come on, Bruce, why the long face?' He didn't appreciate the joke but, having said his piece, he soon stalked off.

James steered me towards the bar and – as I was off the booze – ordered me a large mineral water. Still quite shocked by the vehemence of the comedian's attack, I said, 'All we need now is for Paul Daniels to turn up.' (There had been a spate of humiliating stories about him in *Confidential*, too.)

At that point James glanced towards the door, turned to me and said, 'Don't look now, Chris, but Daniels has just walked in.'

I'd had enough persecution for one night so we agreed that James would create a diversion while I made a discreet exit. As he went off to ask the TV magician to perform some card tricks I began my departure. As it happens, Paul turned out to be a good sport. As I was leaving the cover of one pillar to head towards another, he said – without looking up from his conjuring – 'I can see you Chris, I can see you.'

Despite the presence in the room of angry Brucie, we had a nice time.

It was *Confidential* that brought me back into contact with Paul McCartney. I had not been in touch with the Beatles for some years after what common ground we had was lost when they went through their hippie phase and began paying court to the crazy Maharishi. One day a writer friend who had been to interview the McCartneys at their farm in Sussex called to say that, while she was waiting for Paul to appear, someone in the house told her one of the family's dogs had got into the hen house the previous day and killed a number of chickens. I ran the story making some remark about how, while the McCartneys were vegetarians, their dogs clearly weren't. The day it appeared I got a call from a furious Bernard Docherty, then McCartney's PR man. He said Paul was going to sue. I found it hard to believe that the Beatle I had once considered a friend and who had met his former fiancée in my flat could be so petty.

'Who's he going to sue?' I asked. 'Me or the dogs?'

That only enraged Docherty further. 'How dare you make a joke of this?!'

To which I replied, 'Well, I didn't eat the fucking chickens – McCartney's dogs did according to ****.'

We subsequently got a writ from McCartney's solicitor that included word-for-word my exchange with his publicist. It was clear that the McCartneys had been extremely upset by the whole thing and we apologised in the paper as well as making a settlement with them.

Docherty wasn't the only overbearing complainant to get a mouthful over the years. On another occasion, we learned that Charles Althorp (now Earl Spencer) was selling his house in Holland Park. I sent one of my genial reporters to view it and she produced for the column a nice lead story, describing the interior. It was all fairly harmless stuff and the following day nothing happened until around 6pm. I was about to leave the office when the phone rang. I picked it up to hear Spencer's voice. 'Mr Hutchins,' he began, 'why did you do this?'

It was my job, I told him.

'It's not your job to do this kind of thing. I'm a journalist [he was working for NBC at the time] and I know what the job's all about...'

Determined to wind up Princess Diana's brother, I interrupted: 'Come off it, Charlie [that's what we always called him down at Stringfellow's]. I got my job through ability and we all know how you got yours.'

I can't remember exactly what was said next but I do know there was a very heated exchange. Finally I hung up on him and walked through the newsroom to the editor's office to tell David what had gone on. He was on a call and motioned me to take a seat opposite him. He was grinning at me as he said down the phone, 'I know, Charles, I know what Chris Hutchins is like, but I can't control him. He's a law unto himself...'

Despite our aggressive approach, we only had one serious libel case over the years and that involved Princess Margaret's son, Viscount Linley. In May 1989, we received a tip-off suggesting that the landlady of a pub at Chelsea Harbour had barred him from her premises after he had started spilling beer. We made various checks before running the story, but it turned out to be wrong and, within days of it appearing, Linley's lawyers had served us with a writ. He insisted we admit that we made up the story and pay him damages. As we had published in good faith, we refused to do so and Linley duly instigated the first libel action by a member of the Royal Family to end up in court in living memory.

It reached the High Court in March 1990 and to David Montgomery's delight each day's proceedings were given prominent coverage by all the other newspapers. The jury found in favour of the Queen's nephew and awarded him relatively modest damages of £35,000. In a bizarre twist after the verdict, Linley publicly exonerated James Steen, the reporter sent to the pub to investigate the story, on the grounds that our informant lied to us.

One moment of light relief came towards the end of the trial when Linley's QC, Charles Gray, asked James on the stand, 'How does it feel to work for a downmarket paper?' Ironically enough, Gray was about to earn his crust from that same 'downmarket paper' by representing it the following week in a case brought by Anne Diamond, at that time a well-known television presenter.

It was a story about another member of the Royal Family a couple of months later that led to the start of my parallel career as a biographer of celebrities. A royal source had called to say that the Duchess of York had slipped off to Morocco with one of her daughters. She was staying at a five-star hotel called La Gazelle d'Or in the south Moroccan town of Taroudant. While she flew out with a female travelling companion called Priscilla Phillips, the purpose of the trip was to meet up with a man called Steve Wyatt, the son of the Texas oil billionaire Oscar Wyatt. David was reluctant to run the story because, while it stopped short of accusing Fergie of having an affair, the implication was clear. Despite the good it did the paper's circulation, he may also have felt uncomfortable about the judge's decision in the Linley case. I eventually talked him round, however, and the story ran as the lead in *Confidential*.

Initially, others were reluctant to follow our lead. But when we ran a number of follow-ups – including the fact she had travelled to Morocco on Wyatt's private jet and the fact she had spent four days as a guest at his home in Texas the previous year – rival papers that had initially pooh-poohed the story began to take it seriously. Fergie's Moroccan trip was the first public indication that the Yorks' marriage was falling apart and it laid the foundation for my first book. *Sarah's Story*, the biography of the Duchess that I wrote with my former colleague Peter Thompson (by now a friend again), was published in 1992 and went on to become an international bestseller.

Writing royal books introduced me to an array of new contacts and friends – and put me back in touch with some I had long lost contact with. Into the latter category fell Michael Winner who, as the foremost British filmmaker of his day, was best known for his *Death Wish* movies. I first came across Michael in my early days at the *NME* (where he had also started out) when the paper sent me to Pinewood Film Studios to write a piece about the film *I've Gotta Horse* which he was making with the British rock star Billy Fury. I was in the loo when I heard someone enter the next cubicle and begin vomiting. It was a young actress called Anna Palk – the film's inexpensive female lead – who had dived into the gents because it was the nearest toilet she could find. She later told me that she was sick with nerves after being regularly berated for her performances by Michael. And it was the man himself who followed her in to demand that she return to the set, noisily complaining about how much the lost minutes were costing him.

Despite this unpromising beginning, I grew to like Michael over the years despite his 'awkward' ways. In his determination to ensure that he was not misquoted, he would preface every phone conversation with a journalist by speaking the time and date into his tape recorder so the reporter knew he would have his own taped record of their chat. Once I called him up and, after he had recited the familiar line, I said, 'Thanks, Michael. I only wanted to know what the time was,' and hung up.

On another occasion, I called Michael when Peter and I were working on *Diana's Nightmare*, a dissection of the Princess's miserable existence as part of the Royal Family, and he told me the story of how Prince Edward had persuaded him to invest in a West End stage revival of the 1950s comedy *The Rehearsal*. 'Edward had said, 'All this is going to be wonderful. We'll make a fortune," recalled Michael. "Edward,' I said, 'you are going to lose everything. No company can keep offices and all the staff to put plays on in the West End because it's a very rough business." Against his better judgement, Winner had eventually allowed Edward to talk him round and put some money into the royal venture. 'Bless him,' he concluded. 'I was slightly wrong. I think we lost only 80 per cent of our money.'

Chapter Eleven

WHAT MURDOCH'S BUTLER SAW

M y first meeting with Rupert Murdoch, the most powerful media baron in the world, came a few months into my tenure at *Today*. David Montgomery asked me to go with him and a few colleagues to dine with the proprietor at his London apartment.

On the day in question I had had a difficult time with the column and was in a grumpy mood when we arrived at Murdoch's duplex penthouse in a block sandwiched between the Ritz and St James's Palace. We took the lift to the fifth floor and were greeted at the door of the boss man's apartment by a very tall, slim, well-spoken butler with curly hair, which I noticed was dyed. He led us into what was clearly an enormous apartment with high ceilings. Just inside the door was a large round table with a display of that day's newspapers. Like any good marketing man, Murdoch had ensured that his titles – the *Times*, the *Sun* and *Today* – featured most prominently. The butler led us up a large, sweeping staircase that ended in a huge room with a roof terrace running the entire length of one side.

Murdoch appeared promptly, looking pretty much as he did in photographs, but his manner was not at all what I had expected. He may have been capable of running a vast international media empire but face-to-face in a social situation he appeared to lack confidence to the point of being diffident. This did not stop him being extremely charming, however. I warmed to him when he singled me out to tell me he enjoyed reading *Confidential*. As Murdoch moved on to talk to his other guests, David took me on to the terrace overlooking St James's Park and told me that this was where he and 'Rupert' had plotted the downfall of Princess Michael. (She was having an affair at the time with a wealthy Texan called Ward Hunt and it was exposed in the *News of the World*.)

Dinner was pleasant enough. We were served steaks, which we ate off plates on our laps. As we did so, we could hear the cook bickering with the butler as she passed him the plates. I had expected Murdoch to run his home with the same ruthless efficiency he applied to his businesses but, while he could obviously hear what was going on, he resolutely ignored it. I liked him more by the minute. My mood was not helped, however, by the behaviour of one fellow guest who had clearly done her homework beforehand and was being sickeningly sycophantic to Murdoch. At one point, in an apparent move to end the logjam, he mumbled, 'I see BMW are trying to discourage blacks from buying their cars.'

'At last,' I said, 'something interesting to talk about.' David glared at me and I took it no further. The party dispersed around midnight.

I was back at my desk the following morning when the

phone rang. It was to be one of those landmark calls. The caller gave me an excellent story and when I asked him for his name he said with almost pantomime deference, 'Philip Townsend, sir.' When I said, I didn't believe we'd met, he said, 'We have, sir. We met last night.'

'No we didn't,' I said. 'I was at a private dinner party last night.'

'I know, sir. I served your dinner. I am Mr Murdoch's butler.'

After putting the phone down on my new contact, I made a beeline for David's office to tell him what had happened. David was an unusual combination of dour Ulsterman and mischievous maverick. He rarely imparted much gossip himself and on the rare occasions that he was obliged to use minicabs he would discourage conversation with the driver by announcing, 'I don't talk.' But, like all good editors, he loved stories. He immediately realised the ramifications of me forming an alliance with the proprietor's butler and was acutely aware of the possible consequences. It was clear, however, that Philip could be a valuable lookout in the boss's camp.

'Just be very careful, Christopher,' he said. 'Be very careful. Rupert is not a man to mess with.'

I ran the story Philip had given me the next day and shortly afterwards got another invitation to Murdoch's penthouse, this time courtesy of the butler whose boss (mine also, remember) was away on business. The woman Philip had been arguing with on my first visit turned out to be his wife Penny and, over a supper of Dover sole and a bottle of the chairman's finest champagne, they told me the fascinating story of their downwardly mobile career paths.

They were both the products of families with considerable money and position. Penny's father was Richard Haworth, a member of a wealthy Manchester textile family, who was Master of the Cheshire Foxhounds (his wife was Master of the Bicester Foxhounds) and she had been raised in considerable comfort and grandeur. Philip had been brought up by his widowed mother, who came from the Cobbold brewing family, and spent his youth touring the Continent with her as she frittered away her own multi-million-pound inheritance in casinos. Philip and Penny met at a coming-out ball at Claridge's and were married in the private chapel at Chetwood Prior, on the Buckinghamshire estate belonging to Penny's parents. My rival columnist Nigel Dempster had been one of the ushers.

By this time they were both working on the *Daily Express*, Philip as a cameraman on the paper's *William Hickey* column and Penny as an arts reporter. Philip did well as a photographer in the 1960s, taking portraits of the Beatles, the Rolling Stones, Richard Burton, Twiggy and others of that ilk, but he had always been a frustrated entrepreneur and he left the *Express* to pursue a variety of business interests. It was when the Townsends came badly unstuck on the property market that they decided a radical change of tack was required.

On the basis that as they had once employed servants themselves and knew how it was done, they answered a job ad in *The Lady* for a husband-and-wife team to act as butler and housekeeper to an unnamed employer. Subsequently told to report for an interview at the offices of News International in Wapping, east London, they discovered that their prospective employer was none other than Rupert Murdoch. At the time, the plant was heavily fortified in the wake of the violent print-workers' dispute and they had to negotiate the security cordon before being taken to his office. A queue of newspaper executives was waiting to see the boss but Philip and Penny were led past the line and shown into a cramped office where a harassed-looking Murdoch sat with his sleeves rolled up. 'Take a seat,' he said, 'if you can find one.'

After a brief conversation during which he failed to establish that they had never been in service before, Murdoch explained that he didn't have time to interview any other couples, produced a set of keys and said, 'Perhaps you'd like to look at the place and tell me if you want the job.' He hadn't even looked at their references. Philip and Penny duly went to inspect the apartment and were naturally impressed. Philip called his new employer and asked if they could move in straight away. He agreed and it was Philip who answered the entryphone when Murdoch came home that night. The man who had little time for the Royal Family was almost deferential to his own new servant: 'Murdoch here. Can I come up?'

Philip turned out to be a rather good butler. Greeting guests and pouring champagne was something he had been used to doing as a socialite. Performing the same tasks as a servant merely required a change of tone. But Penny was never comfortable with housework, cooking and conforming to the then Mrs Murdoch's demands. She was particularly upset when Anna Murdoch announced that she would require them to wear uniforms in future and handed over a brochure from an American clothing company called Dornan Uniforms that boasted of how it supplied outfits for below-stairs staff 'from coast to coast'. The uniforms had names like 'Pink-korn Princess' and 'Dinner Belle', and Philip observed that they were the sort of thing he'd seen black maids and butlers wearing in films set in Southern mansions before the Civil War. In a firm letter accompanying the brochure, Anna Murdoch made it clear that they were to wear their uniforms at all times – indoors or out – during working hours. Penny was in tears at the indignity of it all and Philip called and asked me to come round to the Murdoch flat as soon as possible to help him cope with the crisis. They had a couple of vodka tonics from the Murdoch cocktail cabinet and, by the time I left, both appeared to be reconciled to their fate.

Our friendship established, Philip began feeding me stories about his society friends and I had him paid by the News International accounts department, who never seemed to catch on to the fact that the address to which they sent his cheques was the chairman's home. In addition to the material that appeared in the paper, Philip started phoning with gossip picked up during his own conversations with Murdoch or information he overheard as he served food or poured wine. I knew Murdoch read *Confidential* not merely because he had flattered me by saying so at the dinner but also because he'd scribble comments against certain stories before throwing the paper in the wastebasket, from which Philip retrieved it and sent it on to me. He never appeared to twig, however, that he was the source for some of the items.

Or perhaps he did. I recall sailing particularly close to the wind after Philip told me what happened after Murdoch attended a birthday banquet for King Constantine of Greece in the presence of the Queen and Prince Charles at nearby Spencer House. Given his status as the world's most powerful media magnate, Murdoch had been placed at the Queen's table. When he got home, he was, apparently, a bit squiffy and when Philip asked what the Queen was like he said, 'Nice little woman, nothing special.'

I ran the quote two days later without attributing it but baulked at running other remarks he made to his butler that night. 'Actually there were a lot of queens there,' he'd added. 'One was the real thing, the rest were poofters.'

At this, his wife Anna interrupted: 'Rupert, you know you can't say that' (a reference to a recent Press Council ruling). But Murdoch wasn't to be cowed. 'The *Sun* can't say that – I can say what I bloody like.'

It was about this time that warning bells began ringing in David Montgomery's head: 'Christopher, you'll get us both lynched.'

Despite David's trepidation, my visits to Murdoch's apartment became more and more frequent – usually once a week when he was out of town. Sometimes I would even take friends and family along. Jan went with me once, as did James Steen. On these visits I witnessed some strange sights. Once when he was away, Murdoch asked Philip to hire decorators to paint some of the rooms. I walked in to discover a very gay black man up a ladder, painting with one hand and swigging Murdoch's Krug from the bottle held in the other.

The more I learned about Murdoch from Philip, the more I wanted to know. The tycoon I worked for was the most fascinating person I had ever encountered and I was hungry for every morsel Philip had to offer. And his gossip proved to be about as high grade as you can get. One day, he read me the label on a bottle of pills he had come across as he tidied 'Mr M's' dressing-room table. 'To be taken on the morning of surgery,' it said, and a small pamphlet that accompanied the pill bottle advised, 'This operation releases the laughter lines and makes that part of the face look smoother. In 80 per cent of cases the scars disappear after four days.' Although I was hardly in a position to run the story – he was the proprietor, after all – I kept David informed of developments. On the day of his surgery, Murdoch's wife Anna told Philip to pack an overnight bag, explaining that her husband was going into the Harley Street Nursing Home for 'tests'.

'He won't need a great deal,' she said, 'just a nightshirt, a change of underwear and a clean shirt for when he comes out. If anyone rings, just tell them we're away for a couple of days. Whatever you do, don't tell anyone he's in hospital.'

She stayed with him for two nights before returning to the flat to take care of some business. Then she asked Philip to drive her back to the nursing home via an optician's to collect a pair of dark glasses. Philip never did get to see his employer that day as he was instructed to park the car on a meter and walk back to the flat. The Murdochs then drove themselves to Miller Howe, a luxury hotel in Cumbria, but within a couple of days Rupert was bored and he and his wife returned to London. Back in the flat, Philip caught only occasional glimpses of his employer. He wore the dark glasses but they did nothing to conceal the surgical gauze on his face. Soon afterwards, he slipped out to Heathrow and boarded his private jet to head to America.

'Don't worry,' I told David. 'You won't have any difficulty recognising the boss next time you see him. Philip says you can't even notice the difference. The face-lift clearly hasn't worked.'

I was quite surprised to discover that Murdoch was vain enough to have a face-lift at all but I soon learned that he had a capacity for self-improvement that extended to his personal health. I knew that one thing Murdoch and I had in common for a time was an addiction to sleeping pills. Philip told me that at one stage RM's secretary had called from Wapping to ask him to collect multiple prescriptions for Temazepam sleeping pills because her local pharmacist was beginning to suspect her of being a junkie for ordering so many so frequently. Like me, it appeared, the boss was getting prescriptions filled out in several different names. I often wondered if he needed so many for the same reason: to blot out the turmoil in his head. In that regard his need would certainly have been greater than mine.

But unlike me at that time, he succeeded in kicking the habit. Philip called me on one occasion to say that Murdoch had walked into the apartment proudly announcing he'd given up Temazepam. 'I'm into yin and yang and all that shit now,' he'd added. I tried to follow his example. Unfortunately, my addiction was more deeply entrenched and – unlike Murdoch – I was not about to be converted to the holistic prescriptions of a candle-burning Mrs Jonsson in Wimpole Street or the royal jelly recommended to him by Barbara Cartland. Nor, unlike him, was I prepared to take supplies of fresh yoghurt with me when I went on holiday to Greece, which is, after all, the home of the stuff.

Another intriguing aspect of Murdoch's character was his personal thriftiness. When I asked Philip about his spending, he came up with an interesting example. 'He had a suit made at Tommy Nutter's in Savile Row and it cost £1,500,' he said. 'He didn't wear it straight away but took it with him the next time he went to Australia, stopped off in Hong Kong and had a dozen cheap copies made. When I picked up some shirts he'd had made at Turnbull & Asser in Jermyn Street he asked me how much they had cost. When I told him they were £95 each he winced and said he would also keep those unopened until his next Hong Kong trip. He told me, 'I can get them copied at Man Hing Cheong's shop at the Mandarin Hotel for £50 – 20 quid less than that if I can be bothered to walk a few hundred yards down the road."

This behaviour obviously infuriated Anna who once told Philip to go back to Turnbull & Asser to collect a couple more shirts, adding firmly, 'For him to wear, Philip, not to have copied.' The only time Murdoch himself appeared to care whether he was wearing the genuine article or a copy was when he was going to lunch with Prince Charles. 'He gets his shirts made at the same shop and would probably spot a fake,' he explained to his manservant.

Apart from these insights into Murdoch's personal life, Philip also came up with some priceless information about the workings of his business empire. 'I know how interested you are in RM's finances and I thought you'd like to hear this,' he called to say one day. 'As you know, News Corporation is in a terrible financial crisis because of the expenditure on Sky Television. Anyway, Rupert's in the flat at the moment with David De Voe, one of his chief financial aides. They've been going through all the options and Rupert's been trying to get hold of the president of the Pittsburgh National Bank, to which he owes about five million and which is not falling into line with all the others by holding off until things get better. So what do you think he did? He phoned George Bush [senior, who was then president] at the White House, told him of the problem and asked if he could help. A few minutes later – as I was pouring RM and Mr De Voe more coffee – the Pittsburgh National Bank president phoned back and said he'd toe the line. RM mopped his brow, said to Mr DeVoe, 'Phew, that was a close one,' and then thanked me for keeping him fortified. He's such a nice man.'

David lapped up all this intelligence but when the time came that I had some information about Murdoch's plans that might have enabled him to take evasive action, he simply refused to believe it. In January 1991, *Today* was failing to reach its circulation targets and, as group profits were ploughed into propping up the ailing title, David's relations with executives on the group's more successful papers deteriorated. He was told to reduce the number of pages he put into the paper each day but quite often he would call the print works in the late afternoon and tell them to expect a bigger paper than planned. This infuriated senior managers and one day the chief executive of News International, Andrew Knight, walked into RM's apartment and said, 'You know Monty did it again last night.' Murdoch's response was to say, 'Yeah, but he'll have his comeuppance soon. I'm going to tell him in a couple of weeks that he's got to shed more than 40 editorial staff.'

Naturally, Philip had been earwigging and immediately passed on this grave news to me. I in turn reported it to David, who dismissed it out of hand. But sure enough, within three weeks he was calling in journalists one at a time – nearly four dozen in all – to lay them off on Murdoch's specific instructions.

Thanks to Philip, I was also able to tell David the true cost of one particular royal scoop of which he had always been very proud. *Today* had run the first kiss-and-tell story by a member of the Royal Family – Princess Alexandra's daughter Marina Ogilvy's account of how she had met and got pregnant by a working-class photographer called Paul Mowatt. David was particularly delighted that he had obtained the exclusive relatively cheaply. But I had to tell him that, whatever it had cost the paper, Rupert had been obliged to write a cheque for £300,000 to the Prince's Trust after a very angry Princess Alexandra had called the flat and torn into Mrs Murdoch about the *Today* story. Philip had come across a gushing letter of thanks for the donation from Marina's father, Angus Ogilvy. David looked shell-shocked, and the colour drained from his face when I told him. Hell hath no fury like an embarrassed proprietor's wife.

I always found Murdoch to be a man who understood the value of journalists who spent freely on their sources. The butler, naturally, provided a brilliant example of this

223

approach. Philip phoned me one morning to say, 'If you bump into Kelvin McKenzie [then editor of the *Sun*] at Wapping today, don't tell him you know this but he was here for breakfast this morning after a night out with RM and some others at Tramp. Apparently Kelvin settled the bill and when RM asked him this morning how much it came to, Kelvin said, '£330 – but I left £350 to cover the tip.' 'Oh,' said RM, 'so you don't intend going back there then...''

Apart from the more heavyweight gossip, there were many amusing asides. Did I know that, following the marriage of Rupert's daughter Prudence to banker Alistair Macleod in Scotland, Rupert received a flower bill from one of the groom's relatives for £7,850? Another call from the butler's pantry revealed that he had gone into a bedroom occupied by one of Rupert's sisters, who lived in rural Australia, and found her and her husband's washing hung out to dry over the frame of the valuable antique four-poster they had been sleeping in. And when the one-time Israeli Prime Minister, Binyamin Netanyahu, came to stay, his Mossad security men super-glued the locks on the emergency exits, while Netanyahu's girlfriend ran round London on a spending spree, charging all her purchases to their generous host. Murdoch also paid for theatre tickets, a crib for their baby and the hire of an agency nanny.

Then there was the time, at the height of the IRA bomb scares, that Philip phoned me to say he had just called the police after receiving a suspicious package with Murdoch's name and address scrawled on it in felt-tip pen. Later he phoned back to describe what had happened: 'Six police vehicles turned up and they evacuated our building, Lord Rothschild's building next door and the Stafford Hotel opposite. I was the only one told to stay inside – until a bomb expert in a bulletproof jacket turned up, took the package from me, put it in a bucket of sand and carried it gingerly down the stairs. Outside they x-rayed it in Green Park, a large area of which had been sealed off with police tape, and when the x-ray showed wires and a battery they decided it was definitely a bomb and blew it up. I felt such a fool when it was discovered that the package contained the new remote control Mr M had ordered for his TV set.'

This gossip was all very fascinating, particularly given the manner in which it was obtained, but, because the paper I worked for was owned by the man who was the butt of most of the stories, it was rare for any tips such as these to make the paper. One exception was the story of the billionaire peeping tom. 'Paul Getty [who lived in the apartment below] is at it again,' he once told me excitedly. 'As I speak I'm looking at him on his balcony eyeing up the talent in Green Park through his telescope. Why don't you send a photographer round to turn the tables on him?' Within minutes, a *Today* photographer was dispatched to take pictures of Getty as he gazed at who-knows-what through his powerful telescope for publication in a newspaper owned by the man who lived upstairs.

Not for nothing did Murdoch's daughter Prudence once say in his hearing to her father, 'Daddy, Philip's no ordinary butler, is he?'

Despite my intimate knowledge of his personal habits and business strategems, my own personal dealings with Murdoch were strictly limited. Following my sullen display the night I went to supper at his flat, he treated me warily whenever we encountered each other thereafter. I lunched regularly at Wapping with one of his senior lieutenants, John B Evans. Whenever Murdoch approached the table to speak to John, he would nod courteously in my direction but never took things any further. 'What is it with you that he seems so cautious?' John asked me once. I never did tell him about the butler connection, though I always suspected that Murdoch was astute enough to have worked out what was going on but simply chose to let sleeping dogs lie.

Only one person called me at *Confidential* more frequently than Philip and that was Kanga, Lady Tryon. Shortly after the night of the Murdoch dinner, she was photographed with Prince Charles at Balmoral. Princess Diana had always resented the need to sit meekly by while her husband fished but Kanga had no such prejudices. The mini-scandal that arose when the pictures were published was based on the fact that Diana was not in residence at the time. The *News of the World* ran the shots under the headline, 'PICNIC IN THE BUSHES WITH OLD FLAME'. Kanga claimed to have been hugely embarrassed by the resulting coverage that suggested the two of them had rekindled their affair and rang me a couple of days later in tears. 'I'm back in Wiltshire,' she said, 'and the buggers have followed me here. I was out feeding the chickens at six o'clock this morning and they appeared from nowhere with their cameras. Goodness only knows what I looked like.'

The following day's papers confirmed Kanga's worst fears: she did not look good. Her hair was bedraggled and she was wearing no make-up. The *Daily Star* took full advantage, running the picture under the headline, 'CAN YOU REALLY BELIEVE THIS IS DIANA'S LOVE RIVAL?' She called me again that morning. 'What did I tell you?' she said plaintively. 'I bet Diana loved that. Anyway, I've asked Paul [Paul Edmonds, her hairdresser] to come over every morning and make me look good. I'm not even going to step outside until he's done his magic. At least, not while this is going on.'

By this time it was obvious that Charles and Diana's

marriage was breaking down irretrievably and I became convinced that Kanga was actually revelling in the speculation that she was making a comeback in the Prince's affections. Her calls became even more frequent and she gossiped openly with me about Charles. 'He phoned me after that horrible chicken-feeding picture and said he'd cut it out [of the paper],' she said. 'He tells me not to worry about Diana. He's just glad to have some peace and quiet.' I did not believe everything Kanga told me – particularly when she had obviously been drinking and that was becoming the case more and more often.

One night she called me very late and asked me to join her for lunch the following day at Ogbury House, then the Tryons' family home, not far from Stonehenge in Wiltshire. 'And bring Terry [O'Neill], that photographer friend of yours,' she added. She was clearly merry and I wondered what state I would find her in the next day and how I might help her. Before setting off, I wrapped up a copy of the Alcoholics Anonymous 'bible', known as 'the Big Book', and some AA literature before setting off with Terry for Wiltshire. On the journey down I told him about her rambling late-night phone calls – he'd had enough of those from me in my drinking days to know what I was talking about but he was in as cheerful a mood as Kanga had been the previous night.

Set on a hill and overlooking the River Avon, Ogbury House had very attractive views but, with its white-painted walls, it was not a traditional Wiltshire house. Indeed, one visitor described it as 'more of a crossbreed between a Weybridge mansion and Southfork'. Although it was a fine summer's day, fires had been lit to cheer up gloomy rooms – an extravagance of which I suspected the prudent Lord Tryon might have strongly disapproved. The house was filled with exotic flowers, which had clearly not come from the garden, scented candles, expensively bound books, the inevitable family photographs and Kanga's treasured collection of Wemyss Ware porcelain. The obligatory Aga was installed in the kitchen and a table was piled high with what I hope was her entire collection of hats. It was a comfortable home with evidence of a woman's touch in every corner.

We were to lunch al fresco, Kanga announced, as she embraced us. She was heavily made-up and wearing a soft white summer dress, with a plunging V-neck that displayed a large expanse of freckled bosom. It was a sophisticated creation that, quite clearly, had not come from her own shop. Was it my imagination or was the kiss she gave Terry a little more lingering than the one I had received? After all, when she had asked me to bring him along she had added, 'I have to admit, I quite fancy him.'

She had also broken out the silver service for what was supposed to be an informal lunch for three and, despite the fact she knew I would only have mineral water, I noticed that there were two ice buckets with a bottle of Chardonnay in each. Kanga was up for a good time and there was mischief brewing in her deep green eyes. I was beginning to dread what lay ahead.

Over lunch she told Terry (I had already heard the story) how she had had her spine rebuilt after being born with spina bifida. 'I'm a dairy herd on top, an African safari in the middle and a motorway below,' she said, in reference to the combination of cow bone, catgut and cement that had been used to rebuild her backbone.

At the end of the meal she lit a Silk Cut and gave me a mild cigar. 'I got it especially for you. I know it's the sort you like.' Then she giggled and I decided the moment was right to produce the AA literature, casually venturing that she might find it of some interest. Big mistake. Kanga gave me the mischievous smile she used on occasions to deflect any unwanted seriousness and drawled, 'So that's it. You believe I'm an alcoholic? It's really funny you should think that because just the other day HRH asked me why I took so much wine with my food. I told him I drank to drown my sorrows and – rather smugly I thought – he replied, 'Ah well darling, I see your troubles have learned to swim.' What a cheek coming from that family. His grandmother drinks more than me. Would you take her Alcoholics Anonymous literature?

'Anyway, Charles told me that the van-Wotsits and the Palmer-whodos say that I drink secretly and I asked him if that makes them feel better about drinking publicly. I enjoy my champagne. It puts bubbles into my life. Maybe I enjoy it too much but I'm the original too-much girl. I love too much, I do too much and, yes, perhaps I drink too much. But none of it's a problem. So there.' And with that she screwed up the pamphlets before her and threw the 'Big Book' to the ground. The subject was closed.

I knew enough about her circle by this stage to know that the 'van-Wotsits' were the Prince's wealthy land-owning friends, Emilie and Hugh van Cutsem, and the 'Palmer-whodos' were Patty and Charles Palmer-Tomkinson, also close friends of Charles and parents of the high-spirited It-girl Tara.

Alcoholic or not – and in my experience only someone with a drink problem knows when they have stepped over the line of drinking normally – Kanga's behaviour seemed to be closely mirroring my own pattern of the past. Her mood swings were increasingly dramatic and she would go from being full of confidence to feeling worthless. She assured me she rarely allowed others to see her when she felt down, preferring to hide herself away until she felt ready to face the world again. She was also a great believer in controlling her moods chemically and, at a time when I was struggling to give up the sleeping tablets prescribed for me over a number of years, she said that was foolish. 'The doctor doesn't give you those pills for his own good,' she argued. 'You obviously need them. Now take your medicine and if you run out give me a call. I've always got loads of the things.'

I was going through a bad patch of insomnia, but I resisted her offer saying that, if God intended me to sleep that night, I would. But she had an answer to that too. 'God sometimes needs a little encouragement,' she said. 'Let me tell you a tale about a little Jewish man who prayed to Him saying, 'My business is going down the drain. Please God let me win the lottery.' The following Saturday he prayed again: 'My daughter's pregnant and I need to arrange a big wedding, but I have no money now the business is in trouble. Please let me win the lottery.' The following week he was beside himself with despair and prayed, 'My wife is very ill and needs an operation. Now can I win the lottery?' And at that point a voice boomed from the sky: 'Mannie, if you're so desperate to win the lottery, meet me halfway – buy a ticket.' Meet God halfway, Christopher. Take the medicine and you will sleep tonight.'

It was no good trying to convince her that mind-altering substances and me were a lethal combination. Kanga knew best and to all intents and purposes her life seemed to be extremely manageable. But I knew what she was like on her down days – how maudlin she would become and how she was liable to reach out for any royal fix to prop up her own low self-worth. Conversely, on a high she would try to take care of everybody except, of course, herself.

Chapter Twelve

NOBODY'S VIRGIN

British Airways describes itself as the world's favourite
airline and in the early 1990s that was probably true.
But, by the time I'd done my bit with one particular story,
the reputation of its chairman had been badly tarnished, its
head of public relations had been obliged to resign and an
influential consultant had been disgraced. And, of course,
Richard Branson, founder of BA's arch-rival, Virgin Atlantic,
was my new best friend.

The story of BA's dirty tricks campaign against Virgin has
entered British business folklore. Richard himself, various
hangers-on and a number of documentary-makers have all
given their versions of how a dominant carrier sought to
destroy an upstart competitor but ended up having to pay
millions of pounds in damages. One of the few people who
has never written his account of the affair is the man who
was responsible for exposing the plot and that – modesty
aside – was me.

It all started at lunchtime on Wednesday, 23 October 1991, when I took a call from a former *Confidential* reporter called Eileen Wise. Since leaving the column a couple of years earlier, she had worked for Robert Maxwell and Andrew Lloyd Webber, and we spoke occasionally to swap gossip. By now, she was married to the influential PR consultant Brian Basham and the three of us had gone out to dinner on a couple of occasions. By the time I met Brian for the first time, I was already familiar with his reputation. He was known as a smooth-talking but tough operator whose party trick was to bite chunks out of wine glasses. Nothing I saw over those dinners led me to dispute that description. He was certainly charming, but I thought I detected a very tough streak.

That day in 1991, Eileen said that Brian might have a story and she called again a day later, urging me to phone him to discuss the story which, she said, linked Richard Branson to drug-taking at Heaven, a nightclub he owned in central London. When I got round to calling Basham, he did say you could 'apparently buy anything down there in the way of drugs', adding, 'Personally, I'm not interested in what goes on at Heaven. What I am interested in is how Branson runs his operation. Needless to say my client [British Airways] is very interested in that... He'd be in real danger if a story came out exposing what goes on at Heaven.'

When I put the phone down I was quite shocked by what I'd just heard. It was rare for a representative of such a blue-chip corporation to play their hand so openly. His wife had once worked for me and we had become something more than acquaintances but it was presumptuous of him to assume that I would be a willing accomplice in what was quite clearly a smear campaign. It's not being precious to say that my conscience told me that this was something that Richard Branson should know about. I wandered down the corridor to the office of Martin Dunn, who had recently taken over from David Montgomery as editor, to share my thoughts with him. Unlike David – who might well have dismissed my misgivings – Martin was a more relaxed and even-handed individual. After I had outlined my view that we ought to take the side of the little guy, he agreed that I should call Richard and inform him of Basham's approach.

Richard and I had met a few times over the years. Indeed, when he was an up-and-coming music entrepreneur and I was first writing *Confidential* on the *Sunday Mirror*, he had served me lunch on the canal boat in Little Venice where he used to entertain. I knew him well enough not to go through his press office and, though he was tied up when I rang, he returned my call within minutes. He listened intently while I explained what I thought was going on, and who could blame him? At that time, Virgin Atlantic was at one of the most sensitive points of its development. It had just won a hard-fought battle to gain valuable slots at Heathrow, and had also picked up some Japanese routes from BA. But these extensions to its schedules required financing and discussions with potential backers were at a delicate stage. Bad publicity now could break the company.

Richard could barely contain his excitement at what he was hearing. He had long known that BA was working against him behind the scenes but this was the first time he had heard anything resembling concrete evidence. He persuaded me to go to see him that afternoon and discuss the matter in greater detail at his mansion in Holland Park. In all our previous meetings, Richard had come across as an almost happy-go-lucky individual who, I assumed, had built his business through a combination of inspired judgement and shrewd delegation. But that day, I saw a totally different side of him. Armed with a yellow legal pad, he grilled me for more than an hour, all the while making detailed notes of our conversation. He was clearly taking what I had to say extremely seriously.

Basham and I spoke again that Friday and he invited me to lunch 'at my usual table at the Savoy' the following Monday. Over the weekend, while Jan and I were out, Jo took a number of calls from an increasingly agitated Richard. He had something 'vital' to ask me, she said. Before I could call him back, Basham came on to change the lunch venue. He had decided that we shouldn't be seen together in public, particularly since he would be handing over documents, and so instead of meeting at the Savoy he wanted me to go to his house.

As soon as I'd put down the phone on Basham, it rang again. This time it was Richard. He was clearly nervous and, when I heard what he wanted me to do, I could understand why. In that hesitant but persistent way of his, he asked me whether I would be prepared to secretly tape my conversation with Basham. This was something that I was initially unwilling to do. It was one thing to report back what Basham said, it was quite another to make a surreptitious recording and hand it over to the last man who was intended to hear the exchange. Once news of this action came out, it was sure to make Basham an enemy for life. I argued against the proposal for some time but Richard was at his persuasive best. My last excuse had been that I didn't have suitable equipment – a wire – but Richard countered this by saying he would arrange for his right-hand man Will Whitehorn to get that to me.

He called back late on Sunday evening to give me a list of questions he wanted me to put to Basham. Today, reading over my notes of that conversation, it is clear that Richard then viewed Virgin Atlantic's battle with British Airways as a personal feud between himself and its head, Lord King. Top of his questionnaire was: 'How long has Lord King had you working on this case?' 'Why should Lord King be so paranoid about Richard Branson?' (After some thought he had me substitute the word Virgin for his name.) And 'Has RB rubbed Lord King up the wrong way?' He also wanted to know if Basham had – or was in a position to get – a copy of a letter about cuts and belt-tightening he had sent to his airline employees; if Basham's principal purpose was to stop him getting more finance into Virgin; why he had approached me at *Today* and not someone at the *Sunday Telegraph*; if he had anything of a more personal nature on Richard; and if there was someone at BA he could introduce me to who could provide 'more info'.

On the Monday morning, Will Whitehorn turned up at Wapping and, after failing to persuade the jobsworths at the back gate to let him in, I went down to meet him. There, like a wartime fence selling nylons, he offered me a choice of four tape machines, all of which, he said, would record through my clothing, provided I didn't move around too much. I chose the smallest and slimmest model and, with the instrument concealed in my jacket pocket, set off for my 11.30am appointment at Basham's house in north London.

Basham's successful business – he was paid £250,000 a year by British Airways alone – was reflected in his lifestyle. Eileen met me at the door of their handsome Victorian house in Primrose Hill and led me into a large drawing room, where Basham was waiting. He sat cleaning a double-barrelled shotgun. The prospect of the ordeal ahead had already begun to make me feel distinctly uncomfortable but the sight of the gun only made things worse. One of the tips that Will had given me was that, while the tape would automatically switch itself over after 45 minutes, it would do so with an audible click. And so, as Basham briefed against Virgin, I looked repeatedly at my watch to ensure that I wasn't in the room when the switchover took place. After 42 minutes, I asked to use the loo and one of the few things that made Richard laugh about the whole affair is that halfway through the tape you can hear me having a pee.

The contents of that tape proved to be more explosive than either Richard or I could ever have imagined. Basham described Virgin as a 'dicky' business, which was in constant danger of running out of ready cash. He said it was 'scandalous' to give him rights to routes which were 'really big assets' when the driving force behind the company (Branson) was dicing with death as a round-the-world balloonist and the owner of a nightclub where it was 'not inconceivable' that large amounts of drugs were being sold. He said the head of BA's North American operations had told him that Virgin's business was appallingly run, that it had dangerous levels of debt and that maintenance procedures were so poor that 'one day without doubt an aircraft will simply fall out of the sky.'

He compared his work for BA with his brief from Lord Hanson, founder of the conglomerate Hanson Trust. He boasted that he could have done a 'serious job' on ICI 'based on cartels, anti-trust stuff and ... pollution' but said that Hanson had 'formally' told him not to attack ICI. BA appeared to take a different tack. He said he was surprised that the airline's head of PR, David Burnside, was taking the Virgin threat as seriously as he was and added, 'If you blow Branson out, it doesn't make any difference to me as long as neither BA nor I are associated with it.'

Our conversation was punctuated by a number of eccentric

interludes, the most bizarre of which was the time he led me outside to inspect chisel marks on his front door, which – he claimed – had been caused by people working for someone (not Branson) at odds with one of his clients.

By 12.30pm our meeting was at an end and – unable to think of any way of getting out of it – I went for a very uncomfortable lunch with Eileen. As soon as I could get away I drove to a recording studio in Soho where I had the tape copied. When I called Richard's office, I was told by his secretary Penny that Richard had said he wanted me to be put straight through to him but I realised I wasn't ready to speak to him. I wanted to think carefully about what I did next. 'Tell him I'll come over and see him in the morning,' I said.

At his house the next day Richard was at his most solicitous. He busied himself making tea but it was clear that he was desperate to hear what Basham had said in response to the questions he had composed. But I was still unsure whether I would be doing the right thing if I gave him a copy of my tape. Something in the back of my mind told me that it wasn't right to share the information with him before it had appeared in the paper. My problem was that the tape was not audible in parts so, when he offered to have it worked on by sound engineers we did not have access to, I gave in again, handing over the copy I had had made.

Within hours, the soundmen had done their work and the next day Richard biked over a copy of the transcript. When I showed it to Martin Dunn he was clearly excited. But he was also, I felt, intimidated by the prospect of taking on BA. *Today* was, after all, the smallest-circulation daily in the country and its legal budget was tiny compared with a title such as the *Sunday Times*. If BA were to sue for libel and win, it could put the paper out of business. Martin decided to put the paper's investigative reporter, Bob Graham, on the story alongside me. He needed someone to work on the BA side of the feud but it also allowed him some time to weigh up the consequences.

Graham and I spent another week on the story and duly produced a sensational report. It looked as if the scoop would finally be published. It was laid out so that it not only took up the entire front page but also a further seven pages inside. Then Martin had the foresight to inform Rupert Murdoch of the paper's white-hot exclusive. Murdoch apparently concluded that the story was so big and complex that it would never be taken seriously if it appeared in *Today* and ordered Martin to pull it and hand over all the research to our sister paper, the *Sunday Times*. Martin was an incredibly talented editor but relatively inexperienced and I can't help feeling that if David Montgomery had been at the helm we would have run with it, Murdoch or no Murdoch.

On 3 November 1991, the *Sunday Times* broke the story and it spawned a rush of follow-ups, including a *This Week* television documentary, *Violating Virgin*, produced by a man called Martyn Gregory. I was never approached at any point by the makers of this film and I was on holiday in Egypt when it was screened in February 1992. The first I heard of it was when I got home and Jo told me there had been a programme on ITV while I was away about the fight between Virgin and BA and they had used my voice tape 'all the way through it'. She had recorded it but before she played it she warned me I wasn't going to be pleased by what I saw and heard. She was right. I picked up the phone and called Richard's direct line at the office. It was clear from the noise in the background that there was a party going on.

'Chris,' said his secretary, 'this is not a good time to talk to him. He's celebrating. He's just sold the record company to EMI for £560 million.'

'Get him to the phone,' I said, 'or I'll come to him.'

Moments later, Richard came on the line. I thought he sounded tiddly. 'Oh dear, Chris. Are you cross with me?'

'Cross?' I said. 'I'm fucking furious. You've used my so-called secret tape recording for a piece of theatrical television and you didn't even have the decency to ask me. That was my property and it was my life that was on the line when I made it and probably will be even more so now.'

There wasn't much he could say. I was devastated and felt utterly exploited.

By now he had instituted legal proceedings against BA and its chairman Lord King of Wartnaby on both sides of the Atlantic. It emerged that, apart from Basham's smear campaign, BA's tactics had included hacking into Virgin's passenger manifest, cold-calling its clients, telling them that their Virgin flight was overbooked and offering them a BA flight in exchange.

But the tape of my conversation with Basham was the cornerstone of Richard's case. He emerged victorious, winning very substantial damages in the process. But, more importantly, the case irrevocably shifted the balance of power between BA and his fledgling company. A generation of passengers, reared on the idea that BA symbolised all that was good about British quality and service, had had their illusions dashed.

It would be uplifting to report that Richard and I toasted the triumph over corporate sharp practice and forged a lifelong friendship. The truth, however, is that I felt used and it was some time before I could bring myself to see him again. When we did meet for lunch at San Lorenzo on 2 September, Richard was after yet another favour. He was suing BA for libel and wanted me to appear as a witness for the prosecution. All the journalists I know who have been forced to testify in court have told me how traumatic that experience can be. The interrogating counsel does his best to destabilise you in order to discredit your evidence and it is impossible to underestimate the importance of diligent preparation. Did I really want to put myself through such an ordeal for a man who had gained so much from my efforts only to leave me feeling he'd let me down by handing over my tape to the makers of the *Violating Virgin* documentary? When I told him I was not prepared to appear, he became irritable and edgy and when he finished his meal, I said there was no need to for him to hang around. I would settle the bill.

The following evening, he had a letter delivered to my home. It set out at length his claim to the moral high ground. Here is one example of what I would classify as his high-minded guff:

> '*What is at stake is much more than a straightforward libel case. It will also affect other smaller companies in all areas of business in Britain – how far should a giant monopoly be able to use its power to discipline or destroy an upstart?*'

I didn't bother to reply.

In my experience, people such as Richard, who achieve massive success and make small fortunes in the process, rarely do so without cynically using other people. However friendly their public face may be, there is always something in their story that points to an utterly ruthless streak. Having said that, it would have been impossible for him to achieve the success he has done in the space of one short working life without enormous single-mindedness.

The last time I saw Richard face to face was when he invited me to breakfast at Holland Park. We sat in the summerhouse in the back garden of his mansion and tried to resolve our differences over a feast of scrambled eggs, kidneys and bacon. In the 45 minutes we talked I was sufficiently won over to agree to give him a lift to Victoria Station afterwards. Once he was in my car, I asked where he was going and he explained that he had just about enough time to catch a train to Gatwick and board that morning's Virgin flight to Tokyo. Perhaps I was meant to be impressed that this man was travelling across the world without so much as a clean shirt or a toothbrush, but as a veteran of the public relations business, I knew how potent such gimmicks could be.

In subsequent years, Richard developed a weird way of showing his gratitude to me. In his autobiography, *Losing My Virginity*, he described how he was feeling as I spoke to Basham:

> '*I was due to see Tiny Rowland, who was chairman of the* Observer *and Lonrho and had extensive interests in Africa, at the same time as Chris's meeting with [Brian] Basham. If I hadn't been so preoccupied with how the fate of my business was riding on the shoulders of a reformed alcoholic, I'd have taken Tiny Rowland much more seriously ... All I could think about was whether Chris Hutchins had managed to operate the tape recorder, whether the microphone was working, and what Brian Basham was saying. This little chat over coffee*

in a Primrose Hill house was critical to the future of Virgin Atlantic. We would never again have such a good chance to catch British Airways out.'

Earlier in the book, Richard had made much of my disclosure to him of my membership of Alcoholics Anonymous. I had done that because I had been told, rightly or wrongly, that he was drinking heavily on occasions and it was more than my sobriety was worth to get involved with someone who might have a problem and was not addressing it. As it happens, the subject only ever came up once after that when he called to tell me his brother-in-law had a problem with alcohol and he might want to enlist my help in getting him treated. He never did and his brother-in-law subsequently died as a result of drink-related problems.

In April 1992, I discussed Richard with that other great airline entrepreneur Sir Freddie Laker aboard his yacht off the coast of Florida. Unlike Richard, Laker had ultimately been crushed by BA ten years earlier. 'I just hope that Richard Branson is able to heed my warnings about what these giants can do to him unless he keeps fighting every step of the way up,' he said. Fortunately, Richard has and Virgin has flourished while BA's fortunes have suffered, partly as a result.

From the Laker home in Miami, incidentally, I drove down to Key West to interview Philip Burton, the Welsh schoolteacher who had persuaded the alcoholic father of his most talented pupil to allow him to raise him as his own. The two had gone on to become so close that the boy, Richard Jenkins, later changed his surname to Burton and, as Richard Burton, conquered Hollywood and married Elizabeth Taylor (twice). Philip, whose own sexuality was dubious to say the least, turned out to be wildly indiscreet and told me, among other things, the bizarre story of Richard's experiment with homosexuality. 'He told me that, during a wine-drinking session with Laurence Olivier, they discussed whether they had missed out on anything by not being queer,' said Philip, who had moved from south Wales to the gay capital of America's eastern seaboard.

'Anyway, Richard said that he and Larry had gone to bed together to try and discover what they might have been missing, but when little had happened after half an hour, they went to a nearby brothel to vent their frustration on a couple of whores!'

I was back in the US seven months later to cover Bill Clinton's inauguration. Martin Dunne gave me only a couple of days' notice but expected me to get into at least two of the 13 balls the newly installed President would attend on the night of his swearing-in. *Today*'s Washington correspondent said obtaining tickets to the balls would be 'impossible' at such a late stage, but my Higher Power had a better idea.

On the night of my arrival in Washington, I attended an Alcoholics Anonymous meeting held at the Senate. The building had been cordoned off in preparation for the inauguration but when I said I was going to AA the police waved me through. It is no secret that, at AA meetings, members 'share' their problems by talking about them in front of the rest of the group. Spoken contributions normally relate to alcohol problems but people are free to discuss anything that is currently worrying them. When my opportunity to speak came, I shared the problem of my impossible mission. After the meeting, several people approached me to chat and one of them turned out to be a well-known senator, whom AA convention obliges me not to name. He invited me to breakfast in his office at the Senate the next morning and there presented me not only with tickets for two of the balls but also a VIP pass for the inauguration ceremony itself, which meant I was standing just yards from Clinton when he was sworn in. (Not for nothing is AA called the best network in the world.)

One of the balls I went to that night was hosted by MTV and there I saw the legendary Ben E King present Clinton with a new saxophone, which the President then played as his wife Hillary bopped in the wings. Nelson Mandela was there too, as were Chuck Berry, Barbra Streisand and Dionne Warwick. I could not help but reflect on the side benefits of getting sober the AA way.

Later that year I saw Colonel Parker for the last time. Peter Thompson and I were writing a book about Elvis Presley and the Beatles, and the Colonel had agreed to co-operate after warning me that there were certain secrets he wanted to preserve for his own autobiography. Since he was 84 and admitted that he hadn't written a single paragraph, I chose to dismiss the possible competition. Parker had moved to Las Vegas and his instructions about where we were to meet on my arrival there were typically detailed: 'You be seated on the valet-parking boys' bench opposite the hotel entrance. Tell 'em you're expecting your 'uncle', the Colonel. Don't tell anyone where you're goin', Chris, and on no account ever give anyone my address or telephone number.'

At noon precisely, the Colonel's plum-coloured Buick turned into the driveway of the Hilton International, the scene of Elvis's stage comeback 23 years earlier. At the wheel was his second wife, Loanne Miller, a former assistant to the hotel's PR chief, Nick Naff. I climbed into the back seat and, without turning his head, the Colonel looked at me in the rear-view mirror. 'You haven't changed much,' he said. I took that as a compliment since it was nearly 20 years since we had last met. It was not a compliment I could return. He had grown horribly fat, the backs of his hands were almost black with liver spots, the flesh hung in folds from his throat and what little hair he had grew in long wisps from his otherwise bald pate.

When we arrived at the restaurant he had chosen for our lunch, it was clear just how bad a shape he was in. It took him several minutes to walk the 20 yards or so to the entrance, and even longer to get to the table. He was obviously aware of his deteriorating appearance because, when I produced a camera, he shook his head and said, 'No photographs. I don't want people seeing me like this.'

Inside the restaurant, he was annoyed to find that his favourite waitress was off duty and the girl who served us got the Parker treatment when she delivered his turkey soup. 'Where's the turkey?' he demanded, swirling the contents of his bowl with a spoon. 'I usually get more meat than this.' The persecution didn't end there: as the waitress walked away, he called after her, 'You won't get much of a tip.' This was greeted by cold stares from other diners. (Years later I was reminded of that lunch by the restaurant scene in the film *As Good as it Gets*, when Jack Nicholson behaves in a similarly obnoxious manner.) Parker's mood did not improve during the meal as he spilled soup down his monogrammed shirt. Loanne spoke to him lovingly as she wiped away the grease and then fed him his vitamin pills, but I noticed that even she addressed her husband as 'Colonel', never 'Tom'.

The complicated business of eating over, we started to talk. First came the bile. Although he had been accused of taking even more than the 50 per cent of Elvis's income than he was entitled to under the terms of his management contract, that didn't stop him voicing his bitterness about members of Elvis's retinue who had sold their stories. 'One of those guys came to me and told me he'd been offered $100,000 for his story. I said, 'Be sure to write about Elvis bailing you out when they were going to take your house away. And be sure to tell 'em it was Elvis who paid the doctor's bills when your wife was sick.' But they never write that stuff. That's not what they think people want to read about him, right?'

Then came the boasting. He told me the amount he'd been offered for his memoirs if he could ever be bothered to write them, how big his deals had been for Elvis and how much he'd given out of his own pocket to charity. I was beginning to think that from a work point of view this was turning into a wasted trip when Parker surprised me. 'Now I'm gonna take you back to my house and show you a few things nobody gets to see,' he said. Not since our first meeting in 1964, when he had invited me to his apartment in Westwood, had the secretive Colonel allowed me inside his home. Mrs Parker II looked as surprised as me. 'You are honoured,' she said. 'The last visitor he allowed in the house was President Clinton's mother and he thought twice about that.'

The house, on a gated estate, was relatively modest for a man who had made so many millions of dollars. But then he had lost millions, too. Since that night in 1968 when he'd taught me to play craps in the Flamingo's casino, he had singularly failed to exercise the kind of caution he'd attempted to instil in me. He thought nothing of betting $25,000 on the roll of a dice. But, for all its modesty, it was the Colonel's home and I felt privileged to be there. Loanne had done her best with the furniture, and there were some nice prints on the walls and vases of freshly cut flowers. The one thing conspicuous by its absence was a record player. In all the times I was with him, I never heard the manager of the world's greatest singing star either play or even discuss music. Cash, it seemed, was his all-consuming interest.

One room contained all his souvenirs of a career in showbusiness. There were crystal balls ('this one's the biggest in the world'), bric-a-brac from his circus days, around a score of brass and ceramic elephants (his favourite animal), and numerous photographs of himself with various stars and world figures (even an autographed picture of Margaret Thatcher). And there were the mementos of his time with Elvis. So this was Colonel Parker's secret shrine.

Sitting in his swivel chair, he pointed his walking stick at the cupboard behind me. 'Open it up,' he ordered, 'and take a look inside.' As I did so, a bundle of telegrams fell to the floor. 'There's four hundred of them,' he said. 'I sent 'em to everybody when Elvis was in the army. Anybody who was anybody. Famous people on their birthdays, their wedding days, their tour openings. Kept his name alive, not that he cared.' The last remark sounded like the opening of hostilities.

'Do you miss him?' I asked.

'Frankly, no,' he replied. 'There's no point missing what you haven't got. Elvis is dead and buried.'

When I asked whether Elvis was the son he'd never had, he said, 'I have to be honest and tell you that I can't say yes to that one either. I never looked upon him as a son, but he was the success I always wanted. You know, although we were together a lot of years, we never got too close… He had his friends and I had mine. I looked after my money and he took care of his…' So that was it: Elvis Presley had just been a money-making machine for this old man. The world loved his 'boy', but he saw him only as a vehicle for his own ambition. I found the admission depressing.

He went on to talk about Elvis's mother Gladys, who never trusted him. 'I have to say that Gladys Presley was not a well woman and I suppose I was never comfortable around her,' he said. 'But I was managing Elvis not his parents.' From what he said, it was clear that Gladys was no more elated about her son becoming a star than Linda Jones had been about Tom's runaway success. I knew that the Colonel's refusal to take her calls had once led Elvis to rail at him about 'the way you treat my mother'. Parker had always blamed her for introducing Elvis to drugs: amphetamines for staying awake on the road and sleeping pills to bring him down afterwards. I could empathise with that. Hadn't my mother done exactly the same with me? As afternoon stretched into evening, he grew tired and I thought – perhaps hoped – I saw a tear in his eye. 'I'm going to take you back to your hotel now,' he said. 'I don't like talking about Elvis any more and this has drained me. I may see you in the casino later, when I've had a little sleep.'

I didn't see him that night but he called the following morning to say he had arranged for Peter and I to be given a red-carpet tour of Graceland when we got to Memphis. 'Tell the fans I love 'em all just like Elvis did,' he said. 'I get cards from all over the world at Christmas and on my birthday just like Elvis did. Maybe I'll make a record one day.'

This final encounter with the Colonel left me feeling deflated. The man I had once regarded as a role model I now saw as something of an egotistical monster. It was becoming common knowledge that he'd ripped Elvis off but what I considered even worse was the fact that he had squandered a great performer's talent. Parker had not only pushed Elvis into making a succession of terrible films but had held back his musical career by alienating the best songwriters. His greed prevented him paying them enough to keep them and his paranoia was such that some of the composers and lyricists who wrote Elvis's greatest hits were prevented from associating with him for fear that they would become a threat to his authority. On reflection, I realise that Elvis became a legend despite the Colonel not because of him.

Chapter Thirteen

IN SICKNESS AND
IN HEALTH

In the summer of 1994, Jan and I set off with Jo (plus boyfriend) and Dan (plus girlfriend) for a holiday in Italy. Things had been growing increasingly difficult at home and I hoped that a special holiday might help cement relations between us. I had booked two suites at a stunning palazzo in the countryside outside Florence and hired cars for each couple. However, the trip was blighted from the start by a mysterious condition that beset Jo. She developed itching in her legs that was so severe she was constantly in tears from the unrelenting irritation. We took her to a doctor in the village who, unable to suggest either cause or cure, prescribed a heavy sedative that she took during the day as well as at night.

When we got home to Richmond, Jo went to see the family GP who diagnosed eczema. But, in the months that followed, her condition got worse and worse until she was finally admitted to the Chelsea and Westminster Hospital where, the doctor said, she would be 'taught how to deal with the eczema'. Jo had been booked in for four days but three weeks later her doctors were still at a loss to explain what was wrong and sent her to the nearby Brompton Hospital to have samples of her skin analysed.

The result, when it was delivered later that day, was devastating: it came in the form of a summons to a third hospital on the Fulham Road – the Royal Marsden. The name of the hospital alone was enough to tell me how serious the situation was. The Marsden dealt exclusively with cancer patients.

I broke every speed record to be at Jo's side and cuddled her as a kindly doctor there confirmed the news we had been dreading: Jo had lymphoma – cancer of the lymph glands. He said he believed that despite the late diagnosis it had been caught in time and there was every chance of her making a full recovery, but she would have to be admitted immediately and begin an intensive course of chemotherapy without further delay. Poor Jo sobbed in my arms as she digested the news. She was just 27 years old and, as assistant manager of a branch of NatWest, had a promising banking career ahead of her. Now she was destined to spend the next two or three months in hospital, living in the twilight zone familiar to anyone who is undergoing treatment for a life-threatening illness.

It was on one of my twice-daily visits to Jo at the Marsden that I bumped into Kanga on the steps. Unbeknown to me, she had been diagnosed with uterine cancer and was being treated at the same hospital as my daughter. When I told Kanga why I was there, she said, 'Oh, take me to see the darling. Dr Ali's coming to see me soon: I'll take him to see Jo.'

She was as good as her word. That night Kanga and the

society doctor, who had been introduced to her by Prince Charles, called on Jo in the private room she had been given after contracting the hospital infection MRSA at the Chelsea and Westminster. The visit helped to lift Jo's spirits and turned out to be the first of many. Afterwards Kanga, Ali and I went for dinner at a nearby Thai restaurant. Although I wasn't convinced about his unorthodox approach to medicine, I liked the doctor's directness. 'Kanga's incorrigible,' he told me in front of her. 'She drinks, smokes and sends out for burgers and she thinks I don't know.'

Jo and Kanga became firm friends during their stays at the Marsden, and later Jo would visit her at her flat in Cadogan Square and lunch with her at San Lorenzo. There the owner Mara Berni – who subsequently masterminded Jo's conversion to Catholicism – allowed them to have their dogs under the table while they ate amidst the ladies-who-lunch in their jewels and designer clothes. Jo also went on to become a patient of Dr Ali at the Hale Clinic, where he ran his practice.

Prior to one of my visits to the hospital, I spent the afternoon interviewing for *Today* the actor Michael Crawford at the Dorchester Hotel on Park Lane. At one point in the conversation he said, 'You seem preoccupied. Anything the matter?' I told him about Jo and the warmth of his response took me aback and was amazingly reminiscent of Kanga's reaction: 'Oh, the poor love. Do you think it would be possible for me to visit her?'

Possible? I couldn't think of anything more calculated to cheer her up. We agreed to meet at the Marsden the following day and, as he wanted his visit to be a surprise, I promised not to tell Jo he was coming. When the star of *Some Mothers Do 'Ave 'Em* and *Phantom of the Opera* appeared at her bedside, the effect was a joy to behold. Crawford sat with her for the best part of the afternoon and made her laugh the entire time.

On one of his subsequent visits he took his two daughters with him and on yet another occasion he gave Jo a journal in which to keep a record of her recovery. I believe that writing down her feelings, as well as recording the events of each day, helped her greatly in coming to terms with her illness. Crawford's generosity of spirit restored my faith in showbusiness stars – if only briefly.

The chemotherapy was a success and, by February 1995, Jo was well enough for me to take her on holiday. She wanted to go to Disneyworld so we spent two fantastic weeks in Florida. But, when we got back, Jo was told by her doctors that, while the chemotherapy had worked, the only way they could make absolutely sure the cancer would not return was by giving her a second, high-dosage course of the treatment. The first course had been traumatic and painful and this second phase promised to be even worse but Jo agreed to go ahead with it and was booked into the Marsden's sister hospital in Sutton that April.

Earlier that month, I had taken a call from a very angry Colonel Parker. The book I had written with Peter Thompson, *Elvis Meets the Beatles*, had just been published and something in it had offended him. 'Just heard 'bout your book,' he said, 'and I don't like what I hear. What's all this about The Colonel's Secret Shrine [the title Peter and I had chosen for the final chapter]? You've got stuff in there that I intended putting in my book. It's full of my secrets and they were for my book only. I might want to counteract.'

I didn't understand what he meant by that last sentence and I never got the chance to ask him. At that point, he hung up and we never spoke again. I had lost one of my greatest mentors. Of course, he never did write a book and I don't believe he had ever seriously intended to. He had told me 30 years earlier that he planned to write his life story and call it *How Much Does it Cost When it's Free?* but, as so many do, he never got any closer to producing it than picking the title. The Colonel took many of his secrets to the grave with him but I still have a few to divulge at a later date.

In addition to the loss of my relationship with the Colonel, that book cost me a 25-year friendship even more precious to me: that of Terry O'Neill. Terry had had an affair with Priscilla after they had met in the LA clothes shop Bis and Beau, which she ran with designer Olivia Bis. Since in those days we told each other *everything*, I knew chapter and verse about the affair's progress, even down to what she wore for bed on the night they first made love (and how long it took her to get ready for intimacy!). Priscilla had just broken up with Mike Stone and was hungry for love. 'She was ultra-feminine, very gentle and terribly romantic,' Terry had said. 'She was certainly no good-time girl. Before me, there had only been Elvis and Mike which made her a very chaste woman, particularly by the standards of that town and that era.'

He went on to say how their nights together were frequently interrupted by telephone calls from either Presley or Stone. Although he gave me permission to reveal the affair, my account at that time was too detailed and, alas, Terry has never forgiven me. I suspect Priscilla was just as cross.

Jo underwent her second course of chemotherapy and, despite the trauma of the treatment, made a full recovery, thank God. Meanwhile, Kanga's hostility towards Camilla Parker Bowles was beginning to tip over into paranoia. One day in November, after I had picked her up from the Marsden

255

and driven her home to her apartment in Knightsbridge, she called me at the office and asked me to rush back as there was something urgent she wanted to discuss. She had clearly been very unwell when I dropped her off earlier and by the time I got to the flat she was in bed – albeit sitting up. She began by reminding me that I had promised to write a book (to that end I had been keeping notes about our meetings for some time). Then she started ranting about Camilla: how bad she was for Charles and how damaging their relationship could prove. 'If he doesn't get rid of her it could destroy the monarchy,' she said at one point. She accused Mrs Parker Bowles of waging a campaign to win over public opinion by leaking stories to the newspapers that promoted her role as Charles's consort – a role Lady Tryon herself had long coveted.

Kanga said she had been told on good authority that calls to newspaper editors and picture desks, tipping them off about where Camilla and the Prince might be seen together, had been made by Camilla herself. 'You must help me get evidence, Christopher,' she said. 'I have promised Her Majesty that I will get the evidence and she is sending a lady-in-waiting to see me in Wiltshire in a few days' time.' It seemed to me doubtful at best that this would be the case and she must have seen that on my face. She switched her hectoring tone to a more wheedling one: 'Darling, you must help me. I know you can and, if you won't do it for your country, do it for me.' I was beginning to wonder whether my old friend wasn't becoming a bit unhinged.

It was time for me to leave but, aware that I had not yet signed up as an ally, Kanga determined to have another go at me the next morning. 'I will have breakfast ready at eight,' she said. 'Be here.' She was clearly in no mood to brook any opposition.

As I drove back to Richmond, I mulled over the predicament. Kanga didn't just want me to come up with unattributed remarks from people in the know, she wanted tape recordings of individual newspaper executives confirming that Camilla was in contact with them. That night I made several calls to people whose judgement I trusted, asking them – without mentioning names – to what extent I should get involved, if at all. The consensus was overwhelming. 'Don't get involved if you like happy endings,' said one. 'This one sounds as though it's all going to end in tears.'

When I arrived at Kanga's apartment the following morning it was clear that none of her determination had evaporated overnight. I found her singleness of purpose puzzling but eventually concluded that she may have decided that she had made a fatal miscalculation in abandoning any hope of snaring Charles herself. While she had assumed that her marital status precluded any possibility of becoming his queen, Camilla, who was also married, had decided to ignore that particular impediment and it was beginning to look as though her persistence would pay off. This was a prospect that Kanga found intolerable. As she resumed her attempts to enlist me in her cause, it occurred to me for the first time to ask if the Queen really knew what she was up to. Kanga appeared surprised that I should even venture such a question. 'Of course she does,' she replied. 'I told you last night, she's sending someone to discuss it with me. Why do you ask?'

'I just wondered what her reaction might have been,' I said.

'I'll tell you exactly how she reacted. She said to me, "Kanga, you lay mines." Those were her words and in the circumstances, Christopher, I took that to be a compliment.'

Shortly afterwards, Jan and I went to Torquay to see my mother. By now she was in her third old people's home, having been asked to leave the previous two because of her unreasonable demands and her frequent accusations that other inmates and staff were stealing from her. Mum had become increasingly unstable over the years. She had, for example, developed a fixation with the idea that people might think she had AIDS. She had even persuaded her GP to write her a letter that stated that she did not have it, and she carried that letter with her everywhere. When I took her for lunch at the Imperial Hotel, Lord (Lew) Grade was lunching at the next table and I introduced him to Mum, but she wept because for once she did not have the doctor's letter on her to show him. When we left Torquay she seemed more miserable than ever before so I didn't dare tell her that Jan and I were off to Switzerland for a break the following weekend. When I finally phoned to tell her the day before we set off, she said, 'It's all right for some,' and hung up. Those turned out to be the last words she would ever say to me and they saddened me beyond measure.

When Jan and I got back from Switzerland on the Sunday night, I was told that Mum had been rushed to Torbay Hospital after suffering a suspected heart attack. Before I left for Torquay the following morning, I called the hospital to check on her condition, only to be told that she had died during the night. I have to confess that my first reaction was one of enormous relief. My brother, sister and I had put up with her increasingly cantankerous behaviour and wildly fluctuating moods for decades by this point. She would pick fights with everyone from the neighbours to local tradesmen and had played mind games with us ever since we were children. On one occasion, out of sheer devilment, she had even told both Phil and Joan that their spouses were having affairs.

With these mixed feelings running through me, I drove

down to Devon to work with Phil on the funeral arrangements. The next day we were at the undertakers picking out a coffin when I got a call from a friend to tell me that Rupert Murdoch had closed *Today*. Not only had I just lost my mother, but I was also out of a job. Unlike most of my colleagues, however, I felt more relieved at the news than anything else. Since swapping the unpredictability of producing a daily gossip column for the more ordered life of a feature writer, I had begun to feel as if I was on a treadmill. This turn of events would force me to do something more fulfilling.

When the day of mother's funeral arrived, my brother and sister and I found ourselves smiling at each other. All three of us felt free for the first time in our lives. I smiled as I recalled the memory of my mother's hands dancing across the keyboard of a piano with candlesticks to produce happy musical memories, of picking cabbages in the garden on the day before pension day and of trying not to laugh as we knelt beneath the window when the tallymen came to collect their weekly never-never payments. But the three of us were happy in the knowledge that she had been relieved of the demons in her head that had driven her to upset so many people.

As I drove Jan, Jo and Dan back to London along the route we had travelled so many times before, I felt sad that this would probably be the last time we would make the journey together. Ironically, we were crossing Salisbury Plain and not far from the turn-off to Kanga's country home when the car phone rang – it was the lady herself. When she heard I was nearby, Kanga suggested I head in her direction. I explained I had my family in the car and we were on our way home from my mother's funeral, but that only prompted her to suggest that I bring them too, promising to welcome us with glasses of 'consoling champagne'. It didn't seem to occur to her that cracking open the bubbly might not be the most appropriate way to mark my mother's passing. Indeed, she was so insistent on a meeting that I had to promise to visit her a few days later.

By now she had been able to restore the Tryons to their original family home – a Queen Anne mansion at Great Durnford, which lies in a particularly beautiful Wiltshire valley. We had arranged to meet at four o'clock and it was already getting dark by the time I arrived. If I thought she had seemed paranoid when I saw her last, that was nothing compared to the Kanga who arrived back from a visit to Wales by helicopter. Within minutes of clambering from the chopper on the front lawn of what had been for years a private school, I could see that her suspicions of those around her were in overdrive. As darkness fell we had tea in the drawing room – filled again with photographs of her and her family and the Queen with hers – before she insisted we go for a walk. Even though it was a bitterly cold night, she insisted we talk outside the house 'so we won't be overheard'.

'But there's only the butler here,' I protested.

'I once had a conversation with Prince Charles in this room and every word of it was reported back to me. Walls have ears: we must go somewhere we won't be overheard.'

We left the house through the French windows and, wrapped in heavy winter coats, walked arm-in-arm through grounds that swept down to the River Avon, which was all that separated her estate from that of Sting, the rock star with whom she said she had forged a close friendship. When we were some distance from the house, and well out of range of any eavesdroppers, I protested that we had gone far enough.

'No,' she said. 'We'll go into the rose garden.'

We entered the rose garden though a gate in a tall hedge

and, once inside, Kanga locked the gate behind us and then walked round the perimeter, securing the gates on the other three sides. Now I was not only cold but also more than a little uneasy, locked up in the rose garden of a deserted estate on a bitter winter's night with a woman who seemed to be slowly going mad. When all four gates had been secured, she led me by the hand to a summer house, sat me down on a bench and cuddled me like a child. When she finally spoke it was in a dreamy voice that belied the intense mood she was in: 'This is where I come when I want to be alone. I sit here sometimes and watch the sun go down and wonder, 'What if...'.

'What if what?' I asked – as if I didn't know – but Kanga changed the subject. She was anxious, she said, to get down to business. She had convinced herself there was a tape in circulation of Camilla talking to Stuart Higgins, then editor of the *Sun*. 'You must get that tape,' she said. 'You must.' Now it was her turn to sound irritable. 'I have promised Her Majesty you will get it,' she went on, sounding increasingly excited by the task. 'Her lady-in-waiting is coming here specially to collect certain documents and I cannot let her go away without also having a transcript of that tape. Camilla has to be stopped and she has to be stopped now. HRH is potty about her, but he will soon get over it. Good lord, he's made enough derogatory remarks to me about her in the past.'

Once again she appealed to me as a patriot. 'Christopher, you must realise you are not doing this for me,' she said. 'You owe it to your country. The Queen has told me – albeit in a roundabout way – that she will insist Charles put an end to the affair if she can prove to him that Mrs Parker Bowles is manipulating him in the same way as Wallis Simpson manipulated King Edward VIII.'

She went on in this vein for some time, at one point breaking down as if she had suddenly realised that she was essentially powerless. Temporarily spent, she stopped talking and for what seemed like several minutes we sat in silence, the vapour of our warm breath visible in the frosty air. When she next spoke, it was to discuss Jo and her cancer treatment. It was almost a relief to move on to a subject that, while emotionally loaded for me, at least concerned the real world.

By the time we returned to the house, however, I was feeling angry about something Kanga had said concerning Jo's treatment. She took me up to her bedroom where a fire was lit in the grate and – in relation to a point she wanted to make about Jo – asked me to read a passage from a book in the Bible while she sat on the bed. When I told her I had no idea where to find even the book, let alone the passage (the Bible never held any interest for me), she was flabbergasted and said so. I had had enough and declared my intention of leaving. 'But you can't go,' she said. 'I'm having dinner specially prepared and there's a room made up for you to stay in if you can be persuaded to have a drink with me.' My mind was made up, however, and in front of Kanga I telephoned Jo on my mobile and told her I was on my way back to Richmond to take her out for a late supper. Never have I been so glad to leave a house as I was on that occasion. With Kanga ringing repeatedly on the mobile, I broke the speed limit most of the way home.

Following the closure of *Today*, I worked as a freelance journalist and author. One of my first commissions was to interview a very wealthy Englishwoman called Celia Lipton, in Palm Beach, Florida. Jo and I had already decided to repeat the trip we'd made a year earlier and Celia's home was on our planned route. Celia was interesting for a number of reasons. She was the daughter of a well-known British bandleader of the 1940s, Sydney Lipton, and she had married a very successful inventor called Victor Farris, who'd left her £60 million on his death, along with the royalties on a number of his inventions, including the plastic milk carton.

A vainglorious woman who claimed to be 59 when she was 70, Celia used her fortune in the most superficial ways imaginable. She bought the company of the showbiz elite by flying stars halfway round the world for elaborate fund-raising parties, which she financed personally. In a desperate attempt to join their ranks, she ploughed hundreds of thousands of pounds of her own money into recording an album of sugary songs and then advertising it in newspapers and on television when established record companies 'passed' on distributing it. Despite the fact that I had humiliated her in print four years earlier by revealing that of the 40,000 albums she had paid to be produced just 370 were sold, she sent a limo to collect Jo and I from our hotel when we arrived in Palm Beach.

Celia had the best friends money could buy, and to prove it she took us to dine at Mara Lago, the mansion that Donald Trump had turned into a club for fellow local millionaires. I had not been expecting to attend any formal functions on the trip and Tony Miles – now living in Florida – took me to a shopping mall to buy a cheap shirt and tie for the occasion. That night, the three of us had dinner with Trump and his then wife, Marla Maples, a stunningly beautiful woman known as the Georgia Peach. I had met Trump before in New York when I was in the US promoting my biography of the Duchess of York, *Sarah's Story*. He had laid on a suite at his hotel the Plaza for an interview with CBS and was so fascinated by Fergie that he had sat in on the interview and we chatted at length about her afterwards. He was no less attentive at Mara Lago. The evening took a surreal turn when he complimented me on my 'superb shirt and tie' (the set had cost just $15). As far as I could tell, he was not being facetious. Perhaps it had something to do with the fact that he and Marla were dressed as cowboy and Indian.

Next stop was Miami, where we spent a day with old friend and former client Barry Gibb. The eldest Bee Gee was living in a huge oceanside mansion in which he had become something of a recluse. As a member of the Academy (the people who vote for the Oscars), he was sent a copy of every Hollywood film produced before they are released and he would sit for hours day after day watching them in his own private cinema. It wasn't like the Barry I had known in the 1960s, but Jo enjoyed his company and his wife Linda (a former Scottish beauty queen) proved a gracious hostess.

Towards the end of 1995 I had an intriguing meeting with Amanda Platell, a talented journalist and former *Today* colleague who had moved to the *Daily Mirror* (and who was later to become spin-doctor to the former Tory leader William Hague). We arranged to meet for dinner and, as Amanda is a lively Aussie and an entertaining gossip, few topics were off limits. As it happened, her most fascinating tale that night related to her own private life. A few months earlier, she had split up with her boyfriend, a fairly anonymous property developer called Christopher Whalley, who I had met just once at a party at Amanda's former home in Clapham. Having moved a few weeks before, she had called Whalley to invite him round to see her new flat in Hampstead one Saturday evening. Whalley had accepted the invitation on condition that he could watch a particular television programme, after which he would need to make a phone call – in private! 'No problem,' said Amanda. 'Do it from here.'

The first draw of the new National Lottery was being screened live on BBC1 that weekend and Amanda assumed that her ex must have wanted to watch the inaugural show. Perhaps, she mused, he was involved with it in some way. For once the astute Ms Platell was wrong on both counts. In an attempt to lure viewers away from the BBC's milestone programme, ITV had put together a documentary on the life and times of the Princess of Wales. That was the programme Whalley wanted to see and, after watching it in silence, he had repaired to the privacy of Amanda's bedroom to make his telephone call.

'But he left the bedroom door slightly open and I heard some of the conversation,' Amanda told me. 'He was saying, 'Yes, darling. You came across wonderfully well. I promise you people will love you all the more for it.' When he finally emerged I stood there open-mouthed and said, 'That was *her*, wasn't it? You were speaking to Diana."

Whalley admitted he had been and blurted out the whole story. Like Diana, he had become a regular at the Harbour Club in Chelsea, London's most A-list gym. As he walked down the club stairs one morning, he heard a voice say, 'What does a girl have to do to get a man to buy her a cup of coffee around here?' It was the Princess. An astonished Whalley, at first unable to believe she was talking to him, looked over his shoulder to see if there was someone else behind him before realising it was indeed him she was chatting up. They had their coffee, the glamorous Princess and the tall, slim man with matinee-idol looks, and it turned out to be the start of a close friendship. Amanda saw her on-off lover as the successor in Diana's affections to the very-married Oliver Hoare, who Diana had been stalking since he broke off their affair once news of it reached his wife.

Amanda, a journalist down to her fingertips, was clearly bursting to tell the story but she was between a rock and a hard place. As an executive on the *Mirror*, she knew that if the scoop was to appear anywhere it should be in her own paper but it appeared that Whalley had made her promise not to write it. This begged the question: why was she telling me, someone she knew to be one of the, er, more go-getting journalists around? I thought about this long and hard and concluded that she wanted me to place the story. Which girl wouldn't want word to get out that she had shared a lover with the most glamorous woman in the world?

Further evidence that she expected the story to break came shortly afterwards when I heard that, before going on holiday, she had told her secretary, 'If a story breaks about me while I'm away, there are some pictures of me and Christopher Whalley in the top drawer of my desk that might just be useful.' She returned to the office two weeks later to find that her secret was, well, still her secret. In early December, I came to a decision and made an early-morning call to Stuart Higgins, editor of the *Sun*, the *Mirror*'s main rival. He was in his car on his way to work but, when I told him I had a story he would die for, Stuart made a detour to Patisserie Valerie in Knightsbridge, where we met for coffee and croissants. He sat in stunned silence, his jaw hanging open, as I told him the story. Not only did he have the identity of Diana's latest man, but the fellow was the ex-girlfriend of an executive on his paper's leading rival, which appeared to know nothing of it.

'Leave it with me, Chris,' he pleaded. 'Please, leave it with me.'

Now there was an amusing sequel to this rendezvous a few nights later after Stuart called me at home. 'Christopher, it's Stuart Higgins. I need to see you urgently.' I said that was fine by me and he said, 'Name a pub close to your house.' I nominated the Marlborough on Richmond Hill and we arranged to meet there half an hour later. Before I left the house, he phoned again to say that he couldn't find the Marlborough, so I suggested that he come to my home instead. 'Will that be all right?' he asked curiously. I was watching *News at Ten* when the doorbell rang. I opened the door and for the second time in a week I saw Stuart Higgins open-mouthed. He pushed his way past me and – to the amusement of Jan and Jo – walked around the living room banging his fist against his head. 'What a fool, what a fool I am,' he kept repeating. 'I must be crazy. Chris Hutchins? I got the numbers mixed up. I thought I was phoning Christopher Whalley.'

The editor of the world's biggest-selling daily paper had decided to handle the story himself and made a mistake that would have embarrassed the lowliest cub reporter. Not that this setback delayed things for long. Two days later, Stuart splashed with the story of Whalley's affair with Diana and every other paper followed it up. Christopher Whalley was never to be an anonymous property developer again.

In April 1996, I teamed up with my former colleague Dominic Midgley to write a psychological biography of the Princess of Wales. No one was ever likely to improve upon Andrew Morton's authorised account of her life, *Diana, Her True Story*, but Dominic and I felt that her increasingly fragile mental state had never been properly examined. After mapping her life from childhood to the present day by drawing on published accounts and my contacts in and around the royal household, we consulted a range of psychiatrists, psychologists, psychotherapists and specialists on addiction, image and linguistics for their conclusions. The result was a book called *Diana on the Edge: Inside the Mind of the Princess of Wales*.

One of our most startling findings came from Dr Robert Lefever, a leading light in the field of addiction and the founder of Promis, a recovery centre in Kent. After many years of dealing with women and girls who suffered from eating disorders, Dr Lefever had concluded that there was a strong statistical link between bulimia and sexual abuse in childhood. He reckoned that more than 90 per cent of bulimic women had been victims of sexual abuse and that there was therefore a very high chance that Diana had been abused in some way. How could we possibly check out such an ostensibly outlandish suggestion?

After a great deal of soul-searching, we decided no one was better qualified to discuss the matter than Diana's mother, Frances Shand Kydd. We composed a letter, taking care to phrase it as sensitively as possible, and sent it by registered post to her home off the west coast of Scotland. Unfortunately, it appears to have had a fairly devastating effect on Mrs Shand Kydd. On the morning it would have been delivered, she was arrested for drink driving. When her case reached court, as part of her plea of mitigation, she referred to 'an upsetting letter' she had received that day without giving any details of its contents. It failed, however, to sway the magistrate who imposed a driving ban. We never did receive an answer to our letter.

When Dominic and I embarked on our next project, an unauthorised biography of the billionaire financier Sir James Goldsmith, it was our turn to receive 'an upsetting letter'. In response to a request for a meeting with him, we received a letter which began: 'Sir James regrets that his commitments at present mean that he will not be able to meet you to discuss your forthcoming book. He is appreciative of your approach to him.' Fair enough, you might say, only it was written on the letterhead of London's most feared firm of libel lawyers, Peter Carter-Ruck and Partners. We were soon to discover that Sir James had also ordered family members and friends not to co-operate with us but events took a comic turn when we discovered that, by an extraordinary coincidence, his brother Teddy lived on the other side of the street from me in Richmond.

I phoned Teddy and suggested that as we were neighbours I might call on him with Dominic for an exploratory chat. He agreed and over the Darjeeling we talked about the chapter on Goldsmith's early life and agreed that we would show it to him. But, while he proved to be the most charming of men, he refused to be interviewed formally without his brother's approval. A few days later we ran into each other in the street and Teddy looked very worried. 'Jimmy called me from Burgundy on Sunday,' he said, 'and when I told him I had met you he was very cross indeed.'

Nevertheless, we often stopped for little chats in the months that followed and occasionally, if I was stuck with some detail on a particular anecdote, I would run it by him and he was usually helpful. A good example was the story of the artificial grass. When the brothers were struggling entrepreneurs in Paris in the 1950s, Teddy had bought a job lot of it but was having little success in finding customers until Jimmy saved the day. Teddy explained that his younger brother had had it dyed pink, made into gloves and marketed as a cure for cellulite. The idea was that the problem would clear up if women put on the gloves and rubbed their thighs. The gloves leaped off the shelves, apparently. It's not hard to see how Jimmy went on to become a billionaire.

Three years after his brother's death in 1997, Teddy and his wife invited me to their Christmas drinks party. As we stood chatting in his drawing room, he pointed at a nearby bookshelf and said, 'Look, that's your book on my brother up there.' In that case at least, all was well that ended well.

Bridget Rowe, the editor of the *Sunday Mirror*, was on holiday in Spain when she spotted me pontificating about something or other on Sky News and decided I was still sufficiently plugged in to write a gossip column. So, 16 years after Tony Miles had first called to offer me a column called *Confidential*, I was back on the *Sunday Mirror* under the same logo.

Apart from reinstating the column, Bridget made me a special correspondent on showbiz and royal stories. When we heard that Diana had joined a gym called Green's in the basement of the Royal Garden Hotel at the end of the private road that led to her home in Kensington Palace, Bridget asked me to go down and check it out. At the reception desk I enquired about membership and was told that I could sign up for £900. Me being me, I joined on the spot. I hadn't seen the inside of a gym for a long time but having made such a sizeable investment – which I had no hope of recovering from the bean-counters in the *Mirror*'s accounts department – I decided I might as well take the opportunity to get in shape. If I bumped into Diana, that, of course, would be a bonus.

After a few days, I had got into a routine that started and finished with a run. On day five of my new regime, I had just started the closing ten-minute stint on the running machine when I was conscious of someone getting on to the one next to me. I knew instinctively that it was her. When I chanced a glance it was to discover that, although she wasn't looking at me, she was studying the instrument panel on my machine. She set hers a notch faster. By now I was close to exhaustion having worked out for more than an hour and I was in no position to compete with one of the country's best-known fitness freaks. Never one to resist a challenge, however, I set my speed to match hers. She reacted by raising the stakes again. I then had to follow suit and by now the sweat was pouring off me. Suddenly I was involved in an absurd race with the woman who had scowled at me in the Ufizi in Florence and this time there could only be one loser. Fortunately, she had set her machine for a five-minute session and mine had a couple of minutes still to go when she stopped. As she stepped off her machine, she shot me a look that said, 'That'll teach you.'

Not long after I had rejoined the *Sunday Mirror*, I received a flurry of calls from Kanga. I hadn't spoken to her for more than a year but was aware from reports in other papers that her addiction to alcohol and sleeping pills had worsened to the point that she'd checked into a rehabilitation clinic called Farm Place. Her husband said she was being treated for depression. She toppled out of a first-floor window and injured herself so badly that she was permanently confined to a wheelchair. Kanga claimed she had been pushed. Many others reckoned she had thrown herself out, but I have always believed that she had fallen after making histrionic threats to jump unless she was permitted to leave.

After we had caught up with each other's news, she suggested we meet for dinner at the Mayfair Hotel where she was staying. By now, living at Great Durnford was not an option, as the long-suffering Lord Tryon had finally lost patience with her increasingly erratic behaviour. After selling her apartment in Cadogan Square, Kanga was liquid enough to afford a £700-a-night suite at the Ritz and that's where we met.

It was a fine summer's evening in July 1997 and she had supervised the packing of her cases prior to a trip to Australia to visit her ailing mother. She had chosen the Ritz, she said, 'because she comes here' – a reference, of course, to Camilla Parker Bowles. 'Who knows? Perhaps she'll pop in while we're having dinner.' I was already seated at the table when Kanga made her entrance, applauded by other guests as she propelled her wheelchair through the dining room. The first glass of champagne had just been poured – the stint at the drying-out clinic obviously hadn't had the desired effect – when the artist David Hockney came by the table to pay his respects. 'It was Baroness Thatcher the other night,' a beaming waiter told me as he and I looked on. 'Maggie insisted on Lady Tryon joining her table. And Chris Patten [the ex-Governor of Hong Kong] stood up from his table and gave her a deep bow. Everybody loves her.' I think he was right. Kanga was clearly a sick woman, both physically and mentally, but she had shown so much love and care for so many people over the years that her friends were not about to desert her in her hour of need. It was all quite touching.

One of the few people who was not prepared to be seen with her was the one man she most desired to see. 'Did you hear about HRH's people trying to stop me talking to him at the polo the other day?' she asked. 'They stationed a whole line of Royal Dragoon Guards between us at the polo [the Tidworth Polo Ground in Wiltshire]. For God's sake, I was in a wheelchair. I'd only been out of hospital two days and they had all these men in uniforms blocking my path as if I was from the bloody IRA. When I told them, 'I need to see the Prince of Wales, please tell them that Lady Tryon is here. We are old friends,' they looked at me as if I was a green-eyed monster from another planet.'

Kanga said she wanted to speak to the Prince to explain

that a box containing all the letters he had written to her had been stolen. I interrupted to ask whether publication of the letters could turn into her version of Camillagate – the crisis prompted by the *Sun*'s publication of the transcript of a sexually explicit phone conversation between Charles and Camilla. 'No, darling,' she said. 'Not anything as vulgar as that. But very interesting.'

We talked on the phone several times in the weeks that followed, but we were never to meet again. A month after that final dinner, she called in tears to say that her husband had been granted his decree nisi on the grounds of her unreasonable behaviour. She had not taken the divorce as well as I had expected.

'Just five minutes in court and so many years wiped out,' she said. 'He said I'd made him ill with stress. It's so unfair,' she wept, 'so bloody unfair.'

The next time I heard from Kanga she was in India. She called from Delhi in early October to say she was undergoing a course of alternative therapy under the direction of Dr Ali. There was, she said, something I had to know for the 'you-know-what' (by which I assumed she meant the book I had promised to write). 'I had a phone call last night from HRH. He's promised to come and see me here. Isn't that wonderful? He says he'll bring Harry. I want to see him so much. There's so much for he and I to talk about. The Queen is coming here too and my next call will be to Lady Butter to arrange that we meet up. Oh, it's all so exciting.'

I would have been excited for her too if I wasn't now so sceptical of her claims to be in touch with the Sovereign and heir.

Kanga added that she would be back in London later that month, in time to attend a court hearing on 5 November when she would contest her husband's right to the family home. 'I'm determined to get the house and pass it on to my children,' she said. 'I spent more than half a million of my own money doing the place up and getting the gardens nice and I'm damned if he's going to get it all. It was my hard work that paid for the place.'

Typically enough, her last move was to invite me to a party, her 50th, which would be held, naturally, at the Ritz. 'I'll be walking by then,' she said, adding as an afterthought, 'I'll be dancing by then.'

I was abroad when Kanga was flown back to England after being taken seriously ill in India with typhoid – a direct result of having travelled without having the appropriate inoculations. Her condition became critical following surgery to treat bed sores, which had worsened as a result of her refusal to take the advice of Dr Ali's brother Imran (who was overseeing her treatment) to move from her hotel to a hospital where she could be given round-the-clock medical care. The first I knew of all this was when I took a call at home late on the night of Saturday, 15 November, to tell me that Kanga was dead. She had developed septicaemia (blood poisoning) and had slipped into a coma from which she never awoke.

In a statement that reflected the family's relief that she (and they) had been spared further suffering, Kanga's mother-in-law, Dreda, Lady Tryon, said, 'We are very sad, but happy for her.' It sounds superficially callous, but I knew what she meant. Even before she fell from the window at Farm Place, it was clear that Kanga was in a bad way.

A prayer service was held in her memory at the Norman church of St Andrew near Great Durnford. Lord Tryon's mother explained their absence later: 'We are very sad but we could not go to the service because the phone would not stop ringing.' Kanga's fraught relationship with her in-laws was clearly as much to do with a clash of cultures as anything else.

I decided that Lord Tryon would not thank me for showing up at her funeral, given our conflicting interests in his wife, so I wasn't there when half her ashes were scattered on the banks of the Avon. (The other half were taken to Australia, where they were placed beside her late father's grave in Melbourne.) Prince Charles wasn't there either.

Chapter Fourteen

WITH THE PARTING
OF THE WAYS

I was in bed by the time Beechy Colclough called late on the night of Tuesday, 28 January 1998. As an addiction specialist, Beechy was used to dealing calmly with clients' personal crises but on this occasion he sounded extremely agitated. He had just had a call from our mutual friend John Reid. John had phoned him from America to say that he'd had a major row with Elton John. 'John says this could be the end of his relationship with Elton and he needs your help,' said Beechy. I knew what he was referring to. A story had appeared in that day's *Daily Mirror* outlining the hugely embarrassing details of Elton's colossal personal expenditure. Worse, the paper had reproduced a letter to Elton from his accountants, Price Waterhouse, warning that his spending had reached such a point that he was in danger of going insolvent. Quite simply, the money was going out faster than it was coming in.

Although John and I had been friends for years, we had not

spoken for several months and I was in no mood to leap into action at a moment's notice, particularly as he hadn't had the courtesy to call me himself. 'John knows my number,' I told Beechy. 'If he wants to speak to me, tell him to call me. But tell him to leave it till the morning. I'm in bed and going to sleep.'

That said, I was enormously intrigued and, when the morning came, I couldn't wait for John's call to find out what had gone on. The phone rang at around 10am and John was clearly highly charged: 'Elton is convinced the stuff's been leaked to the *Mirror* by someone in my office,' he said, 'and he wants their head on a platter – or mine. But I can't think of anyone at JRE [John Reid Enterprises] who would do such a thing. I'll be honest, I'm desperate.' I said I would see what I could do.

A short time later I was in the office of a Mirror Group executive (not the editor of the *Daily Mirror*, I must point out). He said (as we all do) that it was more than his life was worth to reveal the name of an informant. But straight afterwards he said cryptically that he would have to leave me for a couple of minutes to go to the newsroom. Before doing so, he scribbled something on a piece of paper, looked at me, then at the paper on his desk and left the room.

I picked up the scrap of paper, on which he had scribbled the name Benjamin Pell. It meant nothing to me. At that stage, Pell – who went on to gain notoriety as Benjy the Binman – was relatively unknown. I later discovered that he was a trained solicitor who was making a lucrative career out of picking up rubbish left outside the offices of the representatives of prominent people and then going through the contents in search of stories to sell to the newspapers.

His name meant nothing to John either. 'He's not on my staff,' he said, when I relayed the information.

'Are you sure?' I asked.

For confirmation I contacted another highly placed Mirror Group source, who was able to provide the remaining pieces of the jigsaw. Pell had been paid £3,500 for the documents he'd recovered from JRE's rubbish bags, while the man who had sold the material on his behalf, the publicist Max Clifford (once an employee of mine), had got £4,000.

From his apartment in New York, Reid then called the *Mirror* editor Piers Morgan in a bid to get him to confirm the name of his informant. 'This thing has gone way beyond Elton's embarrassment,' he told Piers. 'It's about the survival of my company.' John went on to tell the editor that he might have to sack all the 30 or so of the staff he employed – enough to trouble the conscience, if not the lawyers, of any editor.

Over the next few days, I took a number of calls from John who remained in New York. Each seemed to begin with the phrase, 'Things are hotting up.' And they were. On one side of the divide, the world's biggest musical star was boiling over with fury; on the other, nervous *Mirror* lawyers were assessing the legal consequences of the paper's revelations and sweating over the scale of any possible libel pay-out. Meanwhile, I learned that Pell and Clifford had also received thousands of pounds between them for an earlier *Mirror* scoop, about Elton falling out with Richard Branson over his refusal to allow the Virgin boss to include the version of *Candle in the Wind* he had sung at Princess Diana's funeral on a memorial album. The letter that formed the cornerstone of that story had come from JRE's bins too.

Things seemed to have calmed down by the time John phoned me from Washington DC on the morning of 6 February. The previous night, he had accompanied his number-one client to a White House ball, where Elton had danced with Hillary Clinton while he himself chatted to one of the Shuttle astronauts. But this proved to be only a temporary lull in what was shaping up to be a serious conflict. A few days earlier, John had started legal action against Pell in a bid to force him to identify his source but that had failed. Meanwhile, the *Mirror* hierarchy was becoming convinced that Elton's anger about the story stemmed from his belief that he hadn't spent the money – someone else had. They were wrong about that. As has been proven since, Elton's accounts were perfectly in order. The problem as I saw it was that while Elton was not ashamed of his extravagance – indeed, he was proud of it – he was appalled to find it being made public in such a high-profile manner.

The plot thickened when Pell gave an interview to London's *Evening Standard*, in which he claimed that he had hacked into JRE's computers, and another to the *Daily Star* in which he claimed to be a computer whiz kid. These claims so confused me that I called him. Pell told me he had conned the *Standard*. He also confessed (boasted might be a more appropriate word) that he had obtained the information about Elton's spending by sifting through JRE's discarded rubbish. He even gave me some other, unpublished snippets of information he had gleaned from the same source. I never did tell him that I was the one who had exposed him.

Soon afterwards Jan and I managed to get away to Switzerland for a much-needed break but when I got back I received yet another call from John. Stuart Higgins at the *Sun* had contacted him to say he'd learned the *Mirror* planned to run a story the following day saying Elton had sacked him, so he would have to do the same in the *Sun*. A source at the *Mirror* told me that the paper had received their tip-off from 'an obviously gay man who said he was a friend of Elton'. While it was to take some time to unpick their 28-year personal and commercial relationship, the story turned out to be substantially true. Elton had decided to dispense with the manager who had taken him from being an obscure songwriter to a global megastar.

John Reid was not the only one to suffer a loss in 1998. In October, Jan left me. Our lifestyles had been totally incompatible for a long time and the disputes that engendered had hacked away at the love we had felt for each other since that August night 40 years earlier. Both council-house kids, we had worked hard to escape our poor backgrounds and bring up two great children, and had enjoyed many wonderful times in the process. But now it was over.

I had been in Brighton for a few days when Jan moved out but, after a visit to the cinema to watch Steven Spielberg's harrowing war movie *Saving Private Ryan*, I felt so depressed that I returned home early to see her and try to reconcile our differences. Alas, when I got there, it was to discover that she had gone and taken all her possessions with her. Her wardrobes and drawers were empty. The house that had been our home seemed abandoned. Her departure must have been planned like a military operation for she had not only found somewhere else to live, but had also carried out her move in a very narrow window of time.

The following evening a solicitor's messenger, acting on her behalf, served me with divorce papers. I was devastated but, knowing Jan as I did, I had no doubt that her decision was irreversible. She was never wrong and therefore her decisions were always irreversible. For days I wandered around Richmond in a tearful haze, desperately hoping to catch a glimpse of her.

I was at a particularly low point when, two weeks later, John and I met for lunch at San Lorenzo. I arrived to find him being consoled by Mara, who later told me she had cried for him and could not believe how ungrateful Elton was. We did not dwell on my impending divorce. Instead I left it to John to tell me in graphic terms how he had had to spend a day systematically sacking, one by one, everyone in his office. 'I asked Gary [the chauffeur] for the keys to the Bentley and drove myself home,' he said. 'I didn't want my driver to see me crying in the rear-view mirror. My face was soaking wet with tears. In all the years I'd known Elton, I'd seen him take on new friends and lovers, give them very generous presents and then just dump them. Cut them dead, out of his life. I never thought it could happen to me but it has.'

Unlike John as he drove to St John's Wood, I did not weep on my journey back to Richmond. But I did weigh up my options and calculated that the time had come to check out in the manner that my father had done. I had had a wonderful life with people like Jan, Jo, Dan, Elvis, the Beatles, Tom Jones and so many others, but all I could see ahead was a fast decline into loneliness and depressing mediocrity.

The decision made, I set about calmly making preparations. In the house I drew the curtains, lit a fire, had a bath and then laid out on the coffee table my stash of sleeping pills. I had 72. That should do the job. Dressed in the bathrobe Jan had bought me one birthday and a pair of pyjamas she had left behind, I put on a CD of love songs, opened a bottle of champagne and swallowed the first two pills. I had the next two in my hand when the doorbell sounded. At first I ignored it but whoever it was proved remarkably persistent. Could it be the police? Even at this tragic stage, my insatiable curiosity got the better of me. I went to the door, opened it and was confronted by two men I had never seen before.

'Mr Hutchins?' the one with white hair asked politely. 'We are from the Vineyard Church. May we come in and have a chat?'

Armed with a copy of the electoral roll, they were on a canvassing mission. Mindful of the AA nostrum that nothing in God's world happens by coincidence or by mistake, I beckoned them inside to hear what they had to say. Once we were in the sitting room, they told me their names – Rob [Sims] and Roy [Harris], funnily enough – and made some complimentary noises about the decor. Then they spotted the sleeping pills.

'What are you doing with all these pills?' Roy asked.

It was a civil enough question and I answered it honestly. By now I'm not sure which of us was the more surprised by their presence in my front room at such a timely moment. Their reaction astonished me: they fell to their knees, closed their eyes, clasped their hands and began to pray. At their invitation I joined them, although I had no idea what it was all about. It was an hour before they left, an hour in which I changed my mind about 'checking out', although I was not sufficiently certain of my decision to agree to their request that they take the pills away with them.

I went to their church that Sunday but, hard though I tried, I could not identify with their school of faith. Clearly, they too believed in a higher power but the fact that their particular brand of belief never became mine makes the manner of their timely intervention all the more remarkable. It was a miracle of sorts, I suppose, although, as the divorce proceedings advanced and Jan's solicitors – who I had come to regard as merchants of misery – did their best to grind me into submission, I was not always grateful.

As the proceedings progressed, I stopped writing, stopped answering the phone and opening the mail, and soaked myself in booze. The only respite was the day I decided to try and put my family together one-by-one. I went out and bought a dog, a Tibetan Spaniel just like Freddie, the one Jan had taken with her, and I named him Charlie.

On a grim morning in March 2000, nothing, I thought, could lift my spirits. My 35th wedding anniversary was looming, and so was my divorce. The prospect of being chatted up by an attractive young woman seemed remote, indeed unwanted. But it happened. Unshaven, unkempt and feeling utterly miserable, I was sitting on a bench in the Terrace Gardens below Mick Jagger's house on Richmond Hill with six-month-old Charlie at my feet, when I was approached by a woman who looked interesting. Pointing at the dog, she asked, 'Is that Freddie?' 'No,' I said, but we got talking anyway. She told me her name was Linda, and the dog she had with her was called BB. It turned out that she knew Freddie because she had often spoken to Jan on dog walks. We chatted for ten minutes or so before going our separate ways.

By chance, we met again the following day, this time in Richmond Park, and Linda said she had told her mother the previous evening that she had met a man – me – who she really liked. 'That surprised Mum because she knows I'm 100 per cent gay,' she said. Then she invited me to call in and have a drink with her any time I was passing the lodge at the Richmond Hill gate to the park. Now it was my turn to be surprised – the lodge was a police house. Linda was a policewoman.

I did not take her up on her invitation but I did slip a note through her letterbox telling her where I lived and inviting her around for a drink. Two weeks later she turned up on my doorstep and together we downed a bottle of champagne before going to the Marlborough to get utterly plastered. Five days after that WPC Linda O'Sullivan and I set off for a memorable five days whizzing around Switzerland.

Because of her sexual orientation it was never going to be anything more than a platonic relationship, but she was my first girlfriend in years. We laughed at the same things and for a while life felt good. Thereafter, Linda would come to see me most nights when she came off duty, usually exhausted after several hours patrolling the park on her police horse, Artie. With Linda at my side, I started going to showbusiness events again. At John Reid's party to celebrate the West End opening of *The Graduate*, she was on great form. Although she was too shy to meet her heroine Kathleen Turner, she got on well with Barbara Windsor, who told others in my hearing, 'I reckon Chris is going to marry that girl. Can you believe it? Him wed to a gay policewoman!'

In the whole three months we were together, we never exchanged a cross word. When we did finally have a row, however, the relationship ended as suddenly as it had begun and we never saw each other again. Six months later, I was called by a friend who urged me to go out and buy the *Sunday Mirror*. The front-page headline screamed, 'QUEEN'S COP IS DRUG DEALER'. Linda had fallen victim to a classic Sunday newspaper sting.

Posing as drug users, two reporters had persuaded her to obtain cocaine and heroin for them and then filmed her inside the police lodge handing over the drugs and accepting £160 in payment. Linda had a heart of gold and would do anything (well, almost anything) for anyone who asked her nicely enough. Knowing her, she probably charged the reporters less than she had paid for the stuff. I knew she was not a professional drug-dealer and subsequently wrote to her solicitors offering to appear as a character witness at her trial, but I didn't receive a reply. She was tried for drug dealing, convicted and given an 18-month sentence. Thereafter, on my daily walk in the park, I would pass the paddock where Artie was kept and see Linda's beloved horse clearly pining for his mistress. It was all horribly sad.

Genuine love, however, was just around the corner. Some friends of mine were discussing me with a group of people who knew a young woman who was on her own and who, they decided, had a similarly impish sense of humour. They decreed that we should meet. Her name was Gerri and she lived just a couple of miles from me in North Kingston. I don't think either of us was particularly keen on being set up, but after a telephone conversation we agreed to have dinner together at Bellini's, an Italian restaurant in Richmond, on the evening of Saturday, 9 June 2001. 'Let's make it early,' I joshed. 'Then if we don't like each other, we haven't wasted the whole evening.'

When I arrived at Bellini's there was only one other diner there – a woman who was far too attractive to be single, far too wonderful-looking to be my date. So I sat at a table on the other side of the restaurant. She seemed similarly indifferent. Some minutes had passed before the waiter who had taken the booking said to us, his only two customers, 'Aren't you supposed to be at the same table?' I was staggered. As it turned out, neither Gerri nor I had thought the idea of a blind date was a good one and we had both considered standing the other one up. It made us laugh. We laughed throughout the meal (particularly at a woman at the next table who resembled Ann Widdecombe), throughout the walk afterwards and throughout every one of the long phone calls we shared over the next few days.

In addition to being beautiful – she has the smiliest green eyes – Gerri was quite the most interesting woman I had ever met. Three nights after that first meeting we went to the London Palladium to see *The King And I*. We left in the interval, not because we weren't enjoying the show but because we had so much to say to each other. We were falling in love.

Over the next few months we sailed on the Solent, drove through Switzerland and flew to Venice, Paris, Dublin, the south of France and the Caribbean. On Boxing Day we travelled to Florida and, laughing like a couple of kids, went on every ride in every theme park we could find. The impossible had happened: I had found someone who had taught me to love again. Blameless, unconditional love. Finally, with an engagement ring on her finger, she took me to meet her family in Ireland.

Fifteen months after that first awkward meeting at Bellini's, we were married in the most moving of ceremonies by the banks of the Thames while a string quartet played favourite (and most appropriate) tunes such as 'A Certain Smile'. I believe I can speak for us both when I write that neither of us has ever been as happy and we remain so to this day. She has no hang-ups about my past adventures, good or bad, and didn't think twice about buying me Tom Jones's latest CD last Christmas. I thank God each night for the timely intervention of the men from the Vineyard Church who were out canvassing for converts the night they saved my life. Without it I would never have met the woman who has taught me to love life again. As they say in AA, never give up before the miracle happens.

EPILOGUE

Shopping in Richmond with Gerri one day in February 2003, I bumped into Adam Faith. He had carved out a successful career as an actor following his decline as a pop star and was then appearing in a play at the local theatre. He didn't look at all well and was limping heavily. I tried to cheer him up and told him Gerri and I had booked seats to see his play.

'Oh great, cock,' he said. 'Be sure to come back [stage] afterwards and we'll talk over old times.'

I agreed but thought better of it later when I recalled how a similar invitation more than 40 years earlier had caused my first problem with Jan. So, in the event, Gerri and I stayed home. Three weeks later, Adam died of a massive heart attack and I deeply regretted not having that final get-together. His death set me thinking of all the other friends and contacts I had lost over the years. Some were victims of their lifestyles, such as Elvis, Keith Moon, Brian Epstein, Brian Jones and

Kanga; others, like Gordon Mills, Colonel Parker, Maurice Kinn, Henri and Maurice Gibb, of natural causes. And who could have predicted John Lennon's fate? As I reflect on the fate of so many of the people I hung out with, I am often amazed that I am still around.

A philosopher once said, 'The young think they're indestructible.' That is certainly true of many people in showbusiness. It attracts colourful, gregarious and confident human beings, but they are not as other human beings. Like members of a self-preservation society, they do their best to socialise only in the company of each other. The hoi polloi must be excluded from the world they have created for themselves – unless they are paying at the door, of course.

But beneath this veneer of confidence in their own specialness lurks an awareness of the fact that it is all, in many ways, an illusion. Fans may revere them today but who knows what tomorrow will bring, and so insecurity is always part of their make-up. The worst thing you can ever suggest to a celebrity is that they might be like ordinary people. If you want to wind up, say, Elizabeth Hurley, ask her if she carries an autograph book to collect the signatures of all the famous people she meets. Try asking Cliff Richard if he was a fan of the Beatles. It would horrify them to be thought of as having the same instincts as the autograph hunters, the fans.

In my various professional capacities, I have had a unique opportunity to observe them at work and at play, but the rule has to be 'Don't get involved.' I did get involved, heavily involved and it almost cost me my life. Occasionally, I still see Rob and Roy from the Vineyard Church as I walk the dogs (I bought Jack, a Papillon, to keep Charlie company during the long lonely hours I am writing this). They ask me how I am and they never seem surprised when I tell them how happy and well I feel. They always pass the same remark, 'It's working then.' And when I say, 'What's working?' they say, 'Our prayers, of course. We still pray for you.'